Project management
for the process industries

Project management for the process industries

Edited by Gillian Lawson,
Stephen Wearne and Peter Iles-Smith

IChem**E**

INSTITUTION OF CHEMICAL ENGINEERS

Published by
Institution of Chemical Engineers,
Davis Building,
165–189 Railway Terrace,
Rugby, Warwickshire CV21 3HQ, UK

© 1999 Institution of Chemical Engineers
A Registered Charity

ISBN 0 85295 406 9

Printed in the United Kingdom by Galliards

Preface

All industry depends upon projects to develop new and improved products and new and improved processes for producing them. Successful projects are the basis for successful companies and the national economy. They therefore need to be completed right first time and on time.

Projects are not successful by accident. From start to finish, projects large and small need concentration on their objectives and attention to their risks, the potential effects on the environment, and the safety, quality, cost and speed of work. They need agreed priorities and realistic planning to make the best use of people and other resources. They need co-ordination, drive and control to deliver the maximum value for money, anticipate problems, manage risks and minimize the effects of changes and mistakes.

These are the tasks of project managers in the process industries. Titles may vary — the title 'project engineer' is often used for smaller projects — but it is the role that matters. 'Project manager' is used in this book to mean anyone with these responsibilities, with whatever title. The role demands skills in dealing with people, time, costs, contract relationships and seeing a project as a whole.

Traditionally project management has been learnt by experience, example and trial and error. That can be too slow, inaccurate and limited in the lessons learnt. Companies and individuals can no longer afford the costs and risks of relying on this alone. Something is required to prepare project managers for the task. IChemE conferences and continuing education courses have developed to meet part of the need. This book is designed to complement them. It is for private reading and to provide guidance at work.

The book is for everyone who has responsibilities for some or all of a project. It is also for all engineers and others who contribute to projects who wish to have a better understanding of the process of producing new processes and products.

The book aims to describe best practice and to give guidance on how principles and techniques can be applied to suit the size, complexity, novelty and urgency of projects. To present the material so that it may be easily digested, the chapters are arranged in three sections, dealing in turn with:

- Section 1 — the typical chronological stages of a project;
- Section 2 — systems and techniques which assist in project management;
- Section 3 — personal and other skills of great value in the process industries.

In practice all aspects of a project are interlinked. Therefore we recommend that you read all the chapters on topics you are not already familiar with.

The chapters include check-lists to help you consider how to apply ideas, techniques and advice to particular projects. There's plenty of jargon, and the 'Glossary of terms' on page 349 is useful. Some chapters give examples of problems met at work, with suggested solutions, but there is no one right way of planning, co-ordinating and controlling every project. There are often alternative ways of dealing with problems, so suggestions found here should not be taken to be absolute answers.

Projects can be challenging, fun and satisfying — if done well. We hope that this book will help you enjoy them.

Gillian Lawson, Stephen Wearne and Peter Iles-Smith
November 1998

The authors

Philip Charsley BSc, CEng, FIChemE, MIPD
Philip Charsley set up in 1998 as an
independent consultant, trainer and auditor
in safety management. He spent 13 years
with ICI in process engineering,
commissioning and operations. Then, in
1982, he joined the safety management
consultancy Technica, and was appointed to
the Board in 1984. His responsibilities
included Hazop services, oil and chemical
plant risk assessments and training in risk
management techniques. When DNV bought
Technica in 1992, he took responsibility for
services associated with the International
Safety Rating System (ISRS).

Richard Collins BSc(Hons), FIChemE
After gaining a BSc(Hons) in chemical
engineering at University College, London,
Richard Collins joined Foster Wheeler
Energy Ltd as a process engineer. He
progressed with Foster Wheeler through
various assignments around the world,
increasing his engineering, commercial and
management involvement, finally moving
into project management in 1985. Since then
he has been project manager for a range of
facilities, including refinery, agrochemicals,
fertilizers, petrochemicals and environmental
projects.

Dinesh Fernando BSc, BEng

Dinesh Fernando is a chemical engineer who has worked in the IChemE's Safety, Health and Environment Department for the last eight years. His main work is the promotion of good safety practice through the *Loss Prevention Bulletin* and various training products. He is currently working on the development of multimedia safety training products.

John Gillett MA(Cantab), CEng, FIChemE, MIOSH

John Gillett is International Safety and Loss Adviser for Zeneca Pharmaceuticals. He worked in process engineering and production for 12 years in the plastics industry. He then transferred to the pharmaceutical industry where he has worked for 22 years in technical management positions. He is a past chairman of the IChemE's Safety and Loss Prevention Subject Group and author of the recent book *Hazard Study and Risk Assessment in the Pharmaceutical Industry.*

Peter Gulliver BSc, CEng, FIChemE, MIMechE

Peter Gulliver retired in 1998 as Divisional Director of Foster Wheeler Energy Ltd, where he had worked for over 30 years. His career included periods in Holland and Thailand, and as General Manager of a newly formed Power Systems division. He was responsible for the introduction of total quality management to the organization. He is a member of the Membership Committee of IChemE and is currently Chairman of the Education and Career Development Committee.

Ian Hymes CEng, MIChemE, CChem, MRSC

Ian Hymes has worked for the past seven years in the Operational Division of Her Majesty's Inspectorate of Pollution which in 1996 became part of the Environment Agency. In the 10 years before joining HMIP he worked in the non-nuclear risk assessment section of the UKAEA's Safety and Reliability Directorate where he became Section Head for Environmental Risk Analysis. He also had a three and a half year spell as a Principal Risk Assessment Officer in the Major Hazards Assessment Unit of the Health and Safety Executive. Prior to this he spent almost 20 years in industry, on R&D, troubleshooting and plant technology in the heavy petrochemical industry. He has been an active member of working groups of the IChemE and an author and lecturer on major hazard topics.

Peter Iles-Smith
BSc(Hons), PhD, CEng, MInstMC, MIChemE

Peter Iles-Smith is Project Engineering Manager for process automation systems supplier Yokogawa, and is responsible for overall project execution and the development of advanced system business. He has been involved over the last 14 years in the identification, design and management of process automation projects in the oil and gas, nuclear, chemical and pharmaceutical industries. He is past chairman of the IChemE Process Control Subject Group and lectures at Cranfield and Newcastle Universities on computer-based control.

Diana Kloss LLB, LLM, Barrister (Gray's Inn)
Diana Kloss is a Barrister and Senior
Lecturer in Law in the University of
Manchester. She is a part-time
chairman of Employment Tribunals and
an independent arbitrator on the ACAS panel.
She regularly lectures to managers at the
Manchester Business School and in the
IChemE's short courses, and is the author
of the textbook *Occupational Health Law*
(3rd edition) published by Blackwell Science.

Gillian Lawson BSc, CEng, MIChemE
Gill Lawson studied chemical engineering
at UMIST while being sponsored by British
Steel. On graduation in 1982, she worked for
Dista Products Ltd, initially in technical
services for pharmaceutical manufacturing,
before moving into project management.
She joined ICI in 1988, managing process
plant projects in Europe. She has since had
many and varied responsibilities in the UK in
project management, including developing
and directing internal training courses. She
is currently managing a production site's
project and design office. Gill is a member
of the IChemE's Council and is a past
Chairman of the Engineering Project
Management Forum.

Jack Loftus BSc, CEng, MIChemE

Jack Loftus's career has been with both client companies and contractors, in process engineering and services, investment analysis, budget co-ordination, medium-range planning, refinery operations and project management. With Lummus Crest Ltd he was successively a Senior Project Manager, Manager of Project Engineering, a Project Director and Director of Projects. In 1987 he joined Glaxo Group Research Ltd as Manager Engineering Services, and he recently retired from the post of Central Engineering Manager, Thames Refinery, Tate & Lyle Sugars.

Derek Maidment CEng, FIChemE

Derek Maidment's early chemical engineering experience was in the food and pharmaceutical industries. Since the late 1970s he has been actively involved in and responsible for the development, implementation and maintenance of quality systems to ISO 9001 for companies in the UK and overseas. He retired from the post of Manager of Engineering, the Wellcome Foundation Ltd, and now acts as a consultant. He is co-editor of the IChemE's publication *Quality Assurance: A Guide to the Application of ISO 9001 to Process Plant Projects.*

Harry Moody BSc(Eng), MACostE, MAPM

Harry Moody is a management consultant. Until recently he was Director of the IChemE's short courses in Project Estimating and Planning. After working in the coal and nuclear industries he gained wide experience with ICI Organics Division in the design, construction and commissioning of process plants. In 1970 he was appointed Engineering Planning and Costing Manager with responsibility for providing a full support service to project managers and their teams.

Peter Thompson

MSc, CEng, FICE, MIWES, FAPM

Peter Thompson is Emeritus Professor of Engineering Project Management at UMIST. He worked with consulting engineers, an oil company, nuclear power contractors, and was project manager on major water supply projects. On joining UMIST he specialized in teaching and research with industry on project management, innovations in contracts, short courses and in-company training. He is joint author of many reports and papers including *Engineering Construction Risks — A Guide to Project Risk Analysis and Risk Management.*

Stephen Wearne BSc, PhD, CEng, FAPM, PMP

Stephen Wearne is a consultant and works with the UMIST Centre for Research in the Management of Projects. After factory training he worked on the design, construction and management of projects in Spain, Scotland, South America and Japan. He was Professor of Technological Management at Bradford 1973–1984. His research has included project team organization, joint ventures, contracts and the managerial tasks of engineers. For 26 years he was Director of the Engineering Project Management short courses in the Engineering Institutions' joint continuing education programme.

Graham Wilkinson BEng(Hons)

Graham Wilkinson is a Senior Cost Engineer at BASF, UK. He is responsible for all cost estimating and project cost control at the largest BASF manufacturing site in the UK, and provides an advisory service to the other BASF UK locations and their US operations. He has worked on projects ranging in cost from £10,000 to £100,000,000. He is a regular speaker in the short courses on Techniques of Cost Estimation run by the IChemE.

Contents

Section 1 – Phases of a project

Gillian Lawson and Richard Collins

Section 1 outlines the typical chronological stages of a project, from the initial objectives and options described through to project completion. The typical project process model it follows is in Chapter 1, with a subsequent chapter on each of the nine stages. Section 1 mentions the systems and techniques which support the management of the project through these stages, and is therefore linked frequently to Section 2. Section 1 uses phrases and terms usually met with in 'design and build' engineering projects, but the principles covered are relevant to all projects, irrespective of type and size. There are many check-lists which can act as useful *aides-mémoire* when managing your own projects. If you are familiar with subjects covered you might like to start by looking at the check-lists.

Additionally, there is a worked example of a typical small and simple process industry project at the end of each chapter, starting with Chapter 2. The example uses typical situations which arise in the life of a project, and which you may face in managing your own projects. The same project example is used throughout, and the lessons you may learn are drawn from the contents of the preceding chapter.

Project principles

Gillian Lawson

1

What is a project?

Most people will call any piece of work a 'project', but what do we actually mean by a 'project'? Do we all have the same understanding? Before we can consider managing a project we need to understand what is meant by the term. What makes it special? Why is a project different from other work?

Consider the situation of a car assembly line. Would you consider the production of hundreds of cars a day off the line a project? Probably not. Would you consider the design and assembly of your own kit car in your garage a project? Almost certainly yes. So what are the differences which make 'projects', large or small, special? Here are a few suggestions:

• The contents of every project are unique. Once the activity becomes repetitive it is then a process.

• A project changes the state of something. This can be either 'hard' (for example, building a new plant) or 'soft' (for example, implementing a new organization structure). It can be changing or decommissioning existing plant.

• A project consists of a number of activities which have to be completed to provide something a customer has requested and is to the customer's satisfaction. The finished project must be what the customer wants.

• A project has defined start and finish points. Ideally, a project has a defined start, but it can be the result of a series of proposals and alternative solutions. Projects which drag on ultimately become processes which are never completed.

• A project requires that people and resources are brought together for its duration to implement the required change, and are dispersed on its completion. Every project has unique requirements which are met by bringing together the appropriate talents, skills and equipment.

THE SAME PROJECT PRINCIPLES APPLY,
WHATEVER THE PROJECT.

What makes a project successful?

In order to stay in business, most industries need to make continual investment in many small and some large projects to improve efficiency, launch new products, satisfy new legislation, keep ahead of the competition — whether to manufacture an existing product to a higher specification or more cheaply, produce a new product, or to reduce emissions to enable existing processes to continue to operate. Typically, this investment and commitment is implemented as a 'project'. In order for the company to remain viable, every project should therefore be managed so that it provides value for money, on time.

All too often people hear tales of what went wrong on bad projects, without considering what makes projects good. So what does make a project successful? Returning to the kit car scenario, what do you think would make it successful?

Here are a few generic suggestions for ensuring successful projects:

• Customer requirements are clearly understood and agreed. Firstly, determine who is the real customer. For a process plant project it may be the plant manager, your boss, or is it the operator who ultimately has to operate the valve you designed which cannot be reached? Then finish the project to that customer's satisfaction.

• Scope of work, and resultant cost estimate and programme with critical dates are agreed with both the customer and the project team. Agreement by all encourages commitment to project targets.

• Risks and uncertainties are understood and accepted by all involved. Timely and appropriate decisions can be made if risks are known.

- People, skills and resource requirements are defined, and are available at the appropriate time. Any delays in involving people and resources can affect the project costs and programme.
- Objectives, priorities and responsibilities are clearly defined for every member of the project team. Members are more committed and efficient if they understand what and when is required of them and others.
- Working relationships are managed in order to produce a committed project team. The sooner a team is committed to a project and confident in its leader, the sooner it will work effectively.
- The right people are informed of the right information at the right time. To be effective, all members of the team need to be confident that they have all possible up-to-date information.
- Safety, quality, cost and progress are controlled through the life of the project, and any changes to agreed scope, costs and programme are controlled effectively. An overspent or late project is usually not deemed successful; the project manager has failed to manage the project.

Why is effective project management important?

For a process company to flourish, it must invest in new projects for new and improved products and processes. No investment by a company, and hence no projects, initially leads to stagnation, then to decline, and ultimately to collapse. Companies must invest in order just to stay in business. More investment is needed if a company wishes to be ahead of the competition. If it is accepted that projects typically involve considerable investment, then it is essential that the money is spent wisely — that is, the projects are managed well, from the very early days all the way through to completion. The effect of investment through projects can be seen in the project investment cycle (Figure 1.1, page 6).

A real or perceived demand usually initiates a project. This embryonic idea may then require further research and development, and can also require support from diverse groups such as marketing and legal services. This typically leads to an initial project proposal, which summarizes whether it is worth pursuing the project, or if it should be abandoned.

On the assumption that the project looks acceptable, the process is designed and developed, and other feasibility studies are carried out. If the project still looks promising, initial design continues, cost estimates are issued and detailed plans developed. It is usually at this stage that the full expenditure for the project is authorized if the project is financially attractive. The project design is completed, equipment, structures and services are procured, the project is constructed, commissioned and handed over to the final user.

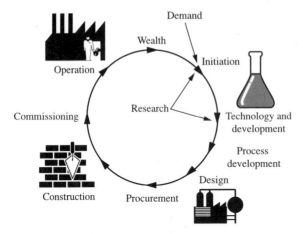

Figure 1.1 Project investment cycle

If the project has been successful, the project will operate and start to deliver its value. The project enables the company to remain in business, generating money to pay bank loans, suppliers, employees, shareholders and so on, and also to invest in new projects to generate the wealth of the future.

Investment in a project requires not only money. Projects usually require significant technical and other resources from the process company, even if much of the engineering is managed and executed by a contractor. If the project is poorly managed, and hence fails to deliver the requirements, this useful and talented resource has been wasted. What else would this resource have been doing instead, which could possibly have been of greater benefit to the company? Likewise with the capital investment — could it have been put to better use on a different project, giving greater and faster returns? What opportunities have been lost? Poor project management can thus be very expensive.

Most operating companies plan their capital expenditure in projects for the next five or more years, covering activities which can be described as sustenance as well as strategic new investments. Project managers are often asked to help to produce these plans by giving very approximate cost estimates and time-scales for potential projects. These approximate figures can be used to shape and influence the strategic direction of the company. Imagine the confusion and lack of confidence, therefore, if a project manager whose previous projects have consistently overrun on cost and time is asked to asked to contribute to these plans. Should these estimates and time-scales be accepted as given, or should senior managers add extra amounts based on previous history? Project managers need to deliver projects to specified costs and time-scales, not just for current needs, but also to assist in planning the future.

How does project management differ from general management?

Some people come into project management from production or general management, and wonder how project management is different, if at all, from their previous role. Here are five paragraphs which show how project management may be viewed as being different:

Managing the 'unknown'

Successful project management relies on the project manager planning for the future — the great unknown — to anticipate problems. In production, for example, the plant and resource team usually already exist, and it is the manager's responsibility to get the best and the most out of them, day by day, month by month. Each project in the process industries has a different technical content, hence the process needs to be developed and designed each time. Thus, in project management, not only does the plant have to be created, but even for small projects, a temporary and perhaps part-time team also has to be brought together.

Managing change

Projects are initiated to bring about a change of some sort — to manufacture an existing product to a higher specification, produce a new product or reduce emissions to enable an existing process to operate. All these require a change from the existing state to a new state. They should not just be thought of in terms of 'hardware'. They can make significant changes to softer issues such as operation manning levels, public relations with local communities and seconding technical staff from other sections onto the project team. Change is greeted differently by individuals and groups. Some are very anxious about any change, seeing it as a threat to their experience, job security and comfort. Others welcome it as an opportunity to improve. These are typical issues to be managed during the execution of a project.

Managing strategically

Project time-scales and objectives are usually longer term than those in production or general management, most of which require immediate action. For instance, breakdowns need repairing today, production levels need to be increased next week, personnel reviews need to be completed next month. Project managers have to think strategically about what are the project objectives, when they need to be achieved, how they will be achieved, and then not be distracted by minor issues. A manager in a production department is not usually a successful project manager as, invariably, the day-to-day short-term production problems demand attention, and the longer-term project needs are not anticipated until there are serious problems.

Managing resourcing

Resources for a project are generally brought together for a particular project, and the team is then disbanded on project completion. The resources are usually from technical departments outside the project manager's direct line management. A project manager therefore does not have the advantage of knowing individuals' strengths and weaknesses well or of being responsible for their management and all that entails. The project manager may also have to compete for the better or limited resources with other project managers, who may have the benefit of leading more interesting or higher profile projects. The management of small or large projects can thus be significantly more complex organizationally than the direct management experienced in production or general management.

Managing completion

It may seem obvious, but a project needs to be completed and handed over to its user. It may be tempting during design or construction to add in a 'little something extra' or to do something in a different way to the plan in order to make the project seem that much better. This is difficult to resist for those from a production or general management background, as 'constant improvement' is usually a significant part of these management roles. Resist a project manager must! A project can be strangled by so many 'little improvements', to the extent that it is never completed and handed over.

Project process model

The project investment cycle in Figure 1.1 (page 6) illustrates how the development and execution of a well-managed project can generate wealth for a company. Figure 1.2 shows stages in the process of specifying, engineering, constructing and commissioning a project. This project process model is typical of many projects in the process industries. The terms and phrases used may vary, but the message is appropriate for most projects. The remainder of Section 1 of this book follows this generic model, covering why the various stages exist, what each stage entails and who is involved with the work.

Further reading

Barnes, N.M.L. and Wearne, S.H., 1993, The future for major project management, *International Journal of Project Management*, 11 (3): 135–142.

Kletz, T., 1993, *Lessons from Disaster: How Organisations Have No Memory and Accidents Recur* (Institution of Chemical Engineers).

Morris, P.W.G. and Hough, G.H., 1987, *The Anatomy of Major Projects: A Study of the Reality of Project Management* (John Wiley).

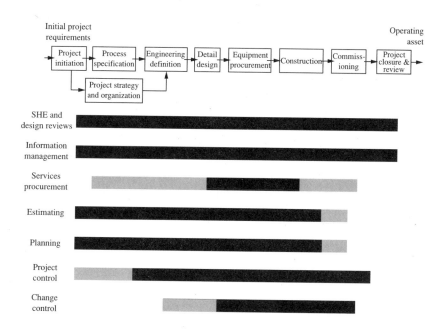

Figure 1.2 Project process model

Project initiation

Gillian Lawson

2

What initiates a project?

Projects start for all sorts of reasons, but for operators in the process industry, there are three main sources:

Opportunity

The possibility to seize the chance to make something cheaper, faster, better or larger than the opposition. For example, the project may be to design and install a plant, start manufacture of a new product, or to change equipment to improve production costs of an existing product.

Problem

Something doesn't work in the way it should, so needs improvement. For example, problems with final product handling equipment may result in upstream production plant having to be run at low output or shut down while problems are resolved. The project could then be to modify the final product handling process and equipment to remove the problem source, or perhaps install a parallel process stream.

Threat

If something is not done, existing operation will be adversely affected. These projects may be part of the company's environmental policy or required by legislation; for example, unless effluent discharge levels are improved, relevant agencies might stop a manufacturing operation.

Why initiate a project?

So, in order to take the opportunity, solve the problem or meet the threat, a 'project' is initiated. But why? By giving the ensuing work the title 'project', those responsible for the problem or opportunity signal to others interested or involved that the problem or the opportunity is sufficiently special to be treated differently from more routine work. This could require related individuals to have different or additional roles to their normal duties during the duration of the project, and perhaps even be moved completely from their existing job. The title 'project' also implies that it is generally understood that there will be expenditure, even if only in terms of man-hours spent on the project. It thus gives the message that those responsible are keen to have the problem solved or the opportunity delivered, and so are committed to the project being successful.

Who may be involved at project initiation?

Project initiator

The person who initiates a project varies from company to company, and from project to project. For an 'opportunity project' it could, for example, be someone in marketing who spots the chance to launch a new or improved product, and is thus keen to get it into production as soon as possible. A 'problem-solving project' may be started by someone in production who has had difficulties with a particular part of the process or piece of equipment. The earlier example of a 'threat-confronting project', meeting stricter legislation on emissions, could be initiated by someone responsible for environmental standards. Who initiates the project at the very beginning is not as important as who they then contact to support and take action on the project.

Management support

All projects require support and ownership by management if they are to succeed. The initiator must therefore very quickly contact the appropriate managers to get the project moving, and unfortunately they may not be too obvious! The obvious managers are those who lead the departments and groups who may be involved directly in the project — process design, engineering, construction, commissioning and so on. Others, though, may need to be contacted in order to lobby for their support — finance, accountancy, safety, environmental, marketing, operations managers whose adjoining plant may be affected by the proposed project, and so on. Who needs to be contacted early varies depending upon the particular circumstances; only experience and seeking advice from others will assist the individual in this task.

Your role

How you then become involved in the project also differs depending on the project and your individual company. You may be appointed to a particular role in the project with appropriate responsibilities by your line manager, or even have to go through a formal interview and selection process. Some organizations adopt a much less formal approach, and you may find yourself gradually attached to a project over a period of time. Your role may be that of project manager, or you may be a member of a larger project team, supporting the management of the project or in a technical position. In these circumstances, it is you who will be providing a service to the project for the ultimate customer.

The customer and stakeholders

But who is the customer? It may not necessarily be the person or group who initiated the project. In the example of the earlier opportunity project, the marketing manager may view the marketing group as the customer or, in turn, the ultimate external purchaser as the customer. In addition, the production managers responsible for producing the new or improved product may view themselves as the customers of the project. Others will also feel that they should have some influence on the project — operating staff, safety, legal, and so on.

Unfortunately, those who should be involved at the project initiation may be reluctant to take part. In the earlier example of the threat-confronting project, one of the main stakeholders should be the production plant or department responsible for the emissions, as it will be their process or equipment which is modified or replaced by the project. However, they may not want the project and be reluctant to assist or become involved as they view it as an inconvenience to everyday operations. Worse still, they may consider it to be something very unwelcome as it has been forced upon them by others. Nevertheless, the project manager should encourage their inclusion from the beginning or risk the 'this isn't what I wanted' attitude, and the resultant rejection or rework at the end of the project.

For larger projects, steering groups may be established. This should be done as early as possible in order to be effective. The steering group is there to direct the project at the highest level, assisting in guiding and in major decision-making. The sooner the group is established, the sooner it can guide the project and the team members towards meeting the objectives. A steering group usually involves managers representing the customer groups and all departments with a substantial interest in any stage of the proposed project. It should always include the project manager. Steering group members can also assist in any internal politicking which may be required on behalf of the project. Numbers of personnel involved should be kept to an operating minimum, otherwise guidance and decisions are slow in forthcoming! The steering group should not become involved in the day-to-day running of the project — that is the project manager's role.

Thus, one of the earliest tasks for the project manager is to discuss, clarify and agree who is the actual project customer and who will 'own' the project, as distinct from those who have a passing interest.

What is the project?

It seems obvious to say that the project objectives — that is, what the project is ultimately to achieve — should be known from the very beginning, but sometimes they may not be too clear.

Taking the earlier threat-confronting project example to reduce emissions. The project initiator may believe that the project objectives are 'to reduce particle emissions to atmosphere by installing cyclones followed by dust filters in vent streams'. But these are not the project objectives; they are a solution. A better definition of the project objectives would be 'to reduce particle emissions to atmosphere to less than x mg m^{-3} by a specific date'.

The final solution may indeed be to install cyclones and filters but, equally, a change to upstream processing or equipment could reduce or even eliminate the generation of the particles at source.

Different groups or individuals may have differing views on the project objectives. Again, the project manager should discuss, clarify and agree the actual project objectives with the real customer and stakeholders, and not just assume that any project brief produced so far is 100% correct. It is of no purpose or benefit to deliver a project to time, to cost and to quality standards if it is the wrong project.

Constraints should not be forgotten — that is, what cannot be done. They should be known in terms of cost, time, quality, resources, legislation and so on. What are the main risks? What is the maximum price the company is prepared to pay for the project and how accurate is the estimate of the likely cost of the project? Are there any particular time constraints, such as meeting shutdown dates, legislative dates and so on? Are there unlimited resources (unlikely!), or will other people's availability and knowledge dictate progress?

Time and money

The benefit to be gained from a threat-confronting project may be that manufacturing can continue because particle emissions have been reduced or eliminated. If so, the financial benefit is an indirect one. Most projects are sanctioned because they promise a direct financial return. Money will have to be expended

13

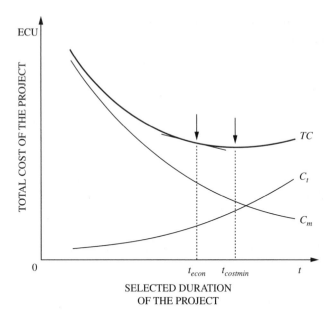

Figure 2.1 Variation of total cost with duration of the project

to engineer and execute the project, but only when it is operating can money start to be earned and the cash flow become positive. Deciding the total time allowed for the development and execution of a project is therefore important.

In theory the total duration of a project is decided after estimating the cost for a range of times and choosing the time at which the present value of income obtained earlier by faster completion equals its extra cost. Figure 2.1 illustrates how total cost varies with the intended speed of carrying out a project. Some costs increase with the time taken, as indicated by the C_t curve in the diagram — for instance, the financing cost of the use of resources. Other costs decrease, as indicated by the C_m curve — for instance, the direct costs of resources. The sum of the two is shown by the total cost TC curve.

The continuous curves in Figure 2.1 are a simplification. In practice the relationships may include step changes at choices in the number of people or the capacity of a range of machines. In principle the relationship indicated between total cost and planned duration provides a basis for classifying projects into one of three categories of urgency:

Minimum initial cost

If the client's requirement is to complete a project for minimum cost, its planned duration should be where TC is a minimum, the $t_{costmin}$ point shown in the diagram. Urgency is zero. This is the condition for investment in services which do not earn money.

Economic duration

If a project is to produce goods or services which are expected to earn money, greater expenditure than minimum cost is usually justified to try to achieve completion earlier than $t_{costmin}$. This point on the *TC* line is where its slope (shown by a tangent line) represents the discounted amount which is expected to be earned per week after completion (the slope of this line is negative, as it represents not cost but income per unit of time). Hence t_{econ} is chosen as the planned duration of the project.

Emergency

If speed overrides all consideration of cost, any attention to optimizing the use of resources is irrelevant. Time is priceless. Only physical conditions and resources limit the speed of work. This is the condition of saving life after disaster, or action to forestall impending doom. Costs are recorded for accounting, but not for control.

Project planning

The objectives of a project should therefore state whether it is to be completed at minimum initial cost, or whether in a faster economic time or as emergency work, in order to guide the project manager in planning the use of resources. These choices are the same as those which apply to deciding whether to 'crash' an activity that is on the critical path for a project — as discussed in Chapter 16. The word 'urgent' should not be used without defining whether it means that work should carried out at its economic speed or whether it means without regard to cost.

The economic speed calculated for a project should of course be changed if the expected future value of the project changes. A consequent decision to increase speed can be properly described as acceleration.

Priorities tend to change during all projects. Projects initially authorized as really urgent tend to incur costs which lead to second thoughts. As a result, the priority may become less haste, more economy. More typically, projects are started after detailed attention to cost compared to benefits. Yet as the work for such projects progresses, completion on time tends to become relatively more important. Extra cost is then incurred to keep to time, often in the form of paying bonuses or paying the costs of overcoming what are claimed to be abnormal hindrances.

Methods of project management vary depending on whether or not the speed of completing a project is important. If minimum cost is the priority for a project, the project manager must not let work start until everything has been detailed and planned. The manager must resist changes and innovations, even from the client. If the project is an emergency, all the critical work for it must be free of restraints on cost. In this rare condition, the project manager usually monitors costs, but only to provide estimates of final cost, not as a basis for control. If urgency only means faster than usual, the project manager must ask what extra may be spent per day to save a day. Then time can be optimized against cost. And on all projects the project manager must also be sensitive to possible changes in the priorities, perhaps before other people are aware of them, in order to recommend changing the priorities in the use of resources.

Starting the right project

On the assumption that the customer, the project objectives and the project manager are known and agreed, it is then time to start looking at possible technical solutions (or options).

For a large or complicated project, there may be numerous possible technical solutions which meet the cost, time, quality and safety constraints. For a smaller or simpler project there may only be one or two possible solutions. There is the temptation at this stage for a project manager to be keen to get on and manage the technically interesting part of the project — the detailed design, procurement and so on — and not to look at possible technical options. This is the time to resist moving ahead too quickly (both from others' and from your own enthusiasm), and to spend some effort looking at possible options, their

advantages and their risks (see Chapter 14). It is at this early stage that the greatest influence can be exerted on reducing cost and execution time and minimizing risks, while improving quality. Indeed, if an ingenious or imaginative solution exists and is not considered at this stage, no doubt it will be thought of at a later date and will then give rise to changes which disrupt the progress of the project.

For a small project, the project manager may take on every role at this stage — the process engineer developing potential solutions, the cost engineer developing very approximate cost estimates (see Chapter 15), the planner producing preliminary simple 'level one' plans (see Chapter 16), the mechanical engineer considering what main plant items may be required, and so on. For larger projects, the project manager may be able to call upon such individuals to assist either part- or full-time in investigating potential solutions. The project manager attempts to assess what other assistance may be required to carry out this preliminary work, and seeks to obtain other resources if necessary. It is often at this stage that operating companies realize that external support is required, and go on to employ contracting or design companies.

There are no fixed rules about who or which skills may be required to assist at this stage but, if in doubt, inexperienced and experienced project managers alike should seek guidance from those around them in the organization. Early action to obtain legal consents may be important, to avoid delay and possible requirements to change the design or add testing or operating procedures later (see Chapter 11 for guidance on statutory obligations). The project manager should not be expected to know all the technical intricacies and requirements of the project, but should be expected to know that if in doubt, ask!

There are usually some administrative requirements even at this early stage, which are often the responsibility of the project manager. The project should be given a formal title, and the title used, so that there is no confusion between personnel when discussing the project. This is especially important if several projects are being executed in the same area or for the same company, otherwise the muddle between the projects can result in something resembling a theatrical farce. The project manager also ensures that any financing to allow this early work to proceed is obtained via the appropriate route. This may result in the project being given a unique identifying project number, which is used whenever discussing the project in order to minimize confusion.

Check-list 2.1 (page 18) presents items for consideration when developing early options. It is suggested that the project manager and client formally discuss and record the items, as the start of the process for achieving a common understanding of the project. Additionally, it assists in the start of the process for ownership and taking responsibility for the project.

Check-list 2.1   Items for consideration when developing early options
(not all topics are relevant or necessary for every project)

Project objectives
- Why is the project being considered?
- What is the project trying to achieve?
- What secondary benefits may be achieved?

Issues
- What concerns are there at this stage (commercial, operational, technical, safety, environmental)?
- What may halt the project, or prevent it from achieving its objectives?
- What may change the objectives or priorities?
- What is the customer prepared to pay? And when?

Options
- Outline the scope of the project.
- Consider briefly each possible solution to meet the objectives. List the advantages and disadvantages of each option. Also consider the effects on any secondary benefits. Note if there are any obvious reasons for rejection or further development of an option.

The possible technical solutions are considered without going into specifics, as it is wasteful to look at each solution in too much detail. Any clear failures are discounted as soon as possible, so that effort can be concentrated on those which remain. Such failures can often be identified due to obvious problems with safety, health or environmental aspects. Potential solutions are examined to ensure that they would meet the agreed objectives of the project:
- to reduce particle emissions to atmosphere to less than x mg m^{-3} by a specific date;

whilst also satisfying any other quantitative and qualitative constraints, for example to:
- cost less than y;
- be available $z\%$ of operating time;
- meet safety criteria;
- cause minimum disruption to existing plant operation;
- meet reliability and maintenance requirements;
- utilize external resources effectively and economically.

There should also be some indication of what is outside the scope of the current project — that is, what will be specifically excluded. Using the previous example:

- any new plant and equipment will not include redundant capacity;
- improvements to liquid effluent discharges from the plant are excluded.

Techniques exist to assist in assessing solutions, and sieving out those which should be rejected. A simple, broad scoring system can be employed based on 'importance factor', where objectives or constraints are given a possible factor out of ten (the highest being deemed the most important). Each solution is then scored out of ten on how well it will meet each objective or constraint; the higher the score, the better it meets the criteria. The score is multiplied by the factor to give the total figure for each. The option with the greatest overall total score is deemed the most satisfactory. The assessment is best carried out by a team of three to five people representing the customer and stakeholders.

Table 2.1 provides an example based on the particle emissions project. It appears at first sight that Option 1 gives the best result, as it has the highest score. It would be an inexpensive project, disrupting existing operations very little, while utilizing a significant amount of external resources. Yet it scores poorly in meeting the target emissions objective. In contrast, Option 3 may score slightly lower, as it is more expensive and would cause more disruption to

Table 2.1   Example of option assessment

Criteria	Agreed importance factor (max 10)	Option 1		Option 2		Option 3	
		Score	Total	Score	Total	Score	Total
Meeting target emissions by specified date	10	3	30	4	40	8	80
Cost < y	8	8	64	5	40	4	32
Operating availability	8	5	40	6	48	7	56
Disruption to plant	6	7	42	5	30	4	24
Utilization of external resources	3	9	27	5	15	3	9
Total score			203		173		201

19

existing operations, but it does go much further in meeting the target emissions and has a better availability once in operation. The negative aspects of Option 3 would only be interim, whilst its positive aspects would be long-term. In reality, Option 3 would therefore not be rejected in favour of Option 1 at this stage. The assessment would, though, allow Option 2 to be rejected, as it scores some 15% below the other two options.

Value engineering (see Chapter 24) can assist in determining the best option. Formal risk analysis (see Chapter 14) can assist in determining whether an option should proceed. Ideally, one solution, possibly two, but certainly a maximum of three solutions continue now for further development, with the goal of reducing the number as time progresses. If the overall project is very urgent, then only one or possibly two options can be carried forward, so that efforts can be focused on implementing the project quickly. For all projects, the number of options should be reduced to one by the time the project reaches engineering definition (see page 59).

On to the next stage

It is valuable to spend time producing a project proposal document, outlining and reviewing what options have been considered and their level of development, recommending which are to be rejected, which are to be carried forward to the next stage, and what further technical, costing, planning and risk assessment work may be necessary. The review document is distributed to all who would be interested in its conclusions and recommendations, so that they have the opportunity to digest and comment upon the proposed project. In producing the document, it is important not just to state what conclusions have been reached, but *why*, which indicates to all that recommendations are based on sound and thorough logic. Check-list 2.2 gives a suggested contents list for the project proposal document.

Remember that the final recommendation may be not to proceed with the project in any shape or form; a poor project should be abandoned at the earliest opportunity, so that resources and money can be redirected towards more gainful work.

Check-list 2.2 Items for consideration for inclusion in project proposal
(not all topics are relevant or necessary for every project)

Confirmed information
- Project title and number
- Project customer or client
- The project manager
- The project's underlying concept and objectives
- Preliminary order of cost estimate, and the basis of its production, and how this compares to sanction budget
- Summary plan with critical milestones and time-cost criteria
- The project scope and any known exclusions
- All interactions with existing utilities, plants or projects
- The anticipated method of project execution — eg, extent of use of contractors
- Summary of any risks
- Commercial, technical or engineering reviews carried out — eg, Value Analysis
- Options which have been rejected

Preliminary information
- Safety, health and environmental criteria
- Legislation, regulatory approvals and consents which will apply
- Constraints on location or layout
- Design life of new assets and anticipated remaining life of any existing assets to be reused
- Specification of products
- Process route, or remaining options to be investigated
- Process or equipment developments required
- Process flowsheets
- Anticipated methods of testing, commissioning and operation (manual or automatic) and maintenance
- Plant availability
- Any provisions for future expansion
- Raw materials, process materials and utilities specifications, and supply source
- Any buildings required, locations and layouts
- Any demolition required
- Information on any assets that are to be reused
- Preliminary information on the control of design and construction risks

Further reading

Brennan, D., 1997, *Process Industry Economics* (Institution of Chemical Engineers).

Maday, B., 1995, How to make a rapid application development fail, *Proceedings, Seminar/Symposium, New Orleans* (Project Management Institute).

Popescu, C. and Popescu, A., 1995, Strategies for project duration reduction, *Proceedings, Seminar/Symposium, New Orleans* (Project Management Institute).

Roberts, L., 1995, Accelerated product development: How long to have a baby?, *Proceedings, Seminar/Symposium, New Orleans* (Project Management Institute).

Wearne, S.H., 1996, Economic urgency in project management, *Project*, 9 (6): 10.

Project example

You are a technical operations engineer working for a small chemical production company, and have told your line manager that you are interested in managing some projects in the future. There is a small project coming along on your particular plant, so it is suggested that you manage it.

Your brief is as follows. Existing equipment is to be used to manufacture a completely new product, WHIZZO. Two existing identical vessels are to be used, A and B. Both are fitted with existing agitators. Liquid Y is added to vessel B, followed by solid Z. They are mixed together, and Z dissolves in liquid Y. Meanwhile, liquid X is added to vessel A.

The contents of B is then to be transferred into A, by a new pump, and then stirred. This results in the production of WHIZZO (see Figure 2.2).

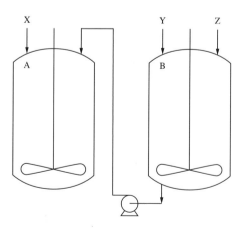

Figure 2.2 Simple flowsheet for WHIZZO production

What are the first things to consider in your new role as the project manager?

Here is a list of suggested actions. This list is not exhaustive, but merely indicates what may need to be considered. It and the similar lists in subsequent chapters are check-lists. Skip those questions which are not relevant to your project.

Project objectives

- Is this viewed as an opportunity project?
- Is the real objective to manufacture WHIZZO, or is it something else? For example, is X an unwanted by-product from another process and is this just a convenient way to dispose of it?
- What is the product specification for WHIZZO?
- Who should you contact in order to confirm objectives and priorities?
- How may objectives and priorities change during the project?
- Is the plant to have spare/redundant capacity included for future expansion?

People

- Who is the customer/owner for this project? Are they aware of their role and responsibilities?
- Who are the other stakeholders in the project?
- Are they likely to assist you in the project, or do they view the project as a hindrance?
- Is a steering group established or to be established for the project? If not, who will give you guidance?
- Are you clear about your role and responsibilities as project manager, and how long it is likely to last?
- Will your line manager support you in this role, or expect you still to be able to give 100% commitment to your existing job of technical operations engineer?
- Do you have all the necessary technical skills to do the project yourself, or what additional resources will you require?
- Where might you obtain these resources, internally and/or externally?
- Will you or others have specific duties under safety and environmental legislation?

Administration

- What, if any, is the official title of the project?
- Does the project already have an identification number?
- What reports on the project are to go to who?
- Is funding required to carry out the early work? If so, how will you obtain it?

Constraints

- Does the project need to be completed by a particular date?
- Do other dates — for example, existing plant shutdowns — need to be met?
- Is there an upper expenditure limit?
- Will you need to contact external legislative bodies, such as the local council, regarding planning permission?
- Will your project have an impact on adjacent plants? If so, how will you minimize inconvenience to them? Will they determine when and how you carry out certain tasks?
- What are the specifications for raw materials X, Y and Z? Are the raw materials always of consistent quality?

Options

- Does existing equipment have to be used?
- Is existing equipment suitable for proposed new duties, or will it need modifying?
- What will you be excluding from the project?
- Does Y and Z mixture have to be pumped, or are there other possible options — for example, gravity feed or overpressure transfer?
- Will you produce estimates and plans for each possible solution?
- Are there any reasons — for example, environmental or safety issues — which may reduce the number of options, or even halt the project completely?
- What are the design and access restraints on the project?
- Have there ever been any safety, health or environmental incidents on similar plants?
- Who will finally decide which option(s) go forward?

Technical

- Is the process batch, semi-batch or continuous?
- What are the interim process conditions — for example, temperature, pressure?
- What additional process or equipment developments are needed?
- How will the new plant be operated? Totally manual, fully automatic?
- Do you have access to technical documentation for existing equipment?
- How good and accessible is the design and other data on the existing plant and services?
- Will you produce a summary project proposal document? Who needs to see a copy of it?

Project strategy and organization

Gillian Lawson

How will the project be executed?

On the assumption that the objectives of the project are known and agreed, and that the proposed project has been given approval to continue to the following phase, the next task for the project manager and team is to determine *how* they will execute the remaining work. That is, how the project can be best managed to ensure that the objectives are achieved. This is the heart of the project manager's role, as it determines the direction of all future work, and thus the likelihood of success. It is this element of directing the 'unknown' future which can make the project manager's role so challenging but so interesting and rewarding.

This plan for managing a project is called different things in different companies — project execution strategy, project management plan (see Glossary for other terms) — but the theme is the same — how the project will be managed.

In formulating the project execution strategy, always remember that there are no absolutely right nor wrong ways to manage the project or elements of it, but rather that considered judgement is necessary for each stage, whatever the size of the project. The way that previous projects have been managed or company routines should be followed only if they were proven to be successful. The project execution strategy is not a one-off piece of work done at the early stage of the project. It is developed, reviewed and enhanced as the project progresses and as new relevant information becomes available.

The preliminary strategy is influenced by the current status of the project. It may be that the project is still being managed by the client company, and it is expected that the remainder of the project will be given to a contractor to manage. It may be that the project has already been given to a contractor, and it is a project manager within the contractor company who will determine the project strategy. Even if the project is to be managed by a contractor, the client may wish to influence the strategy — for instance, by nominating certain subcontractors or stipulating a certain process route which will require interactions with process licensers. Some operating companies have a partner-ship relationship with contractors, where the partnership contractor is used in preference to other contractors, as discussed in Chapter 18.

Producing a preliminary project execution strategy

The first step is to produce an outline or preliminary strategy, based on the limited information available to date. But what needs to be considered? The question which the project manager should always have in mind is, 'How will I ...', and apply this to every remaining aspect of the project. For example, how will I:

- produce an estimate, and then monitor and control expenditure?
- choose a contractor?
- manage the detail design?
- procure necessary plant items?
- deal with any changes within the project?
- get the plant installed?
- get necessary support resources?
- get advice on safety?
- ensure that operating staff are properly trained?
- apply quality assurance to the project?

All the sets of activities needed to complete the project are considered at this stage:

- outstanding preliminary design — for example, option reduction;
- hazard analysis;
- detail design;
- procurement;
- construction;
- commissioning;
- handover;
- project control;
- project organization.

The answers to the 'How will I ...' questions form the basis of the project strategy. Not all have to be considered at the preliminary stage, and not all at any great depth — it depends on whether the project is novel, complex or uncer-tain. For the inexperienced project manager, it is probably best to concentrate on the greatest uncertainties. Also, sufficient time should be given to the thinking process, considering possible future scenarios, and how they will be managed. It is important to resist the temptation to rush ahead. A few hours of thought at this stage can save many hours of work in the future. Now is the time to make use of the lessons stated in close-out reviews on previous projects. Though demanding on time, much can also be learned from taking part in current cross-project audits.

Others who will be contributing to the project should be consulted for their thoughts, comments and experiences, and for their agreement and commitment to the plan. How do they believe that the project or elements of it should be managed? The aim is always to achieve time, cost, safety and quality targets, and make best uses of resources and skills available. For example, should certain elements of design be contracted to Company X because they always meet the agreed timetable? Should a single supplier be used for all pipework, or should orders for pipework packages be placed with the cheapest supplier, even if this results in several different suppliers for pipework? Again, the project manager is not just interested in what they recommend or suggest, but *why*. The type of people who may be consulted for their views on the project execution strategy are:

• project client (remembering that a contract may have already stipulated the strategy);

• managers of contributing groups — for example, process, safety and environmental services, mechanical design, civil design, procurement, construction, plant operations;

Seek suggestions and opinions from others on project strategy.

- those who may not initially be viewed as mainstream project team members, but can advise in areas which could influence the project — for example, financial, personnel;
- those who will become members of project team — for example, control engineer, mechanical engineer, commissioning engineer;
- those who have managed recent similar projects.

The people in the last two categories often have valuable current experience and much useful knowledge. For example, they can bring you up-to-date information on the assessments of the quality and dependability of external design contractors and consultants. Those in the last category are of particular usefulness to inexperienced project managers. They should be able to say what went well in their projects, what they would prefer not to repeat, and of course, *why*. A good project manager always learns from the successes and errors of others, hence this type of information provides a very useful foundation for future projects.

Pre-qualification of vendors and contractors

It may be determined that contractors will assist in part, if not all of the project, and there should be a process for determining which one(s) are to be selected. The pre-qualification of potential vendors and contractors is a process of assessing which have the experience, technical or other resources, financial security, managerial capability, safety standards, quality assurance systems and record of performance necessary for the work. If the results provide a list of qualified potential bidders, the client can then select two or three to invite to bid competitively, with confidence that any of these should be a satisfactory supplier.

The process of pre-qualification should be systematic, to avoid personal preferences and judgements having unbalanced influence. For novel, critical or larger contracts, consider the following facts about every potential bidder:

- work in progress, commitment and turnover history;
- performance on recent projects — quality, schedule, cost and safety;
- attitude to and recovery from problems;
- utilization of subcontractors, partners and other resources;
- size of company;
- resource management structure;
- financial ratios, assets, liabilities;
- credit and bank references;
- experience, qualifications and commitment of line and project managers;
- quality assurance system;

- health, safety and welfare systems;
- training systems;
- staff turnover history.

The factors considered are those which are relevant to the client's objectives and risks, together with those specific to the project such as local knowledge, manpower availability, patents and licences held.

Potential bidders who do not satisfy a minimum standard in every essential factor are eliminated before proceeding to comparison. Pre-qualification should be completed before inviting bids or discussing prices, to avoid the temptation of accepting a low price from a bidder unfit to be given the contract.

When managing smaller projects, and particularly if several are concurrent, it is advantageous to try to treat them as uniformly as possible. This saves time and confusion. Therefore, as much as possible, try to stay with the same type of simple strategy if you have found that it works. For example, taking the earlier project example of reducing particle emission to atmosphere, it could be that a similar project has been managed successfully within the company. Then, the front end engineering package (FEEP, see Glossary) was completed by the production company, but all subsequent work (except commissioning) was completed externally. Table 3.1 (page 30) shows the outline strategy.

If the strategy has produced successful results previously, why change it? The aim when managing projects, and especially smaller ones, is to keep them as simple as possible. Little can be gained from complicated strategies, differing with each project.

There could be a wealth of facts and suggestions at this stage (some possibly conflicting), as to how the project should be managed. The project manager should view all of the suggestions and discuss the advantages and disadvantages with the contributors, and consider which, when fitted together in totality, appear to best deliver the project. Remember that it cannot be totally right or wrong. The project manager needs to consider and distil this information to produce a preliminary project execution strategy with which the manager and the majority of the team are satisfied. Those who have been consulted will want to see their views reflected in the strategy, and will not necessarily be happy if their suggestions appear to have been ignored or altered. The project manager in this circumstance should spend time explaining the reasoning behind the decisions and, even if everyone is not happy, be prepared to move forward with authority, confident that the overall decisions have been correct. The strategy at this stage helps to indicate the type and number of people likely to be needed for the remainder of the project. The strategy also assists in determining how larger projects can best be split down into work packages by work breakdown structure (WBS), as discussed in Chapters 15 and 16.

Table 3.1 Outline strategy for successful similar project

Task	Strategy	Reason
Preliminary design (FEEP)	Internal	Internal resource knows existing plant and can develop interfaces. Location.
Detail design	External contractor X	Insufficient internal resource and skills. X has been cost-efficient and met programme in the past.
Procurement	External contractor X	Can order long delivery items as soon as they have completed design.
Construction	External contractor Y (reporting to X)	No internal resource. X does not have resource. Y has worked for X before with good results. X happy to manage Y.
Commissioning	Internal	Internal resource knows existing plant, and interface with new equipment.
Project control	External contractor X for design, procurement and construction	X will manage costs and programme for areas it can influence.
	Internal for remaining preliminary design and commissioning	Internal will manage costs and programme for areas of responsibility.

The WBS is useful because it breaks larger, complex projects down into smaller 'sub-projects', or work packages. These work packages are more manageable, because they are smaller and simpler. The packages can be treated as projects in themselves with, for example, their own estimate, programme and execution strategy, and always with a 'sub-project manager' responsible for delivering that package. The WBS can be represented pictorially, so that interactions can be seen between each package, and hence how any problems in one package can influence others, and in turn, affect the whole project.

It is useful to issue a document, often called a project execution plan or project implementation plan (PEP or PIP), outlining the preliminary project execution strategy to all those interested, so that they can consider and comment upon whether its recommendations will ensure that the project meets the objectives. As with the project proposal, it is important not just to state what conclusions have been reached, but *why*.

Producing a detailed project execution strategy

As explained earlier, the project execution strategy develops and is enhanced as more information becomes available. Whatever the situation, the original preliminary project execution strategy should be reviewed as the project progresses, detail added as appropriate and also modified if necessary.

The technical data develops concurrently with the management aspects; outline process data become detailed flowsheets and then piping and instrument diagrams, simple equipment data sheets become more detailed, functional design progresses, and so on. It may be that the engineering of the project begins to look more complicated than originally envisaged. Other information may also become available — for example, there may be other projects within the company, and therefore resources you had hoped to use on your project may now be allocated elsewhere. Hence external resources may need to be obtained. Developments such as these could lead to major changes to the original strategy, but it is better to take these into account at this stage, than have to make changes to the strategy later in the project.

The detailed project execution plan is reissued as before if there are major changes, but with luck there will be only a small number of changes. The aim is to have the detailed project execution plan firm, fixed and issued by the time the project is approved by the client to proceed through to execution. Any changes after this stage could adversely affect costs, time-scales and/or quality.

Check-lists 3.1–3.5 on pages 32–34 present items to consider when preparing a project execution strategy.

Check-list 3.1   Items for consideration for inclusion in project execution plan
(not all topics are relevant or necessary for every project)

Summary of project (for the benefit of those new to the project)
- Brief scope of project
- Cost, time and quality targets/constraints
- Overall roles and responsibilities

Design strategy	(see also Chapter 6)

- See Check-list 3.2

Procurement strategy	(see also Chapter 7)

- See Check-list 3.3

Construction strategy	(see also Chapter 8)

- See Check-list 3.4

Commissioning strategy	(see also Chapter 9)

- See Check-list 3.5

Project control strategy
- Project control requirements   (see also Chapter 17)
- Project estimate strategy   (see also Chapter 16)

What type of estimates are required through the life of the project

When the estimate(s) are to be prepared

Accuracy of each estimate

Who will produce estimate(s)

Any assumptions made in estimate(s)

Any exclusions
- Change control strategy   (see also Chapter 17)

How changes are to be managed

At what point in the project the change system is implemented

Who can authorize changes
- Project documentation and administration strategy

How documents are to be managed   (see also Chapter 19)

Summary contract strategy	(see also Chapter 18)

- Summary of contracts relating to design strategy, procurement strategy,
construction strategy and commissioning strategy

Check-list 3.2   Items for consideration for inclusion in design strategy
(not all topics are relevant or necessary for every project)

Front end engineering package
- Input from operating company
- Input from operating site/plant
- Input from research and development departments
- Input from civil, mechanical, control and electrical engineering departments
- Involvement of external contractors of consultants
- Design approval requirements

Detail design
- Input from operating company
- Input from civil, mechanical, control and electrical engineering departments
- Involvement of external contractors or consultants
- Design approval requirements

Check-list 3.3   Items for consideration for inclusion in procurement strategy
(not all topics are relevant or necessary for every project)

- Production of procurement plan
- Procedure for selecting contractors and vendors
- Who will do procurement (internal and/or external)
- Spares requirements
- The need, and system for progressing for all/some/none of the items
- System for receiving goods
- Any special contracts required (eg, secrecy agreements)
- Any special goods or skills required (eg, long delivery items, preferred suppliers)
- Any effect of overseas items (eg, customs, tax, transport, currency purchasing, exchange rates)   (see also Chapters 18 and 23)
- Any requirements for bank guarantees   (see also Chapter 23)
- Stage payment systems
- Any special delivery requirements, and possible effects (eg, ordering before project approved, and potential cancellation implications)

Check-list 3.4   Items for consideration for inclusion in construction strategy
(not all topics are relevant or necessary for every project)

- Who will do construction (internal and/or external)
- Site-based management and organization
- Production of preliminary Construction Health and Safety Plan, and appointment of responsibilities for CDM   (see also Chapter 11)
- Construction programme, and issues which may affect it (eg, weather, time of year, availability of resources, work regimes)
- Availability and skills of management and tradesmen
- Identification and availability of any necessary special skills
- Industrial relations and practices
- Any services, access and facilities required
- Policy on pre-assembled units (PAUs)
- Requirements for transportation, lifting, etc
- Definition of mechanical completion
- System for handover to commissioning, and any support during commissioning

Check-list 3.5   Items for consideration for inclusion in commissioning strategy
(not all topics are relevant or necessary for every project)

- Who will do commissioning (internal and/or external)
- Who will be responsible for training operating personnel
- Site-based management and organization
- Commissioning programme
- Availability and skills required
- Any special services or facilities required
- System for handover from construction, and any support to be provided

What organization is needed for the project?

The personnel involved in the project need to have the necessary skills and to be organized so that the project objectives can be achieved. This is very simple to state, but can be very difficult to attain! Skill in relationships with diverse people is essential for the successful project manager, and is outlined further in Chapter 21.

At this stage in the project, the technical content is usually becoming clearer, and hence the type of people who will be required — commonly 'functional' personnel and management support personnel. Functional personnel typically can be broken down into the following main categories:

- process/chemical engineering;
- civil and structural engineering;
- mechanical engineering;
- electrical engineering;
- control/instrumentation engineering;
- construction (including demolition);
- commissioning;

but other less obvious 'technical' personnel who may be expected to contribute or can influence the project should not be forgotten, for example:

- research chemists;
- safety engineering;
- hazard study leaders;
- plant/production engineering;
- maintenance engineering.

Likewise, there will also be the need for management support personnel, such as:

- project client;
- estimator;
- planner;
- project control personnel;
- purchasing/procurement personnel;
- secretarial and administration;

and again those who may not be so obvious initially, for example:

- legal advisers;
- planning permission/estates personnel;
- accountants.

Within a client organization, where money is made through selling products, the company structure is focused so as to develop, manufacture and market products. Large, well-resourced groups are usually established around research and development, production and marketing. Other functions such as engineering, personnel, legal and accounts are often viewed as supporting serv-ices, and will have the minimum numbers of people and skills needed to carry out their duties. Thus, the organization may not be sufficiently large or strong to provide complete project management activities.

This is in complete contrast to contracting companies, where the emphasis is placed on the delivery of projects. Contractors make their income from successful project management, and their companies are therefore organized to achieve this. They typically have separate groups for each of the main engi-neering functional areas, project managers and project control. The organiza-tion is supported by accounts, legal, personnel departments and so on. Figures 3.1 and 3.2 give typical examples of both types of organization.

The people and skills required vary so much from project to project that it is very difficult to give any definitive guidance as to what personnel are required for every project. Check-list 3.6 (page 38) gives possible organization require-ments. See also Chapter 19 for a review of choices in organization structure.

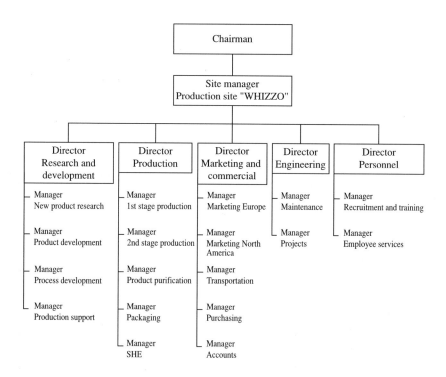

Figure 3.1 Typical organization of a production company

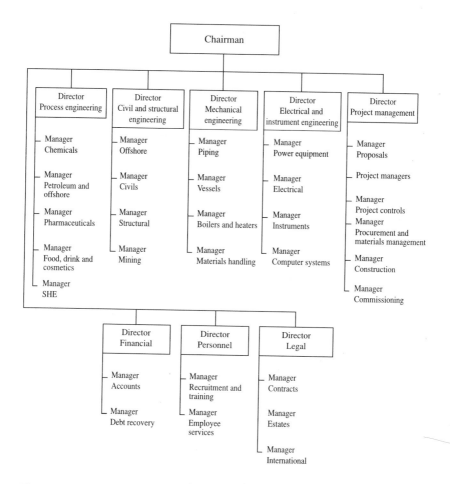

Figure 3.2 Typical organization of a contracting company

Finding the team

The personnel listed in the previous section usually respond to a line manager in a 'functional' structure. The line manager allocates their time and priorities to projects. The allocation of resources and priorities amongst all the project work and other possible demands has to be planned and reviewed regularly by senior management for resources to be available when required. The proposed project execution strategy is used as the basis for structuring the project team. To form the project team, the project manager consults with the line managers regarding the type of people which are required — that is, the skills which are necessary

37

Check-list 3.6   Personnel who may be required by a project
(not all personnel are relevant or necessary for every project)

Project management

Project Manager	Project Engineering
Project Client	
Project Control	Estimating Planning Control Contracts management
Procurement	Purchasing Progressing/expediting Inspection Payment Goods receipt/management
Support management	Steering group Administration and secretarial Accountancy Legal Marketing Estates

Technical

Process engineering	Research and development Process engineering SHE
Civil and structural engineering	Civil/structural Building
Mechanical engineering	Pipework Machines Vessels Materials
Electrical engineering	Low voltage High voltage
Control engineering	Measurement Instrumentation
Construction	Site management Site contractors
Commissioning	Commissioning Operations and maintenance

(for example, engineer rather than draughtsman, or experience in a specific field). Possible numbers of people, start dates, finish dates and percentage of time required are considered. In discussing the project, the line manager is able to get a better understanding of the technical content of the project and so on, and hence the people or groups who are likely to meet the requirements. When individuals do join the project team either full-time or part-time, the project manager then becomes the 'task manager' of that individual, responsible for outlining work requirements.

Where the project execution strategy is to use external contractors, design companies or consultants, the project manager needs to discuss personnel requirements with the contracts manager. Commonly, the contracts manager agrees to be responsible for providing a total service, rather than individuals and/or skills. It is then the contracts manager's responsibility to obtain individuals of suitable calibre at the appropriate time.

Unfortunately, whatever the company, it is exceedingly rare that the right number of people, with the right skills, are available just at the right time. This is where the project manager's powers of persuasion should be used! Most project managers find that they have to make the best of some of the personnel on their team. Weaknesses of groups or individuals should always be considered when preparing estimates, programmes and so on, and allowances made as necessary. An alternative is to obtain the missing skills from an external source, either hiring individuals (which can be time-consuming) or by seeking an overall service, as outlined previously. If such alterations are necessary, then the project execution strategy is revised accordingly.

For very simple, small projects, the project manager may take on all roles, consulting others for advice only, but projects such as these are few and far between. So for the vast majority of small projects, other resources are necessary. Sadly, securing appropriate resources can be especially difficult for inexperienced project managers, junior project managers or those who are managing smaller projects. In some organizations, small projects are viewed as being less important than large projects. Thus, inexperienced or lower calibre individuals are often allocated to smaller projects. Also, if particular individuals are split between projects, they will have favourites, which will get more of their time and attention than others (typically the larger, more exciting projects). Overcoming these problems is again down to the project manager's powers of persuasion, but senior management should be alerted to severe problems which threaten safety, quality or delivery of the project. Estimates, programmes and so on should reflect the honest, not optimistic, strength of the project team.

Roles and responsibilities

Once agreement has been reached between the project managers, line managers, contractor managers and so on regarding the personnel who will be allocated to the project, it is useful to issue a one-page summary 'Who's Who'. This gives brief personal details, such as name, job title, location and telephone number. This simple document can save many hours of searching through project meeting minutes and telephone directories in order to contact someone. Table 3.2 is a typical example of a 'Who's Who' for the project to reduce particle emission to atmosphere.

In obtaining the appropriate resources, the project manager should not just assume that individuals or groups know what is expected of them in a particular project. It is advantageous if the project manager outlines what is required of an individual, so that they and others know what has previously been agreed with

Table 3.2   'Who's Who' for the project to reduce particle emission to atmosphere

Title	Name	Location	Telephone extension
Client company ABC			(Tel: 01234 56(ext))
Project Manager	Andy Anderson	Room 3, office block	1234
Process Engineer	Beverley Brown	Development lab	3357
Civil Engineer	Colin Crowther	Room 6, office block	1357
Mechanical Engineer	Diane Davies	Room 7, office block	1895
Control Engineer	Eddie Edmunds	Room 8, office block	1758
Electrical Engineer	Fiona Fisher	Room 9, office block	1467
Commissioning Engineer	Graham Griffiths	Room 2, site office	5786
Project Control	Harold Harvey	Room 4, office block	1364
Production Engineer	Josh Johnson	Room 8, plant office	6234
Project Client	Karen Kennedy	Room 100, office block	2467
Contractor company X		(Tel: 0171 123(ext) or 0161 987(ext))	
Contracts Manager	Lawrence Lee	London office	9745
Design Manager	Mark Martin	Manchester office	6745
Procurement Manager	Neil Newman	Manchester office	6753
Project Control	Paula Peters	Manchester office	6712
Contractor company Y		(Tel: 0171 567(ext) or 01234 56(ext))	
Contracts Manager	Bob Roberts	London office	2345
Construction Manager	Sam Singh	Site office	9087

the line manager — for example, expected start and finish dates, percentage of time allocated to the project. Consideration should also be given to additional responsibilities that may be necessary to fulfil legislative or contractual roles — for example, 'client', 'designer', 'planning supervisor' and 'principal contractor' under the Construction (Design and Management) Regulations 1994 (CDM), or 'engineer to the contract' under certain contract conditions (see Chapters 11 and 18). It is also useful to explain in a little detail exact responsibilities and the reporting structure, and then to issue a summary document to individuals and their line managers, so that there are no subsequent queries on expectations by either party. How organizations can vary to suit the number, mix and priorities of different projects are reviewed briefly in Chapter 19.

ENSURE EVERYONE UNDERSTANDS THEIR
ROLES AND RESPONSIBILITIES.

An example follows of the type of organization which may exist on a large project. Examples of organization, outline roles and responsibilities, and a resource requirement table (Table 3.3, page 42) are given for the project to reduce particle emission to atmosphere.

Emission reduction project – project responsibilities

Project Manager

Accountable to the Project Client for leading the multi-functional Project Team in the execution of the Company ABC section of the project, to the overall agreed cost and programme. This includes the front end engineering package (FEEP), an estimate for Client approval for the project and commissioning to meet the company needs. The Project Manager must maintain an overview of the total project, including the Company X scope of work, and where necessary, take a positive stance with Company X. The Project Manager must also ensure that communication and co-ordination is maintained between companies ABC and X, the functional groups and individuals. The Project Manager shall act as the Planning Supervisor with regards to the CDM Regulations.

Table 3.3 Resource requirements for the project to reduce particle emission to atmosphere

Title	Expected start date	Expected finish date	Anticipated % time on project
Project Manager	January Year 1	February Year 2	100%
Process Engineer	January Year 1	June Year 1*	30%
Civil Engineer	April Year 1	June Year 1*	20%
Mechanical Engineer	April Year 1	June Year 1*	25%
Control Engineer	March Year 1	June Year 1*	50%
Electrical Engineer	March Year 1	June Year 1*	25%
Commissioning Engineer	December Year 1	February Year 2	80%
Project Control	January Year 1	February Year 2	10%
Production Engineer	January Year 1	June Year 1*	10%
Project Client	January Year 1	February Year 2	<5%

Note: Those marked * will be expected to provide technical support to external contractors from July Year 1 to January Year 2 via regular joint technical meetings

Process Engineer

To provide Process Engineering development, design and input to the ABC scope of supply. Additionally, the Process Engineer is to work closely with X Process Engineers to ensure that the optimum design is supplied by them. The Process Engineer shall be considered to be a 'Designer' with reference to the CDM Regulations.

Civil Engineer

Accountable to the Project Manager for leading the Civil resources, in achieving the agreed Civil costs and programme to produce the FEEP. Additionally, the Civil Engineer must also liaise closely with X on joint Civil issues, and is responsible for providing them with timely information. The Civil Engineer shall be considered to be a 'Designer' with reference to the CDM Regulations.

Control Engineer

The Control Engineer is accountable to the Project Manager for leading all Control resources which are required within the ABC scope of work, to achieve agreed Control costs and programme to produce the FEEP. The Control Engineer is also to provide and manage Control Engineering support for Commissioning where necessary. Additionally, the Control Engineer must liaise closely with X on Control Engineering issues and is responsible for providing them with timely information. The Control Engineer shall be considered to be a 'Designer' with reference to the CDM Regulations.

Project Client

Responsible for the ownership of the project within ABC. A requirement is that the Project Client acts as the prime contact between all internal interested parties on all project matters relating to scope, direction, costs and programme. It is essential that feedback and true representation is made from operational groups. The Project Client shall be considered to be the 'Client' with reference to the CDM Regulations.

Production Engineer

Accountable to the Project Manager and Client for representing production and the plants affected by the project. In particular, to ensure that the relevant department or plant needs and interests are included in the design process, in terms of safety, health and environment (SHE), site policies, infrastructure, operational and engineering standards.

Further reading

Association for Project Management, 1998, *Contract Strategy for Successful Project Management — A Guide for Project Managers on Best Practice for the Procurement of Goods and Services* (APM Group).

Stallworthy, E. and Kharbanda, O.P., 1986, *A Guide to Project Implementation* (Institution of Chemical Engineers) (out of print).

Project example

Good! You have clarified that the objectives of the project are to manufacture WHIZZO, but at minimum capital expenditure, even if this means extending the project duration. It is envisaged by senior management that the project will be complete within six months. You have also been given the technical specification for the product. Production will be a batch process.

Due to the small size of the project, there will not be a steering group, but your immediate line manager will direct you if you have any higher level queries on the project, thus acting as 'project owner'. You have been told that you are expected to spend a maximum of 20% of your time on the project — that is, roughly one day a week — the rest of your time being spent on your technical operations role. Limited funding is available for the early investigative work, but already you are concerned that it may not be sufficient to allow you to complete all necessary preliminary work.

You have also been told that internal people will be available to assist you with early work, but there are not the resources available to carry out process development nor detail design. Your company has a 'preferred contractor' relationship with three companies, who can supply detail design, procurement and construction. You also have an internal construction supervisor who will assist in co-ordination activities during construction.

What should you do next?

Here is a list of suggested actions. Note that this is a guide. It is not exhaustive. It is an indication of what may be relevant to a project.

Project proposal

If you haven't already done so, now is the time to issue a WHIZZO 'project proposal document' or similar to interested parties, summarizing what you believe to be the important technical and managerial issues. Remember to ask for comments to be returned by a specific date — this helps to prevent important items being raised too late.

Project strategy

As the project manager, you should already be thinking of and shaping the future of the WHIZZO project — that is, how will you manage it? Time spent on this activity is time well spent!

Seek advice from those more experienced around you — ask as many as possible.

- Who can assist you with the strategy?
- Is there a standard execution method within the company?
- How have they managed similar projects in the past?
- Were they successful? Why?
- Would they do it the same way again? Why?
- Which individuals, departments or companies would they recommend, and why?
- Which individuals, departments or companies would they not recommend, and why?

What are your greatest areas of uncertainty, either technical or managerial? For example:

- Do you feel that the six months time-scale is realistic?
- Do you feel that 20% of your time is sufficient to manage the project properly, and continue with your other duties?
- Why do you have concerns about funding for early stages?
- What is the best programme for allocating the time available for design, procurement, construction, testing and commissioning?
- Do you have to use one of the three partnership contractors, or is the choice yours?
- Are you confident in their ability, resources, knowledge and motivation?
- If so, is the contractor to carry out all detail design, procurement and construction, or can you choose just certain functions — for example, design and construction?
- Are there long delivery items or materials which need to be ordered before appointing the contractor?
- Will the chosen contractor be free to select his suppliers?
- When can the construction team take over the existing equipment and the construction area?
- Who is to decide what vendors' equipment is fit for purpose? Yourself or the contractor?

Identify the biggest issues and concentrate on resolving those problems as soon as possible, especially where others' expectations may be too optimistic.

Are there standard formats within the company for producing estimates, plans, design drawings, managing changes, inducting contractors and so on? If so, find out about them and be trained in them if necessary. If not, copy any good existing systems.

Who needs to be consulted and who should be briefed on the proposed WHIZZO project execution strategy?

Issue a preliminary project execution strategy document to relevant personnel, and ask for their comments, to be incorporated, as appropriate, into any future improved strategy.

Project organization

As the project manager, as part of thinking of and shaping the future of the WHIZZO project, you should consider who you need to assist you — that is, who to do what and when?

What technical assistance do you need — for example, process design, detail design, commissioning? What services and management assistance do you need — for example, estimating, planning, project control, procurement?

Seek advice from those more experienced around you — ask as many as possible.

- Is there a standard project organization within the company?
- What organization have they used for similar projects in the past?
- Were they successful? Why?
- Would they do it the same way again? Why?
- Which individuals, departments or companies would they recommend, and why?
- Which individuals, departments or companies would they not recommend, and why?

Discuss your requirements with managers of relevant departments.

- Can they provide you with the people with the skills you need, when you need them?
- If not, who do they recommend?

What are your greatest areas of concern, either technical or managerial? For example:

- Who will develop the process design? Are you expected to do it, and if so, do you have sufficient skills and time? Is it possible and appropriate to hire in process engineering specifically for this project? Who would manage this resource — another process engineer or you as project manager? Does the project have sufficient funding in the early stages to do this?
- Who will carry out the detail design?
- Who will be responsible for assessing and decommissioning existing equipment?

46

- Who will be responsible for compiling the safety file (CDM)?
- Who will chase and check suppliers' work?

Identify the biggest issues and concentrate on resolving those problems as soon as possible.

Once people have been nominated, discuss the project, its objectives, your requirements, the strategy, their role and so on with those individuals as soon as possible. This will assist in getting their commitment to the success of the WHIZZO project.

Who needs to know the proposed organization?

Issue a preliminary organization document to relevant personnel, and ask for their comments, to be incorporated, as appropriate, into any future document.

Process specification

Gillian Lawson

What technical information is required?

The development and production of technical information continues throughout the project, to transform the first glimmer of an idea into a constructed and operating plant. The development should provide a good basis for risk analysis in more detail and more accurate cost estimates and programmes. So that the project runs efficiently, technical development runs in parallel to management aspects of the project described in Chapter 3.

The type of technical information required obviously varies considerably from project to project. For example, the type of technical data required for a major civil engineering project — such as construction of a major bridge — is quite different to that required for the installation of a new corporate financial computing system. Likewise, the name given to the data development is quite different from industry to industry, and company to company. Thus, it is typically known as 'process specification' in the process industry, and 'requirement specification' in the IT industry. However, the important feature is that the process is generally the same. There is usually limited knowledge of the current situation, and what information *is* available is often incorrect. But what should be clear is what is required at the end of the project. The project team must then gather correct data from whatever sources necessary, to enable them to add detail and depth to their understanding of the project and so meet its objectives. It is rather like collecting pieces of jigsaw puzzle from various locations without the original picture, and fitting them together until it becomes clearer what the final picture should be.

If, at this stage, there is more than one option still left from the project initiation phase, then they all need to be examined and developed technically, until it is clear that there is one preferred way forward. (Frequently, technical development quickly eliminates options as problems are discovered which were not previously anticipated.)

For example, in the case of a major pipebridge project across a river, the sort of items that the team may need to consider are:

- types, sizes, weights of pipes, operational forces, construction loads, and possible future additions;
- does there need to be access for personnel?
- support soil and groundwater conditions;
- river flow and variations throughout the year. Are there tidal implications?
- possible river crossing positions;
- wind loading;
- availability locally of construction materials;
- is the bridge to be minimum cost, or is it to be a show piece with maximum aesthetic value?
- what river traffic or services, if any, need to pass under the bridge?
- what are the space and other constraints on site?
- how will the bridge be maintained?

By developing these thoughts, the project team starts to get a better understanding of the final design of the bridge. As mentioned earlier, developing and testing the design often highlights problems which were not originally foreseen. For example, computer modelling of possible designs shows that certain types of support columns in the river affect water flow, giving unwanted silting down-river.

It is important that this initial understanding and design is correct, and that the options are reduced to one, as the output from this stage will be used as the basis for all further design work, procurement and construction. These later phases incur much more manpower and expense; hence any errors, omissions or additional options which are carried forward from the process specification can be expensive and time-consuming to remedy in the later stages. The development of project options and technical information throughout the life of the project is illustrated in Figure 4.1.

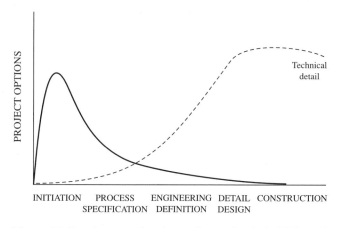

Figure 4.1 Development of project options and technical information

Specification in the process industries

If you are managing your own small projects, then you may have to develop the process specification yourself, perhaps with a more senior or experienced chemical engineer just checking your assumptions and calculations. If you are working as part of a larger project team, then commonly there will be a chemical engineer assigned to your project who may carry out a lot of this work. (These roles and requirements should already have been discussed and agreed as part of the project strategy and organization, and thus there should be no delays in obtaining the necessary personnel.)

An outline process route or routes are usually known from the project proposal, and these can be noted down as simple block diagrams or process flowsheets, clearly indicating main plant items. Taking the earlier example of reducing particles to atmosphere, it could be that two options remain:

(a) Change process dryer so that particles are not generated.

(b) Install cyclones and filters to remove dust.

These can be presented simply as block diagrams as in Figure 4.2, which would be understandable to all those involved in the project.

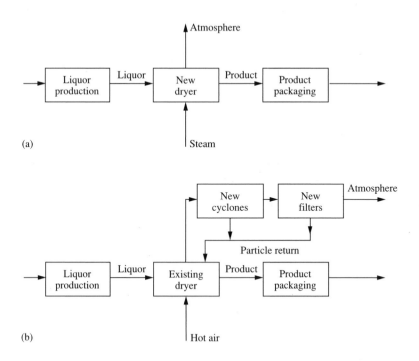

Figure 4.2 Options for reducing particles to atmosphere:
(a) change process dryer; (b) install cyclones and filters.

Simple block diagrams can then be developed into working process flow-sheets, including flow rates, temperatures, pressures and so on, along with a heat and mass balance. Write a process description, outlining in words what is envisaged will happen through the new or modified plant, as this is sometimes more easily understood than the process flowsheet by non-chemical engineers. Preliminary process data sheets can also be completed, briefly specifying each significant piece of equipment (often referred to as a main plant item or MPI), indicating approximate size, materials of construction, access for installation, process conditions and so on. Assistance and advice may be required from a variety of experts — for instance, chemists, safety experts, mechanical engineers, control engineers, materials specialists, operating staff, equipment suppliers — depending upon the innovation and complexity in the project. In some instances, pilot plant trials or tests on existing equipment may be required to assist in developing process routes and conditions.

Safety, health and environmental (SHE) considerations are an integral part of this phase. If left later, SHE needs will cost more, and could delay project approval by statutory authorities. Consider relief requirements, fire protection,

Carry out hazard reviews at this stage to prevent additional SHE costs later.

personnel health protection, environmental impact of the project and so on. This is done via formal studies or reviews which examine potential problems systematically (see Chapter 13) and elsewhere by adopting 'best practice' in design development.

Options should be reduced to one as soon as is reasonably practicable, either for cost, programme or technical reasons, thus leaving personnel involved to concentrate their effort on the favoured solution. Once this is achieved, there may then be the opportunity to optimize the preferred option, such as trying to minimize project implementation cost, minimizing operating plant utility costs, maximizing reaction conversions and so on. This should not become a lengthy task (unless with the client's agreement), otherwise excessive time can be spent in producing the ultimate design rather than one which adequately meets the project objectives.

What may incorrectly be thought of as peripherals should also be considered. For example, what raw materials are required, and to what specification? What utilities are necessary — for example, water, air, purge gas, steam, electricity — and where will the supply source be? Utilities are sometimes forgotten, and this can be very costly and time-consuming if subsequently they are not available from existing supplies, and additional sources have to be provided by the project. Highlight what is included in the project, but especially *what is not*. The break point (sometimes referred to as 'battery limits') between new as supplied by the project and existing should be indicated where appropriate on flowsheets, data sheets and the like.

How the plant will operate should be confirmed — for example, manually, computer-controlled — as this can affect the design and cost significantly. For example, if a vessel is to be pH-controlled by an inline pH meter and adjusted automatically by adding a caustic material, it will need a completely different design than if it were controlled by an operator taking a manual sample from a tap, testing remotely, and then manually adding a caustic material.

In the earlier example of particle reduction, the items needing special attention for development could be:

(a) Change process dryer so that particles are not generated:
- can existing dryer be modified to prevent particle formation?
- can existing dryer supplier provide any guidance, or have experience of the problem?
- pilot plant trials on alternative types of dryers;
- any change to operating costs if alternative dryer utilized?
- are special materials of construction necessary?
- are additional utilities needed for new dryer, and are they available?

(b) Install cyclones and filters to remove dust:

● pilot trials on cyclones and/or filters. Are both necessary?

● confirmation that retained particles can be and are suitable for, returning into process;

● what is to be done with particles if they cannot be returned?

● are special materials of construction necessary?

● are additional utilities needed, and are they available?

It could be possible that both options would give the necessary technical results, but that other factors would lead to one preferred solution.

There can be physical restrictions — for example, it may not be possible to install a new type of dryer in a suitable location, and keep the existing one operational. This would lead to lost production in bringing a new dryer on line, which may be prohibitive.

It could be that utilities are restricted; a new dryer may require additional electricity which could not be supplied with the existing plant power infrastructure. Improving the power supply may then be too costly.

New technology may be advantageous, but can also carry a degree of risk. A new design of dryer may have been proven in pilot plant trials, but senior management may not want to risk it in production.

Issues such as these should be raised by the project team, who also need to have all technical supporting information, but ultimately these types of decisions are the responsibility of the project client.

TRY TO CLARIFY ANY TECHNICAL ISSUES.

As the process specification progresses, it is possible to add detail and hone the process design, so that what were preliminary data sheets, flowsheets, descriptions and so on, become final. The developed flowsheets can then be used as the foundation for producing the piping and instrumentation diagram (P&ID) which incorporates much more of the basic engineering information, such as pipework size and type, indication of valve requirements, control instrumentation and so on. Within the process specification, and every other phase of the project, though, success is dependent upon the right people having the right information at the right time. Refer to Check-list 4.1 for items to be considered when producing a process specification.

The project manager's role at this stage is to act as a driver, co-ordinator, monitor and facilitator, rather than to get involved in the detail of the design development (unless also acting as a technical contributor). The project manager is there to plan ahead to try to ensure that design development, resources availability and costs are progressing to plan, and to take action when they are not. This can be done via discussions with individuals or by more formal progress meetings. The project manager needs to retain an overview of the project, and check that communication and transfer of information between

---

Check-list 4.1   Items for consideration for inclusion in process specification (not all topics are relevant or necessary for every project)

- Process description
- Process data sheets
- Process flowsheets
- Physical property data sheets:
— process materials
— products
— utilities
- Raw materials, process materials and utilities specifications, and supply sources
- Main plant equipment list
- Confirmation of battery limits
- Process and energy interactions with existing plants
- Heat and mass balances
- Protective and relief systems
- Method of operation (manual or automatic)
- P&IDs
- Environmental statements
- Health statements
- Outstanding development requirements or possible issues

---

groups and individuals is happening as it should. The project manager also acts as a focus between the client and the team, highlighting to the client any problems that are being experienced in the project, and taking the lead in seeking answers and guidance as necessary. The project manager feeds this direction back to the team, to enable it to follow the most appropriate course of action.

The client, at this point, is often more interested in anticipated project cost and programme than technical issues, and the project manager also needs to satisfy this demand. Typically, by the time a process specification is complete, the information is sufficient to be able to produce a cost estimate of ±15% to ±25% accuracy for larger projects (less accurate for smaller projects) and to produce a programme of similar accuracy (see Chapter 16). Even at this stage, the client may choose to cancel the project based on estimated costs, projected programme or technical issues.

Drawing all of the information together for the process specification can be a significant amount of work, and hence time and personnel requirements for the work should not be underestimated. Remember that an additional week of development at this stage can save considerable work and cost in later phases of the project. The process specification is issued to those who would be interested in, or need to know, its contents, and it is essential that it contains complete and correct data, as it will be used extensively as the basis for the next phase, engineering definition.

Further reading

Association for Project Management, 1998, *Standard Terms for the Appointment of a Project Manager.*

Institution of Electrical Engineers, *Guidelines on Specification for Computer Control Projects.*

Rase, H.F. and Barrow, M.H., *Project Engineering of Process Plants* (John Wiley).

Project example

You have determined the following strategy for the project:
- Process development will be done internally by yourself, but calculations and so on will be checked by your line manager.
- Other 'front end' functional design will be done by other functional engineers in your company.
- Detail design, procurement and construction will be done by one of the three preferred contractors (which one has yet to be determined by you).

- You will carry out commissioning, assisted by other operating personnel.
- You will have part-time assistance from a clerk for administration.

You have general agreement from management on this strategy and organization.

Unfortunately, you do not believe that the project can be achieved in six months, but that nine months is more realistic.

What do you need to do in your roles as project manager and process engineer? Here are some suggested actions. Note that this is a guide. It is not exhaustive. It is an indication of what may be relevant to a project.

Project management

Try to separate your dual roles, so as to spend sufficient time and effort on each activity. You also need to clarify with your line manager whether you are still expected to spend a maximum of 20% of your time on the project, or whether it has been increased to cover your process development activities. If your time allocation has not increased, then you need to indicate to senior management how this would affect the project.

Why do you believe that the project time-scale is now nine months, a time increase of 50%? The reasons need to be identified. Is it that the original target of six months was an overly optimistic figure generated by senior management? Is it that it was achievable but that there have already been delays? Have there been delays generated by you, now that you are also responsible for process development? Is it that an unforeseen technical problem has now arisen — for example, existing equipment is unsuitable for duty, hence new equipment must be procured, on longer delivery? Is it that others in the internal team will not be able to meet the agreed programme due to higher priority work?

What are you going to do about it? You need to inform your line manager as 'project owner' as soon as possible. Discuss the reasons. You were told earlier that the objective of the project was to manufacture WHIZZO, but at minimum capital expenditure, even if this means extending the project duration. Is this still the case, and hence does the delay matter? Agree what needs to be done. For example, if the delay is due to your dual roles, do you need more time on the project, to work overtime or to hire a process engineer? Do you increase the number of personnel in later stages to reduce the design and construction period? If it is due to perceived higher priority work elsewhere in the organization, then priorities need to be clarified by senior management; your line manager should be able to assist in this process.

You also need to start discussing and progressing the project with others who will be involved at this stage and in the future — for example, on functional design. You should ensure that they understand what is expected of them, and when — for example, design packages, programmes, estimates, input to safety reviews.

It is also worth considering what meetings you may need to hold, such as design development or progress reviews, and arrange them with the relevant people well in advance, as it is often difficult to arrange *ad hoc* meetings at short notice.

Process development

As process engineer, you need to set aside adequate time to develop the process design. Check-list 4.1 on page 54 lists the information required on a typical project.

In this instance, as the project will utilize some existing equipment, and the new process may interact with other existing services and processes, particular attention should be paid to these areas to ensure that they are all suitable for their new use. And remember to get those calculations checked by your line manager!

Thus, as process engineer, you may be expected to:

• Produce a process description which outlines the new WHIZZO manufacturing process.

• Produce process data sheets which indicate process conditions for manufacturing WHIZZO. For example, it may be determined that to achieve the optimum rate at which Z dissolves in Y, it is useful to heat the mixture to 40°C. This could be achieved by inserting a steam heating coil in vessel B. However, to then control the reaction, once transferred into A and mixed with X, it may be necessary for A to be fitted with a cooling water coil, to maintain the temperature at 10°C.

• Create new process flowsheets to show the WHIZZO manufacturing process, and modify those existing ones for services, raw materials and so on which would be affected by the process, to show new uses and interactions. The exact 'cut points' of the project need to be indicated — that is, what is included in the project and what is not — and the flowsheets are often used as a way of indicating this.

You may also need to complete heat and mass balances and consider how they influence, and are themselves affected by, other adjacent processes.

• Complete physical property data sheets for all new process materials — that is, X, Y and Z — and for WHIZZO product. Any existing ones for utilities or services such as steam and cooling water are checked to confirm that they are appropriate for the new process.

57

- Confirm specifications for new raw materials — that is, X, Y and Z process materials — and utilities. The source of these should also be indicated. If they are not existing, there may be major cost in supplying the source.
- Draw up a list of process equipment required. This should clearly indicate what is new and what is existing and, if existing, what modifications are necessary.
- Determine the method of operation of the plant — is it manual, fully automatic or hybrid? If automatic, what type of control systems are to be used? Once this is determined, the flowsheets can be developed in order to produce P&IDs for the new process.
- Consider whether, if the process is to be computer-controlled, a study is needed to form the basis of writing and testing software.
- Consider SHE requirements. Taking safety, for example, how is the new plant to be protected from overpressurization, over-filling, high temperature and so on? Does further thought need to be given to environmental aspects of the new process, products and intermediates? Are there health aspects such as exposure limits which need to be defined? Also, are there any SHE reviews or studies, either formal or informal, which should be carried out at this time?
- Consider if there any process aspects which haven't yet been considered or need further development. If so, bring them to the attention of your line manager as they could affect the project programme, and you could need assistance with them.

Engineering definition

Gillian Lawson

5

Completion of the project 'front end'

Following the completion of the process specification, it should be clear what is the selected project option, and what are the outline technical requirements. Firm and more detailed technical information is then developed to enable a more accurate cost estimate (in the region of ±10%) to be produced, as it is usually at this stage that the client makes the final decision to proceed with, or to cancel, the project. The collation of this data is called many things, including engineering definition, engineering specification, and front end engineering package (FEEP).

The development of the project, both in a technical and a managerial sense, up to this point is referred to as the project 'front end'. It cannot be overemphasized how important the front end is to the success of the completed project. On the assumption that the project is approved by the client, the number of people involved in it, the information generated and the costs of any changes rise dramatically in the subsequent detail design, procurement, construction and commissioning phases. Thus the front end information must be correct (see Figure 5.1 on page 60).

Any errors or uncertainties which pass from the front end into these later phases are expensive and extremely time-consuming to remedy. *If the output from the front end — the engineering definition — is complete and accurate, then the project should be successful. If it is incomplete or contains errors, then the project will fail.*

Who helps to produce the engineering definition?

As further engineering detail and range needs to be added to the process specification, the project team tends to grow at this stage, bringing in additional functional personnel or outside services. Those that are already involved in the project are normally required for more of their time. Again, this should not be

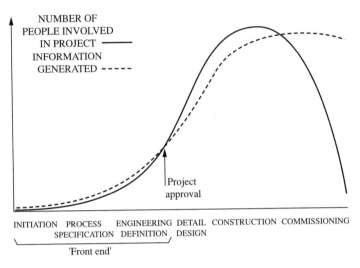

Figure 5.1 How the number of people involved in a project and the information generated increases after the 'front end' stages

unexpected by resource managers if the project organization has been developed and agreed earlier. On smaller projects where you may be the project manager and may have done many of the tasks so far yourself, you will find that you have to discuss many more items with, and have input from, others in the organization — for example, the electrical engineer, the civil engineer, the plant engineer. It is difficult to state here exactly who may make a contribution at this stage, but Check-list 3.6 on page 38 provides some ideas for consideration.

In the earlier example of particles emission from a dryer, it may be that the decision was taken to select installing cyclones followed by filters, rather than changing or modifying the existing dryer, based on technical and economical data. This equipment is to be installed on a new top floor, which will be an extension to an existing building. The installation work can be done while existing plant continues to operate. Final break-in for new plant will require brief shutdown of the existing dryer and associated equipment. Who may now be involved in producing the engineering definition? Table 5.1 lists the possibilities. Additionally, each of those marked * in the table will usually provide cost estimates and programmes for their own functions. Others listed may need only to estimate the cost of their own individual time to be charged to the project.

Table 5.1   The people involved in production of the engineering definition

Project manager	Co-ordinates project.
Client	Gives guidance and makes decisions. Approves changes.
Project estimator/planner	Collates functional estimates and programmes to produce overall project estimate and programme for sanction.
Safety engineer	Gives guidance on safety, health and environmental issues — eg, fire prevention and personnel escape routes. Leads formal studies or reviews.
Chemical/process engineer	Gives guidance on process conditions and specifies equipment performance.
*Civil/structural engineer	Develops structural supports for new plant. Designs building extension.
*Electrical engineer	Specifies new motors, and outlines power sources.
*Control engineer	Develops control systems for new equipment and interfaces with existing control systems.
*Mechanical engineer	Specifies new equipment and piping requirements.
Mechanical designer	Produces plant layouts and pipe routes. Updates P&ID.
Materials engineer	Specifies fabrication materials for new equipment.
*Production engineer	Inputs on plant layout, operating systems, standards. Arranges plant shutdowns and modifications to existing plant.
*Construction engineer	Gives guidance on how design can help construction. Advises on number and scope of contracts. Advises on industrial relations and safety, including CDM requirements.

Continued overleaf

Table 5.1 (cont'd) The people involved in production of the engineering definition

*Commissioning engineer	Gives guidance on how design can help commissioning and special requirements.
*Purchaser	Seeks estimates from potential equipment suppliers. Advises on number of vendor packages. Gives guidance on vendors' responsibilities during construction, testing and commissioning. Contacts design-and-build contractors who may wish to tender for design and installation.
Estates officer	Co-ordinates with local authorities on any building regulations, planning approval, etc which may be necessary.

What information is required for the engineering definition?

This varies from project to project, so the detail of the information to be produced by the individual as listed in the previous example may be completely different for another project, but the type of information required will be broadly the same. Guidance on the type of information contained in an engineering definition is given in Check-lists 5.1–5.10 (pages 62–68). Bear in mind that the lists are quite broad, and hence for smaller projects, only a few points typically will be applicable.

Check-list 5.1   Items for consideration for inclusion in project definition
(not all topics are relevant or necessary for every project)

- Project scope — see Check-list 5.2
- Project location — see Check-list 5.3, page 63
- SHE considerations — see Check-list 5.4, page 64 (see also Chapters 11 and 13)
- Process specification — see Check-list 4.1, page 54 (see also Chapter 4)
- Project engineering — see Check-list 5.5, page 64
- Civil and structural engineering — see Check-list 5.6, page 65
- Mechanical engineering — see Check-list 5.7, page 66
- Control/electrical engineering — see Check-list 5.8, page 67
- Construction — see Check-list 5.9, page 68 (see also Chapter 8)
- Commissioning — see Check-list 5.10, page 68 (see also Chapter 9)

Check-list 5.2   Items for consideration for inclusion in project scope
(not all topics are relevant or necessary for every project)

- Plant capacity and operating patterns — eg, batch, semi-batch, campaign
- Plant availability
- Product quantities, specifications, grades, storage and packing
- Raw materials quantities, specifications, handling and storage
- Building requirements and aesthetics
- Building services requirements
- Plant buildings which may be required — eg, control rooms, switch-houses, laboratories, personnel facilities
- Process plant operation principles and personnel requirements
- Maintenance policy, and what level of spares (if any) to be provided by project
- Plant control policy, including trip and alarm requirements
- Effluent quantities and treatment policy
- Containment principles
- Type, quantity and reliability of utilities
- Planned plant and building life
- Any allowance for future expansion or debottlenecking
- Demolition or clearances of existing plant or equipment required
- Any specific exclusions
- Project programme

Check-list 5.3   Items for consideration for inclusion in project location
(not all topics are relevant or necessary for every project)

- Confirmation of project location
- National and local legislation which will apply to the project, and existing statutory approvals which have already been obtained
- Agreed site and plant layout
- Use of any existing assets
- Services available on-site and off-site
- Site access and security
- Import/export of services and goods

Check-list 5.4   SHE items for consideration
(not all topics are relevant or necessary for every project)

- Confirmation of completion of any formal SHE reviews, including any outstanding actions
- Any SHE reviews yet to be carried out
- Any special requirements — eg, COSHH, CIMAH
- Fire — prevention, detection systems, fire-fighting equipment
- Noise and smell policy
- Any recommendations or special requirements for construction
- Security during construction, and for completed plant
- CDM aspects
- Any special personnel protection requirements
- Health requirements

Check-list 5.5   Additional project engineering items for consideration
(not all topics are relevant or necessary for every project)

- Approved P&IDs
- Agreed layouts for plant and equipment
- List of all main plant items (MPIs), including fabrication materials
- Utilization of any packaged units
- Quotations for MPIs
- Utilization of any pre-assembled units (PAUs)
- Quotations for other equipment
- Any equipment requiring specialist testing
- Any requirements for materials or equipment traceability
- How materials and equipment are to be managed once delivered to site
- Agreed routes for process and utility mains, and any additional pipebridges or supports required
- Any demolition or clearance of existing site and equipment
- Any existing equipment to be reused — condition, modifications or repair required (including who will do it), completeness of supporting documentation
- Any preparation work to be done by plant personnel

Check-list 5.6 Civil/structural engineering items for consideration
(not all topics are relevant or necessary for every project)

- List of standards and specifications to be used (national and company)
- Results of any surveys
- Results of any soil sample investigations
- Confirmation of any existing buried services
- Requirements for new buried services
- Data sheets/requirements for buildings
- Any special buildings or areas — eg, sterile, clean
- Materials of construction — eg, structures, buildings, building finishes, building contents, claddings, fire protection, special finishes, painting
- Loadings for buildings/structures
- Elevations and floor plans for structures and buildings, including any structural analysis
- Any services for buildings — eg, power, heating, drinking water, domestic effluent, HVAC
- Drainage principles, sizes, layouts
- Foundation principles and preliminary specification, including any piling requirements
- Location finishes — eg, pavements, roads, ground, fencing, barriers, landscaping
- Parking (tanker, lorry, car, bicycle) and loading/unloading requirements
- Any rail or shipping requirements
- Additional tasks for construction — eg, temporary removal of existing barriers, temporary roads, acceptable ground loading for cranes

---

Check-list 5.7   Mechanical engineering items for consideration
(not all topics are relevant or necessary for every project)

General
- List of standards and specifications to be used (national and company)

Piping engineering
- Pipe identification list, including to and from locations
- Preliminary piping layouts
- Approved 'break-ins' list
- Flexibility studies required, and method to be used
- Specification of in-line equipment — eg, valves, relief devices, fittings
- Testing requirements
- Lagging schedule
- Any requirements for piping model (3D or plastic)

Vessels engineering
- Approved data sheets for all vessels
- Quotations for all vessels
- Any special vessel requirements

Machines engineering
- Approved data sheets for all machines
- Quotations for all machines
- Any special machines requirements

Check-list 5.8   Control/electrical engineering items for consideration
(not all topics are relevant or necessary for every project)

General

- List of standards and specifications to be used (national and company)

Control

- Control line diagrams (if not already included in P&IDs)
- Approved instrument loop list
- Materials of construction of in-line equipment
- Level of automation
- Any radioactive instruments (may require notification/approval from authorities)
- Control sequence for PLC controlled units
- Control of start-up and shutdown
- Displays and interfaces with operators
- Requirements for data logging, batch records, etc
- System consideration — centralized or distributed, possibility of future expansion
- Quantity, quality and reliability of services to instrumentation — eg, air, power
- Trip and alarm requirements, and test methods/frequency
- Failure modes
- Standby/duplicate facilities
- Response times required
- Any computer requirements
- Environment in which equipment will be installed
- Any analysis equipment, in-line and off-line (including laboratory)

Electrical

- Single line diagrams
- Data sheets for special electrical equipment — eg, transformers, motors
- Area classification
- Earthing requirements for lighting, static and power
- Drive list and loads
- Any requirements for uninterrupted power supplies (UPS)
- Any requirements for voltage dip or peak protection
- Cable layouts
- Electrical distribution and generation
- Trace heating requirements
- Communication system including telecoms

Check-list 5.9   Construction items for consideration
(not all topics are relevant or necessary for every project)

- Construction principles
- Use of package units and PAUs
- Transportation and berthing studies for large or delicate items
- Installation sequence
- Any special arrangements for contractors — eg, hours of work, agreed industry payments
- Any provision of contractor's compound, and any services to be provided to compound
- Any likely conditions which may affect construction — eg, weather, time of year, other work in area, likelihood of emissions from existing plants
- Agreed safe system of handover of plant (or parts thereof) to commissioning
- CDM requirements

Check-list 5.10   Commissioning items for consideration
(not all topics are relevant or necessary for every project)

- Commissioning principles
- Status of preliminary operating instructions
- Outline of commissioning sequence
- Any special materials or equipment required during commissioning
- Radio and communication system requirements
- Level of testing, cleaning, commissioning, etc of package units and PAUs by vendors
- Agreed safe system of handover of plant (or parts thereof) from construction
- Organization of commissioning team, and who will provide resources — eg, client, contractor
- Training requirements for commissioning team
- Condition of plant needed for handover to client

As with all technical information, consider what information needs to be checked and/or approved, and by whom. This assists in eliminating errors and omissions, but should only be done as appropriate, as it can be a time-consuming process, and build unwelcome delays into the programme. Contractors may be asked to obtain approval from clients for certain elements, and the time to complete this process should not be underestimated. Estimates and programmes are often checked and approved by task managers before becoming part of the total project estimate and programme, so that individuals or groups are not committing to unrealistic cost or time targets.

Except on small and quick projects, the project execution strategy and organization should be reviewed. As the technical element of a project develops, initial assumptions may no longer be valid, or there may be better ways of managing the remaining project phases. For example, it may have been assumed originally by the client that all work could be done internally, whereas essential personnel may have since been allocated to higher priority projects. In these circumstances, it may be better to put the remainder of the project out to contract than to wait until internal resource becomes available again. The project execution strategy and organization is modified and reissued to reflect the current plans.

The engineering definition can then be collated into a single package. As this can be a substantial amount of information, the number of copies produced should be limited to those who will actually work on the project in the future — for example, copies for potential contractors — and usually one for retention by the client.

How are projects approved?

In conjunction with producing the engineering definition, the estimate for sanction of the project is assembled. The specific processes and requirements for sanction differ tremendously from company to company, although there are some common themes. Senior management normally want basic information such as:

- reason for project;
- justification for project;
- brief description of what project entails (and any exclusions);
- known risks and uncertainties;
- cost estimate to specific accuracy. Contingencies and reserves to be indicated;
- programme for project;
- execution strategy and responsibilities;
- SHE and Regulatory Authority issues have been covered.

This information is often presented in a written company standard format, sometimes in conjunction with a formal or informal presentation. The rigour of this process often depends on the capital cost of the project, the formality of the system increasing as the value increases. For large projects, it may be necessary to obtain local approval before seeking executive approval. What and who is involved in the sanctioning process, both seeking and granting the approval, should be clarified beforehand. This allows the project manager time to collate information as necessary, and to be prepared if expected to be part of the petitioning team. Where contractors have been involved in the earlier development stages, they too may be asked to provide information for the approval process. The sanctioning process may take some time, particularly if several individuals or layers of management are involved in the approval, and appropriate time should be included in the programme.

YOU SHOULD NOW BE IN A POSITION TO TELL
THE CLIENT WHEN THE PROJECT WILL BE
FINISHED AND HOW MUCH IT WILL COST.

What happens next?

If everything has gone to plan, success! The project is now approved, and is ready to go into detail design.

Frequently, it is at this stage that clients employ one or more contractors to complete the design, procurement, installation, testing and possibly commissioning, if they have not already used contractors for earlier stages. This is done on the basis that internal technical expertise and experience are better for developing the project front end, but that the engineering definition is sufficiently detailed to allow an external contractor or contractors to execute and manage the detail design, equipment procurement and so on. This also means that operating companies do not need to employ large numbers of detail designers, installation staff and other related personnel, but can rely on having these experienced resources supplied by suitable contractors. Again, it is important that the engineering definition is complete and correct, as these other bodies may not as readily identify omissions and errors, or may exploit them to ask for extra time and payment.

If a contractor has already been involved in producing the front end engineering package (FEEP), they will typically continue with the project, completing it through to testing and possibly commissioning. Very occasionally, the client may choose another contractor to complete the remainder of the work. This may occur if, for example, the client does not believe that the contractor has the correct skills or has not been satisfied by the contractor's performance to date.

But what if the project is not sanctioned?

Sometimes projects get to this stage, but are not then sanctioned. There can be numerous reasons, such as:

- costs are higher than expected;
- programme too long;
- insufficient supporting information;
- still too many risks;
- project no longer thought of as sufficient priority;
- client no longer has the money.

If the project owner or senior management have been kept informed of expected costs, time-scales and so on throughout earlier work, then such incidences of non-approval should be minimized. It may be that the project is not totally rejected but sanctioning may be withheld until some future time. Another alternative is that the project team is asked to attempt to reduce costs or programme.

The project team members at this point are often demoralized and disappointed, and it takes good management skills by the project manager to re-motivate the team to look at cheaper or quicker project alternatives. The team, though, must be realistic when considering alternatives, and not merely reduce costs or time without good foundation, just to get the project sanctioned. Typically, if risks are to remain the same:

71

- costs can only be reduced by reducing the scope;
- programme can only be reduced by reducing the scope.

Project example

Well done! You have finished the process design, although it was a little tricky in places, and not everyone was as helpful or as willing as you might have wished. Unfortunately, your line manager was also a little slow in approving your work. As a result, the process design took six weeks rather than the four weeks you had originally planned, but you feel that you can still complete the project in nine months as some work on engineering definition has already started ahead of schedule.

The project needs formal financial approval via an internal sanctioning procedure, with supporting estimates. The project is expected to be submitted for sanction when the engineering definition is complete.

You have already produced a plan for the project, as given in the summary Gantt chart (see Chapter 16).

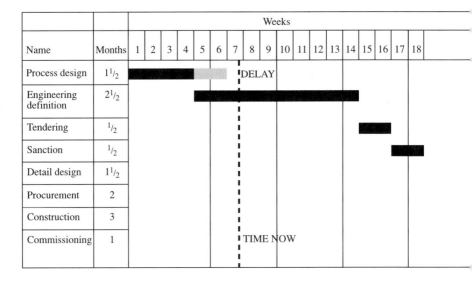

Name	Months	Weeks																	
		1	2	3	4	5	6	7	8	9	10	11	12	13	14	15	16	17	18
Process design	$1^1/_2$							DELAY											
Engineering definition	$2^1/_2$																		
Tendering	$^1/_2$																		
Sanction	$^1/_2$																		
Detail design	$1^1/_2$																		
Procurement	2																		
Construction	3																		
Commissioning	1							TIME NOW											

Revision 1 Gantt chart

What should you be doing as project manager at this stage?
Here are some suggested actions. Note that this is a guide. It is not exhaustive. It is an indication of what may be relevant to a project.

It could be summarized that your role at this time is to 'control the present and direct the future'.

Controlling the present

Spend time seeing and talking to people, to check that they understand the project, that they have adequate resources, programmes of work which meet the project needs and what they are doing is appropriate and efficient. Personal contact achieves far more than letters, memos and telephone conversations.

As the number of people working on the project during engineering definition increases, so does financial investment. Hence as project manager you need actively to monitor, forecast and control costs and progress. Regularly review progress against plan for each function, and chivvy them where it is behind programme. Check how much time is being spent in producing the engineering definition, and whether it is excessive. Also check if any money is

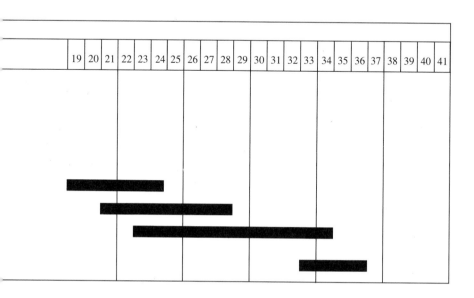

	19	20	21	22	23	24	25	26	27	28	29	30	31	32	33	34	35	36	37	38	39	40	41

being spent against the project externally, and if so what on, and has it got your approval?

If things are satisfactory, then you are fortunate. Unfortunately, in most projects there will be a particular individual or group who are not meeting the project costs and/or programme. Follow this up with the individual or group leader, but if this is unsuccessful, then ask for assistance from your line manager.

Ensure that the relevant individuals and groups are communicating with each other, as they cannot work in isolation. For example, in the case of the heating coil for vessel B, the control designer will need to have its design information from the mechanical designer in order to specify the right control equipment and characteristics.

One method is to visit each design area on a regular basis to check if they have all the information they need. Another is to hold regular design review meetings, which a representative from each functional group attends to review progress and highlight particular problems. This can be very effective, as some issues can affect all functions. For example, if the existing pump is found unsuitable for the proposed new duty and needs to be replaced:

- process would specify new pump characteristics;
- civil function would specify new plinth;
- mechanical would specify pump and modifications to pipework;
- control would specify any necessary instruments and loops;
- electrical would need to specify power supplies;
- procurement would need to purchase pump;
- construction would need to include on installation schedule;
- commissioning would need to include on schedule.

Although you may not need to attend all reviews or studies, you should be satisfied that necessary ones are happening.

As for estimates for the remainder of the project, who will prepare them? Is it something which you expect the supporting functional teams to do? If so, what methods will they use, and are they appropriate? Additionally, as they will not be doing the remainder of the work, they may not feel responsible for their accuracy and subsequent cost control.

If the preferred contractors are expected to produce estimates, then they need to know about the project, so how will you provide them with relevant information? For example, would you give them a copy of the engineering definition in order for them to prepare a tender? If they are to prepare a tender, then time for this activity needs to be included in the programme.

Regarding the sanctioning process, what documentation is required? What documentation may be needed to support the process — such as a summary of the project, its benefits, a programme — and does the information need to be in a particular format? This can be produced simultaneously during the preparation of the engineering definition to minimize elapsed time.

How long may sanctioning take? It is useful to determine how long the sanctioning process may take as it can affect the programme. For instance, if it takes a few weeks, is expenditure (and hence work) supposed to stop on the project? Check the process with the project owner beforehand, so you can consider how you will deal with sanctioning before it happens.

Throughout this stage, utilize your part-time administration assistance as much as possible, as you will probably find that you now need to spend a lot more time managing project activities. All assistance on routine paperwork should be gladly welcomed!

Directing the future

You have earlier decided that the detail design, procurement and construction will be carried out by one of the three preferred contractors. Now is the time to start discussing the project with them, so that they can start preparing for any bidding process, and in turn, you can start the process of determining who will be the successful supplier.

The items for discussion might include:

- project objectives;
- project scope (including exclusions);
- your required project programme and how this fits with their current workload;
- what information will be included in the engineering definition, its format and when they will receive it;
- what you expect the contractor to do — for example, carry out detail design, procurement, construction and any roles under CDM;
- what information you require from them — for example, estimate, programme, tender format, and date by which you need it;
- what type of contract you wish to place on the successful contractor;
- any special procurement arrangements — for example, better terms from certain vendors;
- issues affecting construction, such as needing to meet plant shutdowns.

Any information you receive from the contractors should be fed into the project, such as their views on the programme, and whether the project fits into their projected workload.

You should also look ahead to other requirements — for example, would the project be subject to the CDM Regulations? If so, what actions may you need to take, such as notifying SHE authorities and the company's advisers of the project?

Your modified programme reflects your current information.

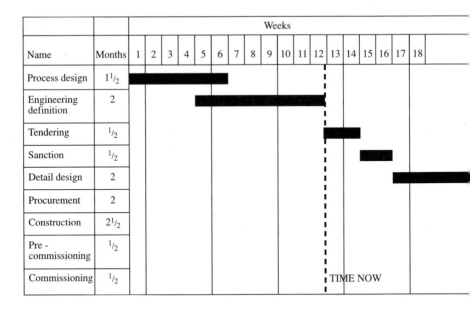

Name	Months	Weeks																	
		1	2	3	4	5	6	7	8	9	10	11	12	13	14	15	16	17	18
Process design	$1^1/_2$																		
Engineering definition	2																		
Tendering	$^1/_2$																		
Sanction	$^1/_2$																		
Detail design	2																		
Procurement	2																		
Construction	$2^1/_2$																		
Pre - commissioning	$^1/_2$																		
Commissioning	$^1/_2$												TIME NOW						

Revision 2 Gantt chart

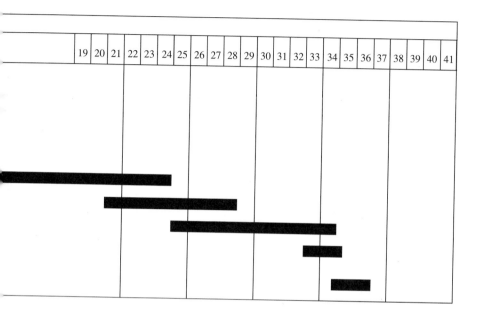

	19	20	21	22	23	24	25	26	27	28	29	30	31	32	33	34	35	36	37	38	39	40	41

Detail design

Richard Collins and Gillian Lawson

Design strategy

The purpose of detail design is to provide the information for the economic procurement and construction of the remainder of the project and also for the testing, commissioning, operation and maintenance of the completed plant.

If principles set out in the previous chapters have been followed, the design strategy will have been decided earlier in the overall project strategy, but at this stage it is worth reviewing that strategy. For example, you may have planned to use an internal resource for the detail design but you may now be in the unfortunate position of finding that a particular resource is no longer available, perhaps because that individual is now working on what is viewed as a higher priority project. In this case, the solution may be to hire in additional resource, or have the particular piece of work contracted to another design organization.

Any necessary modifications should be made to the design strategy before starting detail design and communicated to everyone involved. It may also be appropriate at this stage to re-check the cost-benefit of the project before any large financial commitments are made.

Who may be involved in detail design?

The design strategy states whether internal or external resources are going to be used or perhaps a mixture of both. Ideally, it should be the same individuals that were indicated earlier in the project organization. They are generally from the main functions of civil, structural, mechanical, control/instrumentation and electrical engineering, supported by process engineers, safety specialists, computing and other services. The main personnel who will be involved are as shown in the technical section of Check-list 3.6 on page 38. Co-ordination of everyone working on the project is the responsibility of the project manager, including guiding them on the objectives and programme for their work, but supervision of the detailed design is the responsibility of senior engineers in each particular function. In general, the smaller the project, the fewer the people involved and the easier it becomes to manage the design, as there are fewer interfaces between groups and individuals.

Suppliers of equipment (vendors) also provide detail design information for their pieces of equipment. For standard pieces of equipment, suppliers normally have design data and drawings already available. For specialist pieces of equipment, suppliers need to do the design first. Their contracts normally state that they must then submit data and drawings for approval (see Chapter 18) before they start manufacturing the equipment. Additionally, the project design team is often reliant upon drawings and other information from vendors to enable them to do their design work. Hence, tell suppliers when their designs are to be ready, and whether they should be in any special format — for example, using a particular CAD (computer-aided design) package as opposed to manual drawing.

What is required?

The type of information required from detail design varies tremendously from project to project. What information must be provided from detail design is best agreed by discussions with the users and then the individuals employed in detail design. What information do the designers need from others? What information do they believe they should be producing? Reports and reviews of previous projects and consulting experienced project managers will help. Check-list 6.1 (pages 80–81) gives the type of information which may be produced during detail design.

Where the project has to fit into existing plant or existing operation, time will be required to obtain, check and study records of what was built and subsequent changes to it. For example, what is the condition of existing equipment which may be reused? Are there any special standards or specifications for the existing equipment which the new project must follow? Is the existing information on the equipment up to date or does it need to be reviewed? This checking and measuring of existing equipment can be time-consuming especially if, for example, the design is being done remotely from the existing equipment by a contractor rather than being done internally by the client company. (See Chapter 25 for further comments on managing 'brownfield' projects within existing plants and operations.)

Allow time at this stage for the checking and approval of the design, and for resolving the resulting questions and queries. A design audit by members of another project team or other independent group is useful to question assumptions and exchange ideas. The checking and approval may be done to ensure the

Check-list 6.1	Items for consideration for detail design

Process engineering
- Flowsheets
- P&IDs
- Hazop studies
- Safety and operational reviews:
— operability
— layout for operation/maintenance

Civil, structural and architectural
- Earthwork and site preparation design
- Roads and fencing design/drawings
- Piling calculations/design/layout drawings
- Drainage design/drawings
- Paving and underground services design/drawings
- Floor drainage layout drawings
- Foundation loading diagrams
- Foundation design/drawings
- Structural steelwork design/drawings
- Building plans/sections/elevations
- Room data sheets
- Internal/external detail drawings
- HVAC (heating, ventilation and air-conditioning) specifications
- Plant room layouts

Mechanical
- Equipment design/drawings
- Review of supplier design/drawings
- Plot plans and elevations for piping
- Major pipe routes
- Standard piping details
- Piping general arrangement (GAs)
- Isometrics
- Piping models (physical model or 3D drawing)
- Piping stress analysis
- Piping support details
- Piping material take-off schedule

Control/instrumentation
- Instrument list/database
- In-line instrumentation specification

Continued opposite

Check-list 6.1 (cont'd)   Items for consideration for detail design

Control/instrumentation (cont'd)

- Functional specifications for:
— control systems
— shutdown systems
— fire and alarm systems
— management information system
- Uninterruptable power supply (UPS) specification
- Acceptance test requirements
- Instrument location plans
- Control room layouts
- Console arrangement
- Instrument wiring/connection details
- Power/earthing details
- Instrument cable schedule
- Instrument cable routes
- Instrument piping details
- Instrument housing details
- Instrument loop diagrams
- Trip and alarm test schedules

Electrical

- System calculations
- Single line diagrams
- Electrical area classifications
- Power/earthing layout/details
- Electrical equipment specifications:
— motor specifications
— variable speed drive controls
— transformers
— switchgear (high voltage [HV], low voltage [LV])
— power factor control
- Cable schedules
- Lighting drawings/schedules
- Electrical tracing specifications/drawings
- Telecoms specification/drawings
- Lightning protection specification
- Temporary power supplies design/drawings

Construction

- Layout for construction accessibility
- Construction sequence review
- Heavy lift review

technical competency of the design but may also be a requirement of the client that operating, maintenance and safety staff have the opportunity to influence and comment upon design. Checking and approval has to be a formal process, requiring signatures from the designated 'approvers'. In some companies, and in heavily regulated industries or countries, individuals must have particular qualifications in order to approve designs.

Design stages

How the design proceeds depends on the type, size and novelty of the project. Here is a typical example of how larger, multi-functional projects develop (note that long lead times greatly influence the order and timing of the stages):

(1) The starting point is a proposed layout and information on major plant items as outlined in the front end package.

(2) Foundation and structural design develops based on this initial information.

(3) Major plant items are detailed, giving such information as exact nozzle sizes and positions with flange ratings, locations for instruments, support details, lifting locations, overall weight.

(4) Minor plant items such as pumps and heat exchangers are detailed.

(5) Interconnecting pipework between the plant items is detailed.

(6) Power supplies are designed.

(7) Instrumentation is specified and designed.

A statement of the necessary safety and health standards is needed to guide all stages of design. Throughout the detail design phase, safety standards must be checked. Additional formal and informal reviews may be carried out to check and verify the safe design. Hazard analysis is established as the technique for checking the design for the start-up and operation of the plant, as described in Chapter 13. In Britain and most industrial countries, the law requires attention in design to the safe construction and final demolition of the plant, as described in Chapter 11.

How is design produced?

Detail design is a culmination of ideas, possible solutions, calculations, documents, lists and, traditionally, pencil and drawings. Computer systems are increasingly used to carry out calculations, tabulate lists, check the use of space, produce drawings and generate construction data.

The format of the detailed design is important, not only for the actual production of the detailed design but also for the future operation of the plant. Clients often want design produced in a certain manner or on a certain CAD system to allow storage and retrieval of information on the finished plant, and to enable its operation and maintenance, and any possible future modifications or enhancements. Any such requirements should be specified and agreed before the detail design commences.

CAD systems are becoming more intelligent — for example, certain systems can interpret pipework design and automatically produce a list itemizing all individual pieces and fittings for fabrication. Other systems interpret two-dimensional structural and piping design into a three-dimensional 'model', thus enabling any clashes of pipework, equipment, steelwork and so on to be readily identified. This can also be a useful tool for training commissioning and operating teams about the plant before the plant itself is actually constructed.

CAD systems can help to identify any potential clashes of equipment.
(Reproduced by courtesy of Costain Oil, Gas & Process.)

The project manager's role

For smaller projects, the project manager will often actively be involved in the design process itself, perhaps having one of the design roles. This is in contrast to larger projects, where the project manager's role is much more than the management of the design.

Problems during design occasionally arise due to technical errors or omissions. Problems more often arise between individuals or functional groups due to lack of communication. Thus, one of the prime roles of the project manager is to ensure correct and adequate communication between the individuals or teams involved in the detail design, including internal and external resources. It is useful to have regular meetings with individuals or teams involved and also between the teams themselves, to review progress, assess the resources needed to complete the work and agree actions to solve problems. Such meetings allow any interface issues or minor problems to be recognized and dealt with before they become major problems. (Chapter 22 gives recommendations on the efficient use of meetings.)

THE PROJECT MANAGER SHOULD ENSURE THAT THERE
IS ADEQUATE COMMUNICATION BETWEEN DESIGN TEAMS.

The project manager must agree and control a programme for the progress of the design so that the overall programme is met. It is usual to have a quite detailed programme for the design phase, often based on individual functions, indicating what design they will produce and when it will be produced. The project manager should check that this design is being produced to achieve the programme and take any action necessary if it is not. Often delays or problems in one function or team affect others, causing major delays in the design.

Design progress should be measured against programme and action taken where necessary.
(Reproduced by courtesy of Foster Wheeler Energy Limited.)

The time spent on design should also be measured. An allowance for the time required will have been used to produce the approved estimate for the cost of the project. Any over-run on man-hours or time spent on the design adds to the cost of the project. As discussed in Chapter 17, the project manager needs regular reports or estimates of the cost of man-hours used, the earned value of the work completed and the trends. The systems which can be used are described in Chapters 13 and 14. Reviews of this information at regular meetings attended by senior design staff are useful to stimulate attention on any problem areas.

Changes need to be controlled during this and all subsequent stages. Most late changes are not beneficial to a project. Their potential advantages are usually over-estimated. Their consequential effect on costs, programme and morale are usually under-estimated. The potential effects of all proposed changes on time, cost and safety need to be assessed formally.

On to the next phase

Chapter 7 is on procurement. The procurement of items with a long delivery time often starts long before some of the detail design of the more minor items.

Detail design typically overlaps procurement, and often the start of construction. The design programme is therefore governed by the time needed for delivery times from suppliers, appointing contractors and also statutory approvals which may be required before construction can start.

Further reading

Rutter, P.A. and Martin, A.S., 1990, *Management of Design Offices* (Thomas Telford Publications).

Stallworthy, E.A. and Kharbanda, O.P., 1986, *A Guide to Project Implementation* (Institution of Chemical Engineers) (out of print).

Project example

You received estimates for the remainder of the project from two of the three preferred contractors, 'Aaron & Adam' chose not to bid as their existing workload was too great. The estimate from 'Brown & Black' was about 5% higher than that from 'Cook & Clark', but C&C gave a programme which was two weeks beyond your required end date. Following your line manager's advice, you included the slightly higher cost in your project estimate for sanction.

The project was officially approved yesterday, having taken two weeks to approve as per your previous programme, revision 1 (see pages 72–73).

What should you be doing as project manager at this stage?
Here are some suggested actions. Note that this is a guide. It is not exhaustive. It is an indication of what may be relevant to a project.

If you have not already done so, you should determine who between B&B and C&C will receive the contract for the remaining work, so that work can commence. How will you decide on the company? Check differences in the estimates by talking to both companies again.

- Why was B&B more expensive?
- Do both companies understand scope, risks, priorities and nuances of the project?
- Do both companies understand possible requirements on construction — for example, meeting plant shutdowns, any restrictions on access, working methods and so on?
- Has C&C excluded items, either erroneously or deliberately?

- Does C&C typically offer lower costs initially, hoping to make money later on variations and extras?
- Is C&C's workload down at moment and hence they are prepared to work at slightly less profit in order to keep their personnel employed?
- What are the usual standards of work for both companies?
- Remember to ask others in your company what their opinions are of the two companies and clarify with the project owner that the earlier objectives to manufacture WHIZZO at minimum capital expenditure are still valid, even if this means further extending the project duration.

You decide to use B&B, as their standard of work is usually higher than C&C, they can meet your programme, and the payment terms in their tender were more advantageous to your company.

Arrange for an order to be placed on B&B to complete detail design, procurement and construction as quickly as possible, to keep the project progressing. You should also initiate the briefing and induction of B&B personnel.

Is this the end of your input until commissioning? Certainly not!

Your job as project manager is to ensure that co-ordination and communication between B&B's design team and your own internal team is maintained. You will often find that your team is needed to answer technical queries. Although items may have already been outlined in the engineering definition, they may need further clarification or explanation, for example:

- Standards to be used.
- Documentation and drawing formats.
- Drawings and documents required for operation, maintenance and ultimate decommissioning of plant.
- Information on existing equipment.
- Information for site clearance and preparation, diversion of services, etc.
- Information for safety reviews.
- How new equipment and instruments interface with existing systems.
- How to deal with design changes.

New information which may be required could include:

- What drawings and other information from vendors will be required for acceptance before they commence manufacturing equipment?
- When will foundation and connection detail be required from vendors?
- When will installation, testing and pre-commissioning detail be required from vendors?
- When will operating and maintenance guides be required from vendors?

You need a system in place for dealing with such queries promptly:

- All queries could be directed via yourself but this can be time-consuming for you.
- Queries could be directed to the relevant individual in your team, but this can be harder to control, especially if it may lead to changes in B&B's work scope.

Ensure that there are no delays created by your team in answering such queries which will in turn affect B&B. This can delay the project and hence the benefits it will bring, and also lead to claims from B&B for delays.

You should also satisfy yourself that B&B is progressing the design at the necessary rate:

- You can arrange progress meetings with B&B at the appropriate frequency (possibly fortnightly in this case, due to the relatively short project time-scale). The meetings are held between relevant personnel from B&B and your own team.
- Costs and cost control can be incorporated, so that you can assure yourself that B&B is not exceeding its estimates, and hence your budget.
- You can also cover technical items in meetings to ensure that changes and so on are communicated to the relevant people. Team meetings are also a good way of resolving any outstanding technical issues.

Produce appropriate minutes of such meetings. They can provide a record of what was said, done or agreed between individuals or the two companies. If there are any problems later in the project, they can be used to support or negate claims.

As in all phases of the project, one of the most useful things that you can do is get out and about. Talk to people at B&B, to check if they have any problems or if things are progressing to plan. If you can, visit them in their own premises, as you will then be able to see for yourself what they are doing, their standard of work and their actual progress.

Procurement

Richard Collins and Gillian Lawson

Procurement is the acquisition of equipment, materials and spares and includes services such as design, advice and software, but this chapter focuses on obtaining hardware. As mentioned earlier, procurement typically begins before detail design is complete. Indeed, for larger or specialized pieces of equipment, detail design of the item is part of the successful supplier's responsibilities.

The way in which procurement will take place should already have been considered, if principles given in the previous chapters have been followed (see Check-list 3.3, page 33). It is useful to review the earlier strategy, as other issues may have since arisen. For example, is the same person to be responsible for procurement as per the original plan? Are the deliveries of certain items now critical, so that they will require expediting during procurement?

For each item, a decision is made about who will be responsible for supplying the equipment that is fit for its purpose — for example, client, contractor or supplier.

Briefly, the normal early stages of procurement comprise sending out enquiries to potential suppliers for prices, delivery and technical information, assessment of the returned suppliers' tenders and the placing of orders. There then follows expediting as appropriate, and inspection of goods during fabrication, assembly and testing where necessary, together with the management of associated documentation. Procurement demands a contract between the purchaser and the supplier — further detailed information on contracts can be found in Chapter 18.

Enquiry

Exactly who is involved in the enquiry process varies from company to company, and each has its own system. Typically, a functional engineer responsible for the design of a particular piece of equipment produces the technical specification for the item to be procured. For example, a mechanical engineer normally prepares the technical specification for a vessel, whilst an electrical engineer produces the technical specification for a transformer. The type of specification produced may either be a performance specification — what the equipment is expected to *do* — or a detailed specification — thoroughly detailing *the exact* piece of equipment. The project programme should include specific periods for all this. In certain circumstances — for example, software production — there may be the requirement to produce and test a prototype before any orders are placed. These additional steps should be included in the project programme. Further comment on this appears in Chapter 25.

These individuals may sometimes contact potential suppliers directly, but are more likely to deal with suppliers via a specialist purchasing department within their own company. The advantage of such a specialist corporate department is that it can provide experience, records and a better understanding of contractual term, retain knowledge of suppliers' performance, manage administration and so on.

As part of its role, a purchasing department normally maintains a list of preferred suppliers. The advantages of such a list include standardization of equipment (and thus spares), competitive prices and reliable delivery, and high quality goods and equipment. These preferred suppliers lists are often confidential and any poor performance may result in a supplier being deleted. Also, preferred suppliers may only be on that list for specific categories of equipment; for example, a company may be listed to supply reciprocating pumps but not centrifugal pumps.

The enquiry documentation which is sent to possible suppliers consists of all necessary technical and commercial information, such as specifications, preferred terms of payment, dates when tenders are to be returned and any particular design information required. Remember to include everything which will be required from the supplier if they are awarded the order — such as drawings, test certificates, delivery and off-loading. Otherwise these will become additional expenses and costs later.

Dependent on cost and the importance of equipment to be procured, the enquiry documentation typically goes to up to three potential suppliers, to try to ensure competitive prices from them. Each potential supplier is given the same initial technical and contractual information to keep the process reputable and auditable, and all should receive the same information should any revisions be necessary.

Suppliers may need to contact specialist functional personnel if there are any technical queries on the specification, and hence there should be a system in place to manage such queries. If particularly large or specialized items are being procured, it may be worth having interim meetings with potential suppliers before they submit their tenders, to resolve any technical or commercial queries.

Tender assessment

Potential suppliers will aim to return their tenders by the stipulated date and to the required format. To maintain a reputable system, the tenders should be treated confidentially and neither technical nor commercial information from one potential supplier should be relayed to another.

The tenders need to be assessed both technically and commercially. If equipment covers one or more functions — for example, a compressor unit complete with motor and control equipment — then the offers should be assessed technically by process, mechanical, electrical and instrumental engineers to check that all the equipment requirements are met. The commercial aspect is assessed by the procurement department, which focuses on areas such as payment terms, delivery dates and conditions of contract. Obviously, for minor items the whole assessment is often done by either the appropriate functional engineer or the project manager. In some instances, the potential suppliers may submit tenders which do not meet the original enquiry requirements, usually in either technical details or contractual terms. The project manager then decides whether there is sufficient time to consider these alternative offers (and their potential implications for project design, cost and programme) against the possible benefits. Who needs to consider the non-compliant offer depends on the deviation from the original enquiry — for example, an alternative pump type would typically involve a mechanical engineer and a process engineer; different contractual terms the project manager and someone from the procurement department.

Price is not necessarily the final decider on who will be the successful supplier. Examples of issues which may influence decisions are given in Check-list 7.1 (page 92). Assessments can be done qualitatively or quantitively. Points can be allocated by project team members against tenders, in meeting target commercial and technical criteria. The order is then placed against the tender with the highest points.

There may be some advantage in negotiating final details with the selected supplier. Such negotiations may lead to a reduction in cost or programme, or in improvement in payment terms in favour of the buyer. Such improvements cannot be guaranteed, and there is no substitute for experience in these negotiations. Otherwise, they can produce bad feelings between the vendor and buyer companies, and lead to a poor relationship in the future.

Check-list 7.1	Items for consideration when selecting suppliers

- Programme
- Novelty of equipment
- Complexity of equipment
- Equipment importance
- Supplier location
- Quality requirements
- Degree of flexibility to manage any changes to design or requirements
- Terms of payment — do they suit project risks and priorities?
- Delivery times
- Confidentiality of the project
- The state of the supply market
- Supplier service record
- Standardization of equipment and spares
- Experience of testing and commissioning
- Overall equipment life cycle costs (including spares, maintenance, failures)

Placing of order

Once a successful tender has been identified, the order can be placed for the equipment procurement. Check in advance that all of the requirements have been considered at this stage and nothing has been forgotten — for example, spares, drawing information and technical information.

Most companies have a specific ordering request form, which is completed by the appropriate person from the project team, possibly the project manager for a major item or a functional engineer for the minor items. Usually individuals are able to authorize items up to a certain monetary value; above this level, someone more senior in the organization may have to approve the order. It is useful if the authority levels are checked beforehand so that there are no delays if senior authorities are needed but unavailable. The complete order document contains the specific order request, the agreed commercial terms, the conditions of purchase and any appropriate general attachments, such as documentation requirements and inspection procedures. The purchasing department usually assembles this document and sends it to the selected supplier. Otherwise, an appropriate individual in the project team will have to manage this. The final requirement of any order is the signed and unqualified acceptance of the order by the supplier.

Interim actions

Early in the planning of procurement, determine how important the prompt delivery of each separate item is to the programme, and then consider how much time and money should be spent on progressing supply. For time-critical or major items, it is essential that someone from the project team has responsibility for monitoring progress on the manufacture of the items. Check that the supplier is making a start immediately the order is received. If not, the equipment will be late. In order to keep the manufacture to programme, the project team must formally approve and return design information on time. (See Chapter 6 for comment on supplier design.)

Progressing entails visits to the supplier and actually witnessing that progress is as, or even better than, the supplier's programme. When visiting, the progressor checks that the supplier's production of documentation, design, drawings and so on is as per the programme. These visits can usually be made by someone from the internal purchasing department, the project team or even as a service from a specialist expediting and inspection company. Reports are then issued indicating that progress is being made.

If progress is better than expected, the project team may be able to take advantage of having the unit produced earlier, or else make any extra provisions for early receipt of equipment. Early delivery may in fact be problematic, especially if special access routes or heavy lifting/off-loading equipment are required ahead of schedule. Stage payments may need to be made earlier than expected if linked to manufacturing schedules. Additionally, storage for early deliveries can be expensive to the project. Conversely if progress is slow and behind programme, remedial action can be discussed with the supplier in order to get back on schedule.

For technically critical or major items, always inspect equipment during the manufacturing stages. This enables purchasers to assure themselves that the manufacturer is meeting the technical specifications. Levels of inspection depend on such factors as:

- complexity of design/manufacture;
- criticality of equipment in operation;
- country of origin of material;
- experience/quality procedures of supplier;
- previous good or bad experiences with that particular supplier.
  Types of inspection may include:
- witnessing of positive material identification checks of all materials to be used during the manufacture of the equipment;
- setting up of major welds on vessel bodies prior to welding;
- witnessing of non-destructive examination for major welds;

Always inspect technically critical or major pieces of equipment during manufacture. (Reproduced by courtesy of Gordon McBrearty.)

- equipment pressure tests;
- flow and head tests on pumps.

Further information on testing of software is given in Chapter 25.

Reports are issued again following these inspections, so that those involved in the project can be satisfied that the requirements have been met. In the event that problems arise out of inspection visits, assess the impact so that action plans can be prepared and agreed with the project team. In some instances only the most drastic options may be appropriate — for example, equipment re-design or even cancelling an order and giving the work to another supplier.

It may be possible, to minimize effort and costs, to roll inspection, progress and expediting visits into one. But do ensure that an inspector is not compromised into accepting unsatisfactory quality of work in order to meet the programme! As part of the contract, it may have been agreed that stage payments be made, for example, against the handover of finished design data or drawings or on completion of certain aspects of the manufacturing process. Each such stage payment should have specific criteria for acceptance. Progress and technical inspection visits help to check that the stage requirements have been met and hence payment is due to the supplier. The purchaser has a duty to make such payments when satisfied that the stage criteria have been met.

Transportation and off-loading

The co-ordination of shipping of equipment and materials from suppliers is of great importance, especially if there is a tight schedule or the order involves handling of large loads, extensive sea freighting or importation through customs.

There is an advantage in including the transportation, off-loading and associated insurance and customs as part of the supplier's work, as the supplier often has experience of all these operations, and normally has systems and personnel in place to manage them. Depending on the size of equipment, transportation may be a major task and involve, for example, arrangement of road closures and police escorts for large equipment. The disadvantage is that the supplier charges for doing this work and taking the risks, possibly making it more costly overall to the project. Any special delivery requirements — for example, to a specific site entrance or at a time of day — should be stipulated well before transportation begins.

Timing of delivery should be considered against when the item will actually be installed. If it is not to be installed immediately then safe, secure storage should be arranged to prevent damage or loss. This may not be too difficult for small items. For large items, however, arrival at site should be co-ordinated wherever possible with installation. Otherwise off-loading, storage and re-handling costs can be very expensive.

Delivery of large pieces of equipment may require road closures and police escorts.
(Reproduced by courtesy of BOC Limited and ICI plc.)

Closing orders

The purchaser checks that goods, equipment, spares and documentation have been completed as per the order and then arranges for payment of outstanding invoices. In some instances, the final invoice is not paid at this stage, as it is linked to the successful operation of the equipment. This may be several months hence and many suppliers are unlikely to agree to such a retention payment. Further comments on items relating to money are found in Chapter 23.

It is unlikely, if appropriate procedures have been followed, that the supplier will try to claim for extra payments, justified or otherwise. Any such claims should be examined systematically and paid where valid.

Further reading

Association for Project Management, 1998, *Contract Strategy for Successful Project Management.*

Project example

The project is now into its fifth month, and you have been checking progress against your programme revision 2. So far B&B has been making good progress on detail design, ready to start procurement. On closer examination, it has been found that the motor on existing vessel A is not adequate for the new agitator duty. Additionally, there are concerns that the new pump will be on a longer delivery than first thought. B&B has come to you for guidance.

What should you be doing as project manager at this stage?

Here are some suggested actions. Note that this is a guide. It is not exhaustive. It is an indication of what may be relevant to a project.

You need to have the agitator motor and its paperwork thoroughly checked to confirm whether or not it is suitable. But this may be easier said then done!

• Depending on how well the motor has been maintained, its working environment and similar factors, it may be difficult to read any information on the motor itself.

• There may be difficulty in finding documentation.

• You may be fortunate that your company has retained all the original project documentation from when the vessel, agitator, motor, etc, were first installed. But beware! The original motor may have long since failed and been replaced by a different unit, with different properties.

• You may be able to contact the manufacturer with the motor's serial number, to obtain the necessary information.

If after following these routes, it is determined that the motor is suitable, then the problem is solved. But if it is not suitable for the new duty, what do you do?

• You need to get someone either from within your own company or B&B to specify a new motor as quickly as possible, and identify any preferred manufacturing companies.

• Additionally, get someone to check if the specified motor is a standard unit which your company may have as a spare, If so, this may take some of the urgency out of the situation, although you will need to replace the spare unit.

• Costs for a new unit, its delivery and so on need to be determined, as they will affect your project programme and cost control. Can you afford the new motor? Will you need to get more senior authorization to purchase one because it is outside the original project scope?

• The delivery period of the unit may well affect your programme by extending into commissioning, so are there ways of reducing the consequences? For example, is it possible to carry out commissioning using the existing motor, and replace it with the new one at the very end of

97

commissioning? Can the suppliers reduce the delivery time if you are prepared to pay a premium?

Remember, though, that this may incur additional work to B&B's original scope, hence they will expect to be paid for it.

Determine why the new motor requirement was not identified earlier. Was it an error or oversight by someone? If so, who? By someone within your own company or by B&B? Does it imply that the agitator motor for vessel B may also be unsuitable? You need to find the root cause of the error to prevent it occurring again and also, if it was due to B&B, to ensure that you do not pay for its errors.

With regard to the pump, B&B has been contracted to provide procurement, and hence it should follow up deliveries with the supplier. If there is a problem, then B&B should resolve it directly with the supplier, take any contractual action necessary and modify its own construction programme to deal with the situation. However, you are the project manager, with responsibility for delivering the project; if you can assist, then do so. For example, if the manufacturer is a preferred or frequent supplier for your company, then you or your purchasing department may be able to exert some pressure on the supplier to meet your programme.

Continue with your cost control and planning for the project, incorporating these changes into your financial and progress reports, so that you can predict when the project will finish, and how much it will cost.

You should also be looking ahead to the next phase of the project — construction. What sort of things should you be doing now to ensure that construction runs smoothly? Make sure that:

- B&B knows of any restrictions on ways of working on the plant — for example, requirements to wear certain protective clothing, permits-to-work, any prohibited materials or methods and so on.
- Plant personnel understand what will be happening to the existing plant.
- Plant personnel understand the scope of any decontamination on the existing plant, and when this should be carried out.
- Dates and types of shutdowns are known.
- Your construction supervisor will be available and understands the role requirements.
- The safety file is complete and approved to hand over to the contractor and safety, health and environment authorities so that construction is not delayed.

Construction

Richard Collins and Gillian Lawson

8

Construction is the site preparation, provision of services and foundation work to enable the fitting together and installation of equipment. Depending on the project, it may also require as a first step the demolition of existing plant and removal of underground services and facilities. Construction typically starts whilst procurement is still going on, and even when some peripheral detail design remains. Of all of the project phases, construction often includes the largest number of people and the highest expenditure, and thus this phase can present the highest risk of all the project phases. Due to the complexity and size of the construction phase, it often has a dedicated construction manager or construction engineer who treats this phase as a project in itself. But always remember that the project manager usually has the overall responsibility for delivering the project. The project manager should not just hand over construction to someone else as this would be a shirking of responsibilities.

Success at this phase is very much dependent upon the thought, time and effort put in by the team during the earlier stages. Thus, if the project team has considered construction throughout earlier design and procurement, and the construction manager has been actively involved in the earlier thinking, the construction manager should have a much easier job to manage. Moreover, in the UK — as is now the requirement under the Construction (Design and Management) Regulations 1994 (CDM), except for very small projects — construction cannot be started until the safety file has been accepted by the principal contractor. (See Chapter 11.)

Construction strategy

During design and procurement phases, further thought should be given as to how construction will be managed and executed, and any earlier strategies examined for current validity. For instance, a client company may already have partnerships or alliance arrangements in place. The partnership contractor will have already carried out design and procurement and will also carry out the construction. For large projects, part of the construction strategy is to consider how best to break the construction down into manageable packages — for example, based on process phases or equipment location. For smaller projects it may be possible to consider the whole construction as one package. The strategy selected should follow the project's objectives — for example, a minimum cost objective may produce a different construction strategy from a minimum programme objective. (See Chapter 2 for comment on the effects of time and money, and Chapter 25 for construction implications for different types of projects.)

As process plant projects normally involve several functions, it is usual for several companies to be involved in construction, each covering its own trade. These companies do not necessarily have direct contracts with the employing company, but may be subcontracted through other firms. Some multi-functional installation companies also exist and this can be useful as they can be employed as a management contractor and, in the UK, be capable of the role of principal contractor under the CDM Regulations. Another option is to use one contractor specializing in a particular trade but who, in turn, contracts out to other companies for the other trades. Occasionally, for smaller projects, the client company may have an installation department which expects to be used for the installation. This is becoming rarer, as client companies believe that they can no longer afford to run such departments, and external installation companies are now used widely. Chapter 18 includes a review of these choices.

During earlier project stages, it is possible just to have an approximate idea of the likely organizations who will carry out construction. However, as design progresses the project manager and construction manager need to start selecting the construction companies. This is so that the successful companies can start their preparation — for example, preparing their site base, assembling a skilled workforce, carrying out inductions, securing equipment in their scope of supply, and so on.

The main construction management team needs to interface with many interested parties during construction. These are likely to include managers of any adjacent working plant, other construction teams on the same site, neighbouring residents, statutory inspectors and commissioning teams. The construction strategy should include how these interfaces are to be handled and what the communications processes will be, so as to minimize confusion and thus delays.

Material and equipment arrive at the site throughout the construction period. Items that will not be installed immediately need to be located in a compound for security reasons, and preferably in a warehouse to minimize deterioration due to weather. The construction strategy includes how this material and equipment is to be controlled, for example:

- method of receipt of goods;
- storage in right environment;
- storage in retrievable location;
- release for correct use;
- associated paperwork systems.

These will all reduce delays from loss or damaged equipment or safety issues due to installation in the wrong location. It does not matter whether this materials management is carried out by the construction management team or by contractors, as long as the system is in place and communicated.

Think about the extent of off-site versus on-site fabrication and assembly. Advantages of assembly off-site include:

- measurement, fabrication and testing in workshop conditions, as opposed to on-site where they may have to be carried out in open air;
- complete units delivered to site, and hence less likely to lose smaller elements;
- the possibility of starting assembly earlier.

The disadvantage is that large items have to be transported, which may be more difficult, risky and costly.

The construction strategy also considers the construction programme — for example, how long it will take realistically to complete the work, if there are any major milestones to meet such as existing plant shutdowns, access and tie-in opportunities, and the time of year the construction will take place and hence the likely effects of weather.

Towards the end of construction, parts of the erected plant are handed over for commissioning. How this is done needs to be discussed and agreed between team members — for example, will it be done on a plant by plant or equipment basis, or rather on a process route basis? The physical completion of the plant at handover is also agreed so that there are no areas of confusion. As there are possible safety implications if there are areas of confusion, a formal handover procedure including appropriate documentation is preferable to an informal process. These items are included in the construction strategy.

It is also determined at this stage who or what type of organization will actually construct the project. As in the main project strategy, the roles and responsibilities during construction are defined so that everyone involved knows what is expected of them and when. The construction manager obviously has a leading part in this phase, being involved with more detailed elements of construction. However, the project manager still has overall responsibility for delivering the project and should not shirk that responsibility at this stage.

Likewise, the design team members still have a role during construction. They should be available for technical support, answering queries such as:

- why is this instrument located here? Will it be OK in this position to make access easier?
- type A valve is on long delivery — will type B valve suffice?

These queries need answering promptly so as not to delay the construction. The construction manager often has a team of construction supervisors overseeing day-to-day details of the installation. These supervisors may be from the main management contractor or from the individual installation companies, but wherever they come from, they should understand their roles. Depending on the project size, there may also be planners, estimators or quantity surveyors to assist in determining construction progress and costs.

As per the main project strategy, the construction strategy is reviewed periodically and modified as necessary, and then communicated to all concerned.

Safety in construction

Historically, safety performance during construction throughout industry as a whole has been poor and this has been a major driver in the implementation of safety, health and environment (SHE) legislation. In the UK, CDM emphasizes the importance of considering the safety of construction during design. The typical types of hazards within process plant projects which may influence construction safety and should therefore be considered during design are:

- need for demolition of existing equipment;
- size/weight of equipment;
- materials of construction;
- source of equipment (local/imported);
- access routes to and within the site;
- schedule for delivery/construction;
- cranes available;
- soil-bearing ability for heavy cranes/trucks;
- method to be used for heavy lifts;
- interactions with existing plant/tie-ins;
- construction site location in relation to existing hazards such as overhead power lines, buried services, other live services and open water.

Wherever possible, remove the hazards. Where this is not possible, minimize the risk and consequences.

The client company itself may have additional hazards or safety requirements which may not occur in other operating companies. For example, there may be risks from toxic releases or potential flammable atmospheres. To

Access routes within site may be difficult — equipment too large to negotiate a corner is lifted over a pipebridge.
(Reproduced by courtesy of BOC Limited and ICI plc.)

minimize risk, client companies will therefore have safe systems of work in place to prevent unsafe situations. The safe systems may include:

- site induction and specific plant inductions;
- permits-to-work;
- restricted access to enclosed or partially enclosed environments;
- searches for underground services before excavations are permitted;
- wearing specific protective equipment in certain areas;
- standby personnel for specific activities;
- restriction on the use of electrical equipment in certain areas;
- limitations on the use of ladders;
- work on existing equipment restricted to internal workforce only.

These requirements and restrictions should be fully discussed and a common understanding reached between the client and the installation company well before starting at the site. Otherwise, they could adversely affect execution strategy, cost, programmes and so on.

ACCESS MAY BE DIFFICULT
DURING CONSTRUCTION.

Construction programme

Due to the complexity of construction, quite a detailed programme is required if the construction is to be managed effectively. The programme is developed from a higher level plan covering the main activities. For a process plant project, the main activities are typically:

- demolition of any existing redundant plant or buildings;
- site clearance;
- establishment of temporary construction facilities;
- soils improvement/piling;
- underground civils;
- above ground civils/structures;
- main plant item installation;
- pipework fabrication/erection;
- instrument installation;
- electrical installation;
- painting;
- insulation (thermal and acoustic).

Construction starting with a clear site …

through to main plant item installation …

and finishing with painting and insulation.
(Reproduced by courtesy of BOC Limited and ICI plc.)

Tie-ins/connections to existing facilities are usually done, where possible, when an existing plant or service is already due to be shut down and hence may occur at any stage in this process. The plan becomes more detailed and for some critical items, such as those involving existing plant shutdowns, may become an hour-to-hour programme.

There are generally a lot of interdependencies during construction, and hence progress is monitored frequently and action taken as necessary. Slippages against time for seemingly minor items can very soon impact on much larger items.

Management of contractors

The majority of large process plant construction projects are undertaken with multiple contracts using specialized contractors in the required trades. A client company may already have a list of approved or preferred contractors, just as the suppliers list for equipment and materials. This list is based on criteria such as:

- workforce skills and quality of workmanship;
- previous safety performance;
- previous cost performance;
- previous programme performance;

- technical capability;
- established contract conditions;
- locality to construction site.

The client company may wish that these preferred contractors are used or may allow the main contractor to select its own. In this situation, the main contractor undertakes an enquiry, evaluation and negotiation as with equipment and materials. Again this system should be undertaken in a fair and auditable manner. Before construction contracts are actually awarded, pre-award meetings are often held with each selected contractor. These ensure that all aspects of the scope and systems to be implemented are agreed by all parties, and that any contentious issues are fully resolved before the contract is awarded. It is also the last time to present revised design documents to the contractor without encountering the dreaded contract change.

Where a contractor needs to establish a base at the client's site, allow time for this mobilization. It may require provision of any temporary facilities such as:

- offices and furniture;
- telephones, fax machines and computers;
- site transport;
- power, water and drainage;
- canteen, changing rooms and toilets;
- security arrangements;
- material storage/warehouse facilities;
- site labour camp.

Industrial relations can play a major role during construction and hence should be managed considerately in order to keep the workforce content. There are many opportunities in the site environment for dissatisfaction of the workforce:

- remote site with poor living conditions;
- difficult working conditions;
- discrepancies in payment;
- lack of adequate site facilities;
- large, crowded groups of people;
- loss of bonuses due to delays or aborted work;
- differences in conditions of employment with neighbouring employers.

The subjects which may be considered and agreed beforehand by the client, contractors and any subcontractors include:

- application of any local/national agreements;
- hours of work;
- arrangements for overtime or weekend working;
- any special payments — for example, for dirty working conditions.

Management of contracts

The contractors' performance should be monitored early and regularly to check the construction is progressing to plan and, if not, that appropriate action is taken. First, check that the contractor has a good programme and methods worked out in detail, including time for placing subcontracts. Items to consider monitoring include:

- manning levels are as agreed;
- construction equipment is available;
- work is to the correct quality;
- safety requirements are being met;
- productivity;
- claims for contract extras;
- meeting the agreed programme.

In most instances, a discussion at site management level will suffice to resolve any problems. Failing this, it is possible to take the problem to a higher management level with the contractor organization, in order to reach an acceptable solution. The next level for resolution includes delaying payments or applying any damage liabilities within the contract. Any such apparent cost savings are then applied to overcoming the problem in some alternative manner — for example, giving additional work to another contractor.

The worst scenario is for the matter to develop to the point that a contractor is removed from site and/or legal proceedings are started. Were it to deteriorate to this stage, it is clear that as the project manager you have already missed one of the project aims, and there is no way of recovering fully from the impact of the contractor's failure.

The contractor may submit claims for extras to the contract. These should be assessed and dealt with quickly — that is, either approved or rejected. Failure to complete this in a timely manner usually results in additional problems caused by:

- those with first-hand knowledge of the details being transferred to other work at the end of their assignment to your project;
- the simple loss of memory over time.

Any prolongation of conflict over claims for extras inevitably leads to bitterness, and reduces motivation and effort within the affected parties.

Even in the best-managed projects, there are usually changes during construction. A system to control these changes should be agreed in the contract, to prevent the contractor being instructed to undertake additional or changed work prior to approval by the appropriate person within the project team. To achieve this, the system incorporates:

- accurate verification of contractor payment entitlement, whether it be based on percentage progress or measured quantities of work;

• up-to-date and accurate forecasts of final contract value.

Towards the end of each construction contract, preparations should be in hand for the contractor to complete outstanding punch-list work rapidly, in order to release systems to the commissioning group in the previously agreed system. The contractor then submits a final account for the services and to close up the contract without undue delay. Any money retention or performance bonds are cancelled in accordance with the contract terms.

Further reading

European Construction Institute, 1993, *Client Management and its Role in the Limitation of Contentious Claims* (ECI).

Project example

Construction has now started on the project. The existing equipment has already been shut down and decontaminated as required, and services isolated. You now know that a new agitator motor is required; it has been specified and is on order. It will be installed after commissioning. The pump manufacturer has confirmed that the pump delivery will meet the programme requirements. What are the issues for you at this stage?

What should you be doing as project manager at this stage?
Here are some suggested actions. Note that this is a guide. It is not exhaustive. It is an indication of what may be relevant to a project.

In construction, achieving safety must be planned and monitored. You should therefore satisfy yourself that all safety requirements are being met. How might you do this?

• Issue the safety file and check that the contractor understands it.

• Identify who in B&B (as the principal contractor) is responsible for implementing safety amongst all its employees and any subcontractors' employees, and for maintaining the safety file.

• Get regular reports from your construction supervisor and from B&B.

• Arrange for safety audits on the construction.

• Visit the site regularly and actually check yourself that safety systems are being followed.

If safety issues are raised, then follow them up and ensure that actions are implemented. For example, what would you do if you saw someone working at height and reaching from a ladder, and you thought this to be unsafe? You should arrange for that particular task to be stopped immediately, and a better method implemented — for example, scaffolding erected — so that the work could continue from a safe platform.

If any safety incidents do arise, then it is important that they are fully investigated to determine the cause and hence recommend preventative measures. Reports should be widely publicized in order to share learning and to prevent similar incidents happening again.

As the project is being constructed within an existing operation, there are certain issues which may arise which would not on a greenfield site. For example:

- Access to the plant may be difficult due to other process operations.
- There may be restrictions on, for example, types of equipment which can be used, conditions for burning or welding.
- Permits-to-work and entries into vessels may need to be issued by operations personnel. This may not be their own priority, and so delays can arise if they are unhelpful.
- Storage of installation equipment may not be possible at the installation site, so it may take time each morning to assemble equipment at the start of the day.
- Security at the installation should be considered. Are operating staff likely to pilfer goods that are not locked away?
- Noise generated during installation could cause great annoyance to operating personnel in the vicinity, and typically they would not hesitate to complain.
- Operating staff may try to interfere with the installation if they feel it is being done inadequately.

So what should you do in these circumstances, as all are likely to lead to delays in the construction? Some of the more routine issues could be dealt with by your construction supervisor.

For others, you may need to discuss the problems with production management, to try to resolve the issues. Explain the consequences — delays and additional costs to the project and, ultimately, additional expenditure for your company. If matters do not improve, then you could ask your own line manager to follow it up with senior management.

Variations or changes may be submitted during construction by B&B, so what should you do with them? Implement a system for managing them, considering for instance:

- Safety aspects are checked and understood before any change is made.
- Identification of how the change will affect project cost and/or programme.
- Methods for approving such changes before they are made.
- Whether your construction supervisor can authorize changes, and if so to what expenditure level. Above this, do you authorize them?

You still need a system in place and your team available to answer any technical queries which may arise at this stage.

You should be obtaining up-to-date and detailed programmes and method statements for all remaining work and getting regular feedback on progress on problems from both B&B and your construction supervisor. How would you do this?

• Make sure you have informal discussions and meetings, as well as formal reports. You need to know how both progress and costs compare to plan, and what effect variations are having on the project.

Continue with your own cost control and planning for the project, incorporating B&B's information into your own financial and progress reports, so that you can predict when the project will finish, and how much it will cost.

You should also be preparing for the next phase of the project, commissioning, as you will be acting as commissioning manager. What preparation is needed?

• Prepare your detailed commissioning plans, identifying what sections you will commission, when and how.

• Re-check that the current construction programme allows you to commission the sections in your required sequence.

• Ensure there is a system for formally handing over sections from construction to pre-commissioning.

• Start training any operating and maintenance personnel who will assist you in commissioning.

• Check the new equipment to ensure that it is being installed to the correct standards and specifications.

Commissioning

Richard Collins and Gillian Lawson

Commissioning entails bringing the 'dead' constructed plant to life, and producing product to the design quantity and quality. In certain companies or for larger projects, commissioning may be split into sub-stages, typically called handover, pre-commissioning and commissioning. Thus, handover and pre-commissioning often start when some of the equipment or systems are still being constructed, and hence safety is of paramount importance.

Commissioning strategy

The way the plant is to be commissioned should have been thought about earlier in design, to check that systems can be started up safely and with the necessary instrumentation. For larger projects, commissioning may have been in the scope of the main contractor, or may fall to the client. For smaller projects, the plant may be commissioned by the project manager, or preferably by someone who will finally manage or operate the equipment.

With larger projects, the commissioning strategy considers how best to break the task down into manageable packages under the work breakdown structure — for example, based on process phases, process material or equipment/plant location. Conversely, it may be possible to consider the commissioning as just one package for smaller projects.

The strategy also considers the commissioning programme — for example, how long will it take to complete the work realistically? Are there any major milestones to be met, such as:

- cooling water available to enable commissioning of dependent equipment;
- steam available to allow cleaning of other equipment;
- compressed air available to enable instruments to be tested;
- first process phase completely commissioned first, so that first stage product can be used as feedstock for second phase commissioning.

The commissioning requirements and programme are fed back into the construction programme before it is finalized, and well before construction commences. Thus, items which need to be commissioned first are constructed first.

Check-list 9.1   Items for consideration at the construction/commissioning
interface

- Completion of outstanding construction work
- Completion of reservations or punch-list items — that is, defined installation
activities
- Any testing, witnessing, hazardous area and electrical inspections and tests
- Clarification on packages of work, systems or plant items
- Operation of permit-to-work system
- Induction of new persons to site or plant
- Training of commissioning teams
- Identification of live services, utilities and process fluids
- Control of access and egress — normal and emergency
- Isolations, boundaries and notices
- Changes to any existing site practices — eg, smoking, carrying of battery
equipment, wearing of personal protective equipment
- Check that all parties agree on the definition of any local terms or phrases — eg,
'mechanical completion', 'clean', 'pre-commissioning'
- Any involvement of suppliers in commissioning
- Phasing and priorities in commissioning of systems
- Support expected from construction — eg, construction management,
construction supervision and labour, temporary services, accommodation
- Handover of safety file

As described in Chapter 8, the system for handover of parts of the plant from
construction is discussed and agreed early. There should also be clear agreement on the stages (if any) within the commissioning itself — for example,
mechanical completion, pre-commissioning, commissioning on process materials — and the scope of each stage. Check-list 9.1 gives examples of items to
be considered and agreed at the construction/commissioning interface.

The commissioning team interfaces with many interested parties, including
the construction team, contractors, managers of adjacent plants, and managers
of utilities to be used. Again, how these interfaces are to be managed should be
agreed and communicated, to prevent confusion later.

The commissioning team
The roles and responsibilities of those involved in commissioning need to be
discussed, agreed and communicated. For larger projects, a commissioning

manager is often appointed quite early in the project. This allows the commissioning team the opportunity to understand fully the design criteria, the construction and their effect on construction, and feed back any amendments required. Additionally, it gives the commissioning manager the opportunity to start planning the commissioning, and assembling the supporting commissioning team as soon as possible. The scale of this operation may obviously be less for minor projects. If the basic process is owned by others and licensed to the project, in some instances the licenser will provide the commissioning team, or at least have a representative within the team.

Depending on the project size, the commissioning manager may have a support team to assist in commissioning, Ideally, the commissioning team consists of people with relevant training and experience of all stages of commissioning who have worked together before. This typically includes a balance between those with theoretical and practical ability. As a rough guide, the technical staff requirement is about twice that for normal operation. The support team may come from the contractor organization, the client company or an appropriate mix of both. It may consist of management and/or operating staff who will ultimately operate the plant. This is often viewed as a good way for the final owners to understand the plant that they will receive. If this is not the case, then it is worth checking whether one of the additional responsibilities expected of the commissioning manager is that of training the ultimate operating personnel in running the plant.

Commissioning of plant often requires the systems to be started up, operated or shut down at any time of the day or week; it is very rare that commissioning can be done during typical day working hours. Thus, in assembling the commissioning team, numbers of personnel should be available to provide total 24-hour coverage, using shift systems as appropriate.

Remember that the project manager still has overall responsibility for the project, irrespective of the size of the commissioning team, unless an EPIC contract has been placed (see Chapter 25 for further information). If not employed as part of the commissioning team, members of the design team should still be available at this stage to answer any technical questions. Further, the construction team should be available to assist with any modifications identified as essential by the commissioning team (following all necessary safety assessments and so on).

Commissioning programme

A detailed commissioning programme is required if the commissioning is to be well managed, and this is especially true for complex activities. The commissioning programme is linked to the construction programme, to ensure that the pieces of plant or process systems are constructed in the most appropriate order. The typical phases of commissioning for a system are:

- confirmation of mechanical completion (equipment installed and physically tested);
- confirmation of completion of remaining 'punch-list' work;
- handover from construction;
- pre-commissioning checks and tests;
- pre-commissioning on water or inert substances;
- commissioning on process materials.

CONSTRUCTION SUPPORT MAY BE NEEDED DURING COMMISSIONING.

Handover from construction

Mechanical completion is the stage at which that part of the plant has been fully installed in accordance with the agreed design intent but no live testing has been undertaken. All modifications to the design which have been made during construction should be recorded in 'as built' documentation. This documentation reflects what actually exists, and is communicated to all relevant groups, thus superseding all previous versions of the documentation.

Some aspects of the plant may not yet have been installed — for example, catalysts — pending further preparatory work during pre-commissioning. Typically, equipment will have been cleaned out. Vessels, heat exchangers and the like, and interconnecting pipe systems will have been pressure-tested, either hydraulically or pneumatically. Electrical and instrument wiring will have been tested to confirm continuity and correctness of signal routing, but normally none of these systems will have been supplied with power.

When this state is reached, mechanical completion has been achieved and formal certificates can be issued. Such certificates normally define the part of the plant to which the certificate relates, possibly referring separately to the different disciplines — for example, civil, structural, mechanical, instrumentation, electrical.

It is common practice to effect mechanical completion with limited but well-defined work outstanding. This is often referred to as 'punch-list' or 'reservation' work, and typically allows for completion of painting and insulation in some areas, together with removal of residual scaffolding after commissioning is complete, thus minimizing later re-work costs. For example, a design change may have caused a delay to the delivery of a piece of instrumentation, in which case it is agreed that this can be installed later. Such outstanding items are clearly listed on the mechanical completion certificate as reservations. Suitable systems should be in place for this outstanding work to be completed by construction at the appropriate time, and to ensure that any commercial implications are taken fully into account.

Additionally, it should be understood what documents — such as data sheets, flowsheets, installation manuals, operating and maintenance instructions — are required for commissioning of the plant. Often, this is carried out as part of the preparation and issue of the project data book to the client. The project data book is the bound collection of documents which provide the client with a full definition of the 'as built' plant. The format, indices, contents lists and number of copies of the book are agreed early in the project. This enables the correct number of copies of vendor data to be stated on purchase orders, to be followed by the gradual build-up of the data books. This initiative is in the best interest of the project manager, because the project manager is the first person on the project, and the last person to leave it, and if the data book is not complete, guess who has to finish it! Check-list 9.2 (pages 118–120) shows the typical contents of the project data book.

Formal safety systems should be in place to ensure that the status of equipment and process are known during commissioning.
(Reproduced by courtesy of Conoco Ltd and David Lee Photography Ltd.)

Pre-commissioning

Pre-commissioning is the work undertaken after mechanical completion in order to prepare the plant for receipt of feedstocks, and to allow for introduction of utilities.

The work required includes:

- flushing of piping systems to remove residual debris;
- installation of final components of in-line instrument components;
- dry-out of refractory in furnaces;
- fill with catalyst;
- power to electrical and instrumentation systems;
- full instrument circuit checks through the control system;
- confirmation that trip systems are working;
- enlivening utility circuits and building services;
- checking rotation of pump motors;
- running pump circuits on water.

Check-list 9.2   Typical contents of the project data book

Process engineering

- Process description
- Plant capacity
- Feedstocks, raw materials, intermediates and product specifications
- Physical property data for process materials, products and effluents
- Services and utilities specifications
- Process conditions
- Process flowsheets
- Mass and energy balances, with utilities consumption
- Gaseous, liquid and solid effluents
- Process data sheets for main plant items
- Control philosophy
- Calculations
- Sampling requirements
- Relief streams
- Protective systems
- Hazard study reports
- Environmental reports
- Health reports

Design information

- Drawing register
- Engineering line diagrams/P&IDs
- Layouts and general arrangement

Civil, structural and architectural

- Building information, including HVAC details
- Drainage details
- Floor loadings
- Foundation details
- Calculations
- Lifting gear and beam schedules
- Room data sheets
- Structure and building finishes
- Steelwork and structural drawings

Continued opposite

118

Check-list 9.2 (cont'd)   Typical contents of the project data book

Mechanical
- Piping:
— drawings including isometrics and GAs
— in-line fittings data sheets and schedules
— fluid conditions
— pipeline specifications
— pressure relief valves, bursting discs, overflows and vents
— pressure testing and cleaning
— insulation/painting specifications and schedules
- Vessels:
— equipment data sheets
— drawings
— calculations
— equipment schedules
— test certificates
- Machines
— equipment data sheets
— drawings
— calculations
— equipment schedules
— test certificates
— lubrication schedule and maintenance manuals
- Furnaces and boilers:
— equipment data sheets
— drawings
— calculations
— equipment schedules
— test certificates

Continued overleaf

Check-list 9.2 (cont'd)	Typical contents of the project data book

Control/instrumentation and electrical
- Instrument list/database
- In-line instrumentation specifications
- Control loop diagrams and lists
- Instrument wiring/connection details
- Power/earthing details
- Instrument cable schedule
- Instrument cable routes
- Trip and alarm test schedules and methods
- System calculations
- Single line diagrams
- Electrical area classifications
- Power/earthing layout/details
- Electrical equipment specifications
- Electrical cable schedules
- Lighting drawings/schedules
- Electrical tracing specifications/drawings
- Lightning protection specification

Other inerts rather than water may be needed for flushing, due to potential chemical reactions or to prevent wetting of subsequent dry systems, such as powder handling equipment.

Approved procedures and resources are applied to this stage, including the prudent application of a permit-to-work system to ensure that work is done without risk to personnel, the plant or the environment. Where any final modifications have been identified by the pre-commissioning team, and carried out by construction, such modifications are recorded in the final 'as built' documentation.

The pre-commissioning activity releases the plant for commissioning by section or area in accordance with the previously agreed commissioning plan.

Commissioning

Commissioning is almost the final stage in the project, and involves the introduction of feedstock to establish the plant as an operating unit. Commissioning is usually undertaken in a stepwise manner, gradually bringing in each section of the plant to full operational capacity. To be successful, it requires the provision of an experienced, skilled team and extensive measuring and monitoring activities above those which are required in normal operation. A significant amount of training of the team under the direction of the commissioning manager is usually required over a substantial period before actual commissioning starts.

For each section of the plant in turn, and in a pre-arranged sequence to secure progressive start-up through the process route, the commissioning team carries out the start-up activities. These activities are typically:

- purge systems of traces of flushing water and/or inerts to dry them as necessary;
- introduce feedstocks or purge materials and circulate them around as complete a system as possible using process equipment as appropriate — for example, pumps and compressors — following the manufacturer's instructions;
- bring the system up to near operating pressure as necessary;
- commission furnaces and other heating systems, and bring the system up to operating temperature at a controlled rate;
- adjust instrumentation as necessary and transfer to automatic control as appropriate;
- switch plant trips to live positions as appropriate;
- introduce or circulate feed to the equipment at process conditions — for example, reactors, distillation columns;
- route initial products to flares or intermediate storage for later recycle to the process;
- take readings from instrumentation to monitor the operation at each step and compare to the design or expected readings;
- take samples of feeds, intermediates and products for analysis, and compare with design or expected values;
- undertake initial maintenance and mechanical adjustments as necessary — for example, hot bolt tightening at flanges, cleaning out of temporary strainers.

The plant is checked to ensure that it meets its flowsheet operation with regard to feedstocks, products, utilities and chemicals. Further, to confirm that the plant operates to required environmental legislation, it is important that measurements are obtained to ensure that the plant meets the noise, liquid and gaseous emission standards.

Commissioning usually culminates in a performance test run, which is performed in accordance with any previously defined operating parameters as per the design basis, or any contractual obligations for the plant. After a successful test run, the plant is often awarded an 'acceptance certificate'

Check-list 9.3   Information which may be required for the acceptance process

- Operation and maintenance manuals
- Building operation manual
- Project data book
- 'As built' drawings
- Calibration certificates
- Factory test certificates
- Guarantees
- Commissioning test results
- Documentation for any registered system — eg, pressure vessels, lifting equipment
- Safety data

---

confirming that the client agrees that the plant meets the agreed operation requirements. Sometimes, provisional acceptance certificates are awarded when some minor requirements have not yet been met, but will be corrected later. Check-list 9.3 carries information which may be required for the acceptance process. Close-out activities can then commence.

The client, however, is usually just starting a long and interesting relationship with the new plant, endeavouring to understand it, keep it on-stream for the maximum possible time, and to improve its operability, efficiency and safety, health and environmental (SHE) performance.

Further reading

Horsley, D. (ed), 1998, *Process Plant Commissioning*, 2nd edition (Institution of Chemical Engineers).

Project example

Construction is still continuing on the project as you move into pre-commissioning. You are concerned that the new pump has still not arrived from the manufacturer, and that construction is a few days behind programme. You have started to produce a 'punch-list' of outstanding work, which needs to be completed before you start commissioning.

What should you be doing as project manager and commissioning manager at this stage?

Here are some suggested actions. Note that this is a guide. It is not exhaustive. It is an indication of what may be relevant to a project.

Progress all actions needed for delivery of the pump with B&B and with the manufacturers with great urgency, and get assistance from others to exert even greater influence on them. Get B&B to use contractual provisions if necessary, in order to get the pump delivered. Ensure that pressure is maintained on the manufacturer until the pump arrives. Meanwhile, assess the detailed programme for installing the pump once it does arrive, for example:

- Berthing of the pump onto prepared foundations/plinth.
- Mechanical alignment and pipework connection.
- Fixing to plinth (and allow time for curing as necessary).
- Electrical connection.
- Testing rotational direction.

Determine the best way to tackle each step in order to minimize elapsed time. For example:

- Could the installation be carried out so that curing is done overnight rather than waste day time?
- Could time be saved by using additional people? Possibly not in this instance as it is a simple task, requiring few people. Also, limited physical space may inhibit the use of more than a couple of people.
- Could the work be scheduled for installation at the weekend or on overtime?

Likewise, resolve how you want B&B to catch up to programme and to complete the punch-list items.

Initially, you should determine and agree why there have been delays:

- Are they due to B&B errors or inefficiencies?
- Are they due to your own company? For example, waiting for permits-to-work or shutdowns on services to allow tie-ins, not to predetermined programme.

Where the cause is due to B&B, then it would typically be responsible for completing the work to original time and cost (dependent upon contract terms). Where the cause is not due to B&B, then you would need to assess the additional cost to the project of overtime and/or additional resources against the benefit of keeping to programme. If you already have a good change control and cost control system in place, and hence know exactly how much you have spent so far, it is easier to judge such situations.

What is still your top priority at this stage?

- Safety has priority throughout the project, and this phase is no exception.
- Do not be tempted to rush yourself or others into finishing off jobs. This can

lead to poor quality workmanship or errors — for example, fitting wrong gasket materials or the wrong size gasket leads to greater problems in future, such as leaks.

• Take time to consider any changes to the construction plan in order to assess how this may affect the commissioning sequence. For instance, if water connections are completed late, then this may mean you cannot flush clean other equipment.

• Follow your agreed formal handover process for sections of plant from construction to commissioning, so that you know the state of all pieces of equipment — for example, motors confirmed electrically 'live' or 'dead'.

• If there have been any changes to the process or equipment during construction or commissioning, then ensure that these changes are incorporated into all relevant documentation, so that 'as built' information truly reflects what is there.

You should be able to proceed with your pre-commissioning and commissioning as per your programme, assisted by trained plant personnel. Complete any outstanding training requirements. Remember to carry out any necessary measurements such as noise emissions or test runs.

Also at this time, collate the project data book and safety file, bringing together all the relevant, current information for the future operation, maintenance and decommissioning of the plant.

Project closure

Richard Collins and Gillian Lawson

The project is only satisfactorily completed when it achieves the purpose agreed with the client and is accepted by the client. It is necessary to close a project to ensure that any further expenditure on the project is stopped, but closure is not normally carried out until any remaining activities or required work has been completed, and associated invoices paid. Thus, the project manager has to co-ordinate actions to correct design faults before closure. The project manager may also be asked to manage new needs highlighted once the plant is in operation, but if they are outside the original scope, they need not be completed before starting project closure.

Close-out

When it is thought that the time is right to start closing the project, this should be communicated to all the project team members, so that they have the opportunity to finish off items under their responsibility and control. Activities which may remain and should therefore be completed include:

- project fully accepted by client;
- transfer of documents to client (for a more complete list see Chapter 20);
- safety file completed and handed over;
- surplus material disposed of or sold;
- purchase orders and contracts finalized;
- all invoices paid;
- all guarantees met;
- liquidated damages paid;
- performance bonds cancelled;
- project accounts reconciled;
- any special project bank accounts closed;
- project insurance policies terminated;
- any property leases cancelled;
- special telephone links cancelled;
- project records which are not required rehoused or destroyed.

Project review and report

There remains one very worthwhile task — to review the project. This enables all those involved to reflect on the project performance; what went well and should be repeated, and what did not go so well and should be avoided in other projects. A lot can be learned from sharing experiences from a project.

The format and content of the report differ from project to project, and organization to organization. However, the general intent of the report is to summarize the project activities and methods of execution, and to capture the good and bad parts of the project management. The successful methods and failures are examined and the reasons investigated. What were their causes? What risks were foreseen, and what could have been foreseen? *Why?* Thus, statistics, perceptions relating to client satisfaction and any lessons that have been learnt are documented and shared for future reference. Check-list 10.1 (page 128) suggests topics for inclusion in the review.

The personnel that are usually asked to contribute to the review are:
- the project manager;
- the client;
- representatives from each of the main functional design areas — process, civil, structural, mechanical, instrumentation and electrical;
- contractor organizations;
- purchasing;
- suppliers of significant pieces of equipment;
- construction contractors;
- construction management team;
- commissioning team.

At its worst, the report is a collection of meaningless data of little value, but at its best it provides a co-ordinated view and can be the basis of corporate decisions on how to do things better. Such activities can secure and improve safety, quality, cost and programme features for future projects and thus enhance perceptions of clients and the general business role with regard to project management in the process industries.

One final activity remains for the project team. Celebrate the end of a successful project with an end-of-project party!

Project example

Congratulations! Last week you handed over the completed plant to operations, and they have been producing WHIZZO to planned throughput and quality. The project was within budget, but a week late due to the pump delivery and construction delays (this was accepted by your line manager).

A PROJECT MANAGER GETS GREAT SATISFACTION
IN SUCCESSFULLY COMPLETING A PROJECT.

Have you now finished your tasks as project manager?

Here are some suggested actions. Note that this is a guide. It is not exhaustive. It is an indication of what may be relevant to a project.

It is certainly not the end of your tasks! There are still some items to be finished off — such as financial closure of the project. It is unlikely that you will have received all invoices yet, so closure may not be possible for a couple of months.

If you had a robust system in place for dealing with changes and variations from B&B, then its claims should have been dealt with at the time. Any outstanding claims should now be resolved as quickly as possible. You may also have decided to take indirect action against the pump manufacturer via your contract with B&B for the late pump delivery, and this may take time to resolve.

Inform others when you plan to close the project. Aim to get outstanding items completed as quickly as possible in order to close the project to prevent further costs being added.

You should also complete a project review and report, to summarize and share the learning from the project. Ask those who had a major role in the project to contribute to the review. Review what went well and why, as well as the causes of and the lessons learned from the problems, for example:

- Why the initial six-month programme was not realistic.
- Why the need for a new agitator motor was not identified earlier.
- How B&B performed.

Check-list 10.1   Suggested topics for inclusion in the project review report

---

Summary of project
- Project purpose
- Summary of risks identified, and any actions taken
- Project scope, and any changes
- SHE requirements, and how these were met
- Client, contractor and subcontractor interfaces
- Any new technology
- Any new management systems introduced

Project organization and performance
- Project organization
- Project control strategy
- Contract strategy
- Contractor's performance
- Design performance and productivity:
— process
— civil, structural and architectural
— mechanical
— control/electrical
- Procurement
- Construction performance:
— productivity
— safety performance
- Commissioning

Deviations from project estimates and programme, and reasons
- Project costs for all phases
- Project programme, and milestones met
- Project man-hours
- Use of project reserves

Client's review on performance

Conclusions and recommendations

- Why the pump was delivered late, and whether the manufacturer should be removed from the preferred suppliers list.
- Which management systems worked well, and which others could be improved — for example, change control.

Lastly, ensure all those who contributed to the project are properly thanked for their effort and input.

Section 2 – Tools and techniques

Stephen Wearne

The ten chapters in Section 2 review systems, tools and techniques relevant to project management.

The sequence of chapters is not in order of importance of the subjects covered. As indicated in Section 1, the use of any appropriate tools and techniques should be considered at every stage of a project.

The chapters include check-lists for project managers. The chapters do not specify universal methods and rules. They describe choices and give comments on their potential advantages and disadvantages for different projects.

Statutory duties – health, safety, welfare and the environment

11

Diana Kloss, Ian Hymes and Stephen Wearne

Most developed nations have laws which are designed to regulate the safety of people at work. As the welfare of the workforce is seen by enlightened nations as both a moral and an economic issue, these laws are strengthened by a system of inspection and by legal proceedings against those who transgress. Clearly, the effectiveness of legislation must depend to a large extent on how stringently the law is enforced. The number of inspectors, and frequencies of inspection, differ markedly from state to state. The European Union has a Committee of Senior Labour Inspectors which consists of representatives of labour inspection and enforcement bodies of the member states to try to agree minimum standards of inspection and enforcement throughout the European Union.

In the United States, the Occupational Health and Safety Acts impose duties on the Federal Department of Labor and the Department of Health to set standards of occupational health and safety. The Occupational Health and Safety Administration (OHSA) is responsible for the administration of the legislation. Equally important is the US National Institute of Occupational Safety and Health (NIOSH) which undertakes research.

The European Union

The safety of workers has been an important part of European Community (EC) policy since the foundation of the Coal and Steel Community in 1951. The European influence on the law of health and safety has become paramount. As the standards of safety and the investment demanded from employers to protect workers differ from state to state, it has always been accepted that health and safety at work is a proper subject for Community initiative. Economic integration must not be achieved at the price of placing workers at unacceptable risk. The Single European Act (in Article 118A) permits Directives on improvement in the working environment to be agreed by a qualified majority of the member states. However, no state may be ordered to reduce its safety requirements, and regard must be had to the costs of implementation for small and medium-sized undertakings.

Though European law has not always been accepted by the UK Government, which followed a policy of deregulation, the UK Health and Safety Commission in 1989 said that, 'the EC is in effect emerging as the main engine of law-making in safety and health'. In the EC the UK Government have abstained from voting on some Directives and actively opposed others, but if a matter is classified by the European Court in Luxembourg as falling within the category of health and safety at work, the UK Government has to implement a Directive which has obtained a qualified majority in the Council of Ministers.

United Kingdom law

UK health and safety law is now incorporated in the Health and Safety at Work, etc Act 1974 (HSWA) and Regulations and Approved Codes of Practice (ACOPs) made thereunder. The old statutes like the Factories Act and the Office Shops and Railway Premises Act have been replaced by the Workplace Regulations 1992 and the Provision and Use of Work Equipment Regulations 1992 (PUWER).

The HSWA introduced a number of important changes:

- it applied to all places of work;
- it was untechnical: the employer must do that which is reasonably practicable. Detail was added in Regulations and Codes of Practice. What is 'reasonably practicable' depends upon cost-benefit analysis;
- it involved a duty to consult with worker representatives (safety representatives) appointed by a recognized trade union. Where there is no recognized trade union, safety representatives are appointed by all the workers;
- it gave important new powers to inspectors to issue prohibition and improvement notices (the employer can appeal against a notice to an employment tribunal);
- it imposed duties not only on the employer but also on senior managers and individual employees (Section 7). Occasionally criminal prosecutions are brought against individuals where there has been a very bad incident or the inspector wishes to make an example of someone;
- it imposed duties not only on employees but also on third parties, including contractors and the public both on and off site.

UK Regulations and Codes of Practice

In the UK, statutes such as the HSWA are amplified by UK Regulations ('Statutory Instruments' or SIs).

An Approved Code of Practice is one approved by the UK Health and Safety Commission. It is presumed that a failure to follow the recommendations of an Approved Code of Practice constitutes a breach of the criminal law unless the defendant establishes that he complied with the law by some other means (Section 17, HSWA).

Penalties

The burden is on the defendant in criminal proceedings to show that he has done what is practicable or reasonably practicable (Section 40, HSWA).

There is no action for damages for breach of statutory duty for breach of Sections 2 to 8 of the HSWA. Breach of Regulations made under the Act are actionable in the civil law so far as they cause damage, except where the Regulations provide otherwise (Section 47, HSWA). Most Regulations do not provide otherwise, but Regulation 15 of the Management of Health and Safety at Work Regulations 1992 and Regulation 21 of the Construction (Design and Management) Regulations 1994 provide that there is no civil action for breach of most of those Regulations.

Where the Health and Safety Executive or local authority investigate in connection with a possible criminal offence, Section 28 (9) of the HSWA permits them at their discretion to furnish to any person who appears to be likely to be a party to any civil proceedings arising out of any accident or occurrence a written statement of relevant facts observed in the course of exercising statutory powers.

Recent developments in health and safety law include an increase in potential penalties — in the magistrates' courts up to six months imprisonment and a £20,000 fine. The Crown courts (judge and jury) can imprison for up to two years and impose an unlimited fine. Most prosecutions are brought in the magistrates' courts, because the expense of bringing proceedings there is far lower than in the Crown court. There have been prosecutions for manslaughter in cases like the Zeebrugge ferry disaster. It is necessary to prove gross negligence. A company can be prosecuted for corporate manslaughter.

Deregulation and self-regulation

In recent years, the policy of the UK Government has been to scrutinize health and safety laws closely in order to weed out unnecessary Regulations which are seen as a restraint on competition. A policy of self-regulation by large employers has led to the introduction of the 'safety case' idea, whereby the employer is responsible largely for policing his health and safety policies. (Offshore Installations (Safety Case) Regulations 1992; Railways (Safety Case) Regulations 1994.)

...WEED OUT UNNECESSARY REGULATIONS...

Implementation of European Directives

The UK Regulations which implement EC Directives follow a similar pattern, with which British industry first became familiar in the Control of Substances Hazardous to Health Regulations (COSHH) 1988, updated in 1994. Even more important are the Management of Health and Safety at Work Regulations and Approved Code of Practice 1992, implementing EC Directive 89/391. These relate to all employers and all kinds of hazards.

Employer's duties: Management Regulations 1992

Under the Management of Health and Safety at Work Regulations:
- the employer must make a suitable and sufficient assessment of:
— the risks to the health and safety of his employees to which they are exposed while they are at work; and
— the risks to the health and safety of persons not in his employment arising out of or in connection with the conduct by him of his undertaking, for the purposes of identifying the measures he needs to take to comply with law.

The self-employed person is also under a duty to assess risks to his own health and safety and to that of others;
- the assessment must be kept up-to-date. The assessment must be recorded where the employer employs five or more employees;
- the employer shall make appropriate arrangements for planning, organizing, monitoring, control, etc, of preventive and protective measures;

- every employer shall ensure that his employees are provided with such health surveillance as is appropriate;
- every employer shall appoint one or more competent persons to assist him, and shall make arrangements for ensuring adequate co-operation between them;
- every employer shall establish and where necessary give effect to appropriate procedures to be followed in the event of serious and imminent danger;
- every employer shall provide his employees with comprehensible and relevant information on the risks, the preventive and protective measures, etc;
- where two or more employers share a workplace (whether on a temporary or permanent basis) each such employer shall:
— co-operate with the other employers;
— take all reasonable steps to co-ordinate the measures he takes to comply with the law;
— take all reasonable steps to inform the other employers of risks to their employees' health and safety arising out of his activities;
- every employer shall ensure that employers of persons from an outside undertaking working in his undertaking are provided with comprehensible information on the risks to those employees' health and safety;
- every employer shall, in entrusting tasks to his employees, take into account their capabilities as regards health and safety and provide them with adequate health and safety training;
- employees are required to use safety equipment, follow safety instructions, etc, and to inform their employer of work situations which give rise to serious and immediate danger or disclose 'gaps' in the safety cover.

Construction (Design And Management) Regulations 1994 (CDM)

The UK Construction (Design and Management) Regulations 1994 (abbreviated to CDM, formerly CONDAM) implement European Directive 57/92. ·

The CDM Regulations apply to construction, demolition and dismantling work. Under the Regulations designers and contractors have to be selected on the basis that they are aware of their health and safety duties and will allocate adequate resources to them.

The Regulations impose on the client the duty to select and appoint a 'planning supervisor' and a 'principal contractor' for a project. Figure 11.1 (page 136) illustrates the relationships and flow of information required between all parties.

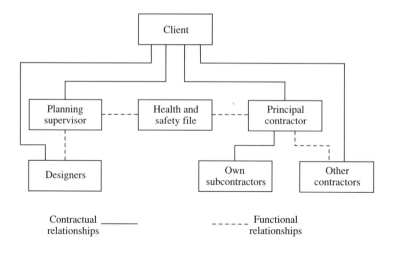

Figure 11.1 The relationships and flow of information between parties

The planning supervisor

The duties of the planning supervisor include:
- ensuring that construction health and safety requirements are met in design;
- ensuring that particulars of a project are notified to the health and safety authorities;
- preparing a health and safety plan for the project.

The person appointed must be competent and have adequate resources. The client may appoint the project manager, a consultant or any other person as the planning supervisor. A member of the client's staff may be appointed.

The principal contractor

The duties of the principal contractor include:
- maintaining the health and safety plan;
- ensuring co-operation between all contractors on health and safety;
- ensuring that everybody on site complies with rules in the plan.

The contractor appointed must be competent and have adequate resources. It can be the main contractor for constructing the project, a management contractor or a specialist in construction health and safety.

Designers

Design must comply with the health and safety standards required by law. The main duties of the designer under the CDM Regulations are to:

- alert the project manager to the client's duties;
- consider during design the hazards and risks which may arise to those who will construct and maintain the works;
- design to avoid risks to health and safety throughout the life of the project;
- reduce risks at source if avoidance is not possible;
- consider measures which will protect all workers if neither avoidance or reduction to a safe level are possible;
- ensure that drawings, specifications, operations and maintenance instructions and so on, include adequate information on health and safety;
- pass this information to the planning supervisor so that it can be included in the health and safety plan;
- co-operate with the planning supervisor, and where necessary other designers involved in the project.

Under the CDM Regulations, the client has a duty to appoint designers who have the competence and resources needed for their duties under the Regulations.

Construction start

Under the CDM Regulations the client has the legal duty not to permit construction to start until the principal contractor has prepared a satisfactory health and safety plan.

Control of Substances Hazardous to Health Regulations 1994 (COSHH)

The COSHH Regulations were originally introduced into UK law in 1988, and were updated in 1994. They derive from European Directives.

Prior to COSHH, there were Regulations relating to particular substances — for example, asbestos and lead — but the new Regulations apply to all hazardous substances other than those already covered by legislation, including dust and biological agents. For certain substances, occupational exposure standards or maximum exposure limits are fixed by delegated legislation (see Schedule 1, COSHH Regulations, EH40 (HSE Guidance Note)). The occupational exposure standard is the level of exposure to which, on average, it is permissible that the workers should be subject. The maximum exposure limit is the upper limit above which workers should not be exposed.

The COSHH Regulations introduced into UK law for the first time the obligation on the employer to undertake a comprehensive risk assessment of the substances to which his employees, and others on his site, are exposed.

Employers have duties to those directly employed, to the employees of contractors, and to those within the foreseeable area of risk, like members of the public both on site and near the site. The Regulations impose a duty to prevent or control exposure to hazardous substances, to monitor controls, and to provide health surveillance, information, instruction and training to employees. Personal protective equipment should not be a first line of defence: engineering controls are the first priority, and protective equipment the back-up.

Where any ill-health effects are likely from exposure, the employer must undertake health surveillance of his employees. This may be done by a doctor, nurse or other responsible person (for example, a supervisor), depending on the complexity of the task. Records of health surveillance must be kept for at least 40 years.

COSHH assessments should be undertaken only by competent persons and records should be kept. The assessments must be regularly updated.

Injury at work: compensation through the civil law

The civil law of tort provides compensation for those injured at work. An action may be brought against the employer for:

- negligence;
- breach of statutory duty.

The latter is used where there is a specific duty imposed by statutory regulation or the regulation imposes strict liability (liability is not dependent on proof of negligence).

The employer has a duty at common law (law not covered by statute or regulation) to take reasonable care to provide:

- safe plant and equipment;
- safe fellow employees;
- safe system of work.

(The employer has to insure against liability to his employees (Employers Liability (Compulsory Insurance) Act, 1969.)

There are special rules about defective equipment (Employers Liability Defective Equipment Act, 1969). The employer is responsible for defects in equipment supplied to employees for use at work even if the defect is not due to his fault but to that of the manufacturer. The manufacturer has to compensate the employer.

In recent cases the courts have begun to develop the employer's liability for failing to protect the employee's mental health, as well as his physical well-being.

Social security benefits
Social security benefits are available to employees injured in an accident arising out of and in the course of their employment and those contracting a disease prescribed by the Secretary of State for their employment. All benefits over five years must be deducted from any damages awarded to the employee and paid to the Department of Social Security by the employer.

Environmental considerations

Is the proposed process a Prescribed Activity?
The initial question to be addressed by the project manager is whether the proposed process is prescribed for regulatory control, either by the Environment Agency or the Local Government Environmental Health Department. This can be determined by reference to SI 472 1991, the Environmental Protection (Prescribed Processes and Substances) Regulations (as amended). Each Section in SI 472 1991 is subdivided into Part A (Environment Agency control) and Part B (processes prescribed for air pollution control by Local Authorities). The subdivision is primarily determined by the technical complexity of the process in question. Some Sections have nil Part B entries and some have nil Part A entries.

By way of an example, say that the proposed process is one which uses an amine. We find that the main reference to amines is under Section 4.2, 'The Manufacture and Use of Organic Chemicals'. If the proposed process makes a chemical through the use of the amine and if there is potential for the release to atmosphere of the amine then paragraph (d) refers. Thus we now know that an application must be made to the Environment Agency for an Integrated Pollution Control (IPC) Authorization to operate the process, as illustrated in the logic tree shown in Figure 11.2 (page 140).

Proposed changes to IPC regulation
All EC member states are required to implement the requirements of the IPPC Directive 96/61/EC concerning Integrated Pollution Prevention and Control. The Directive dated 24 September 1996 set a time-scale of three years for complying with this requirement. It seems likely that all present IPC processes will be subject to IPPC but some additional sectors of industry will be caught. Refer to the Directive for further details.

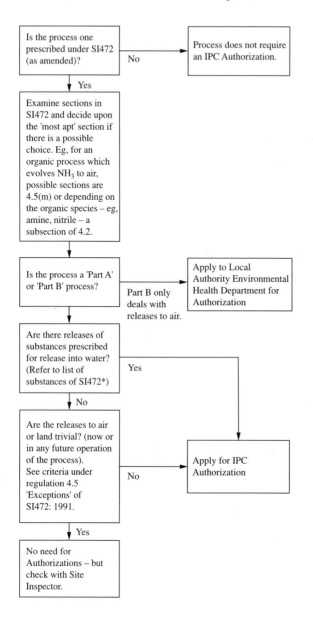

Figure 11.2 Logic tree for the need for an IPC authorization

* Notes:

(1) Must consider the whole process from raw materials. Process per se, intermediate products and final products. (2) Also any ancillary operations — eg, CO_2 absorber. (3) Consider significant impurities: mercury in caustic soda if larger quantities used; PCP in loomstate cloth (section 6.5(b) of SI472 1991 refers).

Minimization and abatement of releases from the process

The project manager must review the techniques which are available for operation of the process — for example, what are the alternative chemical routes? and what are the options regarding releases to the environment? The latter are given high priority in the Environmental Protection Act 1990, with reference to Best Available Techniques Not Entailing Excessive Cost (BATNEEC) and Best Practicable Environmental Option (BPEO). These now well-known acronyms are the bases for regulatory thinking. BPEO is the consideration of which environmental medium or media into which the releases from the process are discharged with the aim of minimizing the net consequential adverse effects on the environment. This entails a review of disposal to land, to water with or without on-site treatment of the effluent, and releases to air probably following abatement such as filtration, scrubbing or incineration and so on.

There is information on BATNEEC/BPEO in the Chief Inspector's Guidance Notes for Inspectors (CIGN) series — the relevant CIGN for the example of the 'use of an amine' is number IPR4/2, 'Processes for the Production and Use of Amines, Nitriles, Isocyanates and Pyridines'. It is also useful to obtain an Application Pack from the Regulator as this gives broad guidance on what to address in the Application. The CIGN series also specifies those substances identifiable as inherent in the particular processes which are prescribed for release to land, water and to atmosphere.

The equivalent series of guidance documents for the IPC Part B processes is the Secretary of State's Notes — for example PG6/1(91), 'Animal By-Product Rendering'.

What is the extent of the Prescribed Process?

It is important for the project manager to appreciate that the process includes all operations from raw materials handling through to intermediate and final products and wastes handling. In cases where there are ancillary operations which support the prescribed process but which may not actually partake in the process chemistry, these must not be forgotten. For example, take a process involving a stage for removal of carbon dioxide. There might be two options for doing this, one being the use of an alkanolamine and the other being the use of an alkaline arsenate solution. Neither option theoretically consumes the carbon dioxide removing agent but history tells us what the consequences may be should the pressure vessel containing the agent rupture. A simpler example of ancillary operations is the use of an old coal-fired boiler to supply process steam to the new IPC process. The Authorization would take account of the emissions to air from the old boiler which may find itself the object of an improvement programme which would probably have engineering implications.

141

Consultations by the Regulator

When an application for an IPC Authorization is received by the Environment Agency, a copy of it goes to certain relevant statutory consultees. These may include the Ministry of Food and Fisheries (MAFF), the sewerage undertaker, the Nature Conservancy Council (NCC) and the Health and Safety Executive (HSE), as well as consultees within the Environment Agency. There may be some objection to a proposal — for example, by the sewerage undertaker to the choice of a scrubber unit for, say, fluoride-containing fume instead of, say, a ceramic filter. This could be because the sewage treatment works can not tolerate the spent irrigation liquor. Thus it is not simply a question of deciding on engineering alternatives without reference to the BPEO as reflected by the stances of the statutory consultees.

The MAFF and the NCC have a particular interest if there is a Site of Special Scientific Interest (SSSI) sufficiently close as to be affected by emissions. Emissions to air containing concentrations of a pollutant of concern, but perhaps not so high as to automatically require abatement, or more efficacious abatement, may be dealt with by increasing the height of the chimney. Air dispersion calculations using conservative (that is, pessimistic) assumptions about the concentration of the emitted pollutant may convince the Environment Agency's Site Inspector that an increase in height may be the appropriate solution.

The need for an Operator to demonstrate compliance with release limits in an Authorization may involve considerable planning and expenditure. Sampling equipment (possibly of a continuously operating kind), the means of access to such equipment, provision of sampling flanges and ports, and miscellaneous items such as dataloggers and protective purge air may be involved.

Abatement equipment

Design of abatement equipment may possibly be left to an external specialist, but data generally need to be provided on the worst case duty for the abatement. It is worth considering that there may be more than one worst case to take account of. For example, the worst case dust loading for the combined emissions from several foundry crucibles must clearly be determined if, say, a bag filtration unit is required. But what is the effect of running the appropriately sized bag filtration unit with only 10% of the furnaces operating? There have been major difficulties when dew point problems in cooler fume ducts have been overlooked, particularly if hygroscopic substances are present.

Civil actions for compensation

In addition to statutory controls, persons injured by an act of pollution caused by negligence will be able to sue the wrongdoer for compensation, as in AB v

South West Water Services (1993), where the introduction of aluminium sulphate into the system at a water treatment works led to hundreds of successful claims for damages.

Further reading

Bahu, R., Crittenden, B. and O'Hara, J. (eds), 1997, *Management of Process Industry Waste* (Institution of Chemical Engineers).

Garner's Environmental Law, loose leaves (Butterworth).

Kloss, D.M., 1998, *Occupational Health Law*, 3rd edition (Blackwell Scientific Publications).

Control of Substances Hazardous to Health Regulations, and Approved Code of Practice, 1988, updated 1994 (HMSO).

Construction (Design and Management) Regulations 1994, and Approved Code of Practice (HMSO).

Environmental Protection Act 1990 (HMSO) and the Environmental Protection (Waste Management Licensing) Regulations, 1994, SI 1994 No 1056 (HMSO).

Management of Health and Safety at Work Regulations 1992, and Approved Code of Practice (HMSO).

Revised IPC Guidance Notes for the Chemicals Industry:
Large Volume Organic Chemicals, ref S2 4.01
Speciality Organic Chemicals, ref S2 4.02
Inorganic Acids and Halogens, ref S2 4.03
Inorganic Chemicals, ref S2 4.04

Technical Guidance Notes series, HM Inspector of Pollution (HMSO).

Quality assurance

12

Derek Maidment

The purpose of any process plant is to manufacture products cost-effectively. The quality of the plant and the associated utilities has a direct influence on the quality of the chemical product and also the reliability and safety of operations. This is true of projects large and small. A quality assurance system is the means of achieving these objectives and also, most importantly, getting it right first time.

Principles of quality

Quality

A simple definition of 'quality' taken from the *Oxford Dictionary* is 'the degree of excellence'. Quality has been expressed in many other ways, the more frequently quoted examples being:

- fitness for purpose and use (Juran[1]);
- the totality of features and characteristics of a product or service that bear on its ability to satisfy stated or implied needs (ISO 8402[2]).

Although describing the same topic, these two examples have a somewhat contrasting approach. Juran described 'fitness for purpose' as the sum of certain concepts — quality of design, quality of conformance and the abilities. The latter include usability, reliability, safety and maintainability. This is a simplistic approach but begins to give breadth to the understanding of the meaning of quality. The process engineer can recognize that these identifiable features are essential for the successful design, construction and commissioning, or alternatively refurbishment, of any process plant.

Quality assurance

Quality assurance is the activity of providing independent assessment to give confidence that the quality function is being performed properly. In ISO 8402 it is defined as all those planned and systematic actions necessary to provide adequate confidence that a product or service will satisfy given requirements for quality.

The function of quality assurance should not be an afterthought and under-taken retrospectively on project completion. It requires review and considera-tion at the commencement of a project or contract. This establishes the levels of quality required, the planned inspections, verifications and any other necessary actions. When complete this documented evidence gives confidence that the quality objectives have been achieved.

The quality system

Every organization should have a quality system that enables engineers to organize, plan and co-ordinate their projects. The quality system consists of a range of advisory documentation for deciding:

• the level of quality required for the project and for individual items;
• the documentation necessary (viz standards) to achieve this quality level;
• a means of comparison between expected and achieved levels of quality (the acceptance criteria);
• a review of the quality system to benefit future projects.

Figure 12.1 shows a total quality system which encompasses all the stan-dards, procedures and other documentation needed to execute the range of projects that the company expects to undertake.

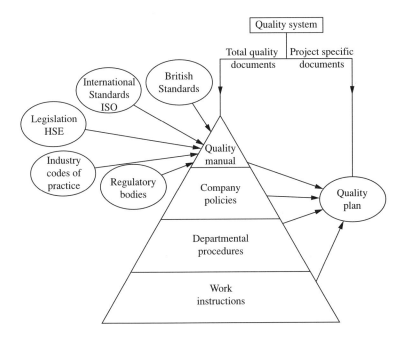

Figure 12.1 Quality system

It is from this totality of documentation that the project manager and his team must select the appropriate standards and procedures to meet the quality requirements of the project. This is perhaps best explained with the example of the installation of cooling water pipework. Normally this pipework is manufactured in carbon steel, requiring the minimum of inspection since the installation presents little risk. However, should the duty be for a nuclear facility, then a failure would present a serious hazard. In this example, the quality requirements for each of these installations would be significantly different. In both applications it would require engineers to make careful decisions to ensure that the installation is cost effective and safe.

The quality manual covers all the company and departmental standards, procedures and works instructions used in the total organization, both on site and off site, with regard to quality assurance. It references appropriate international and British Standards and any other industry-recognized codes of practice. The manual is often based on corresponding Sections 4.1–4.20 of ISO 9001[3]. The quality manual sets out the quality policies, procedures and practices within the organization. It does not necessarily contain these documents, but states their existence and location.

It is from this totality of company documentation that relates to quality that the relevant documents are selected to prepare the quality plan. The quality plan sets out the specific quality practices, the resources available (material and manpower) and the sequence of activities relevant to a particular plant project. The documentation must be simple and is often in the form of check-lists. The required levels of quality, in the form of acceptance criteria and applied standards, are agreed at project conception and certainly prior to contract or detailed engineering design.

Quality standards and legislation

Safety and quality are complementary. If after construction and commissioning the plant as designed is fit for purpose, it will be safe and reliable. Therefore, a process plant that achieves the specified quality requirements will also be safe for chemical manufacture.

UK, US and other legislation can make compliance to national or international standards mandatory, as discussed in Chapter 11. More frequently, engineers have to judge which standards apply to individual projects. If a serious occurrence were to take place and it could be demonstrated that the design and installation complied with recognized industrial standards, it is unlikely that any prosecution would result.

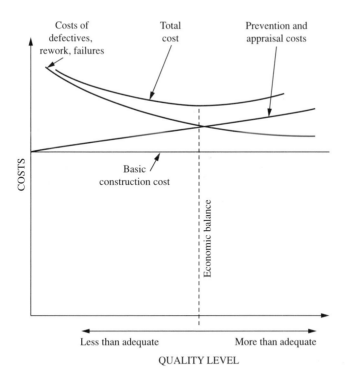

Figure 12.2 Economics of quality assurance

The cost of quality

Establishing and monitoring a quality assurance function incurs cost. These costs include administration, inspections, preparing and updating the quality manual, and the cost of training and auditing. These are quality-related costs and are incurred in the implementation and maintenance of the quality system.

Two important facts must be understood with regard to the costs associated with quality:

● quality assurance activities cost money to operate;

● plant failures can create a safety hazard, cause environmental damage and reduce profits.

A balance is thus needed between ensuring that the quality costs are kept to a minimum and minimizing the risk of failure. Figure 12.2 (based upon BS 6143[5]) indicates the relationship between quality cost and risk of failure. To achieve the right balance for a project, the cost of quality assurance must either be known or estimated. This includes internally incurred expenditure (agreed by apportionment), external inspections and other identifiable costs.

147

Creating a quality culture

Patience and determination are needed to create and develop a quality culture within client, contractor or other organizations. It is only when everyone appreciates the advantages of operating a quality system that the benefits become apparent. Project team members will then promote its use. Many a system has failed at birth due to the large amount of paper that the organization has generated and christened 'the quality system'. If the system is difficult to understand and unwieldy to use, its operation will be compromised. It will be replaced with a paper front that purports to deliver compliance. This will be meaningless, of little value and eventually abandoned since it serves no useful purpose. Therefore, a successful quality system is simple to operate, requiring the minimum of documentation to give traceability. In essence, the system should comply with the KISS concept — Keep It Short and Simple.

If the KISS concept is strictly applied, it ensures that the documentation is precise, easily comprehended and understood. More importantly, the paperwork is kept to a minimum, resulting in only the essential information being collated and registered. To be successful, the KISS concept must percolate throughout the organization in an endeavour to achieve total quality management (TQM). This objective will only be met by an investment in time and manpower:

- time to train employees;
- time for the introduction of new methods and ideas;
- time for people to recognize the benefits;
- time to improve the quality system.

For TQM to be effective, directors and senior management must demonstrate commitment. They must take its introduction seriously, understand its concepts and be determined to succeed. If senior management expect others to show dedication to TQM while they themselves pay lip service to its establishment, it will be impossible for the organization to generate a quality culture. TQM should be promoted in all activities and at all levels. It needs active commitment by every individual and department to ensure continuous improvement with the objective of meeting the customer quality needs.

Maintaining the quality culture

Once a quality culture and a common commitment to TQM have been established, it requires consolidation and improvement by regular assessment. This can be achieved by teamwork and understanding of the quality system. The following techniques can be applied to meet this objective.

Training

When faced with what engineers initially perceive to be unnecessary paper-work, it is essential to explain the real benefits of a good quality system. There-fore, the company must make resources available to train people in the operation of the system. This includes every individual from senior manager to office junior — in fact, anyone who contributes to the engineering quality. In addition, it includes skills training for craftsmen (for example, welding). It should be broad in concept, addressing a wide range of issues that can impact on quality. New recruits should have, as part of their induction course, a quality awareness programme. This enables everyone to have a better understanding of the benefits of the system and to operate as a team.

Coaching

One of the most cost-effective methods of encouraging individuals in the appli-cation of quality is by more experienced managers, engineers and technicians coaching junior and recently recruited staff. If senior engineers are enthusiastic about the need for quality, this will strongly influence their subordinates. If, however, they are less than totally committed, this will have a detrimental effect. Senior members of the project team must ensure that even routine proce-dures such as approval of design drawings are in place and operated.

Auditing

The way to monitor progress in the attainment of TQM is by careful internal auditing. This enables management to determine any real improvements. Auditing may be seen by some as a policing tool and perhaps seen as threat-ening. Therefore, the selection of auditors is vitally important. They require adequate training, but as they gain experience the information received from the audit will be of more value. The purpose of the audit is to establish how the quality system is being implemented and, if deficiencies are found, what corrective action must be taken. An audit is meaningless if discrepancies are identified and no action taken.

There are four essential elements of an audit:

- training for effective auditing;
- audit schedule;
- procedure for audit;
- corrective action.

By far the most effective way to promote and maintain quality within an organization is by encouragement. The project team members are greatly moti-vated if they perceive that the senior management understand and believe in the philosophy of TQM.

The quality cycle

It is extremely important to set the quality levels to meet the process needs, as this minimizes the risk and maximizes the cost-effectiveness of the completed project. Various industries require different defined levels of quality to ensure fitness for purpose. For example, the material handling of aggregates presents minimal risk when compared to the handling of toxic materials within the pharmaceutical industry. In the latter, ongoing documentary evidence is necessary to satisfy the requirements of regulatory bodies such as the FDA (Food and Drugs Administration) to prove the process plant has been validated. The need for validation usually only applies to high risk process plants, such as nuclear and pharmaceutical installations. It is therefore up to the client at project conception, and then again at the quality plan stage, to decide if plant validation is appropriate.

As indicated in Figure 12.3, the quality system must be implemented and operated during the life cycle of the project from conception to commissioning. It continues through to production and maintenance. The engineering design should be based on the specification as issued by the client. This must be a meaningful and accurate document which clearly defines the client's requirements. If it is ambiguous or unnecessarily complicated, the final results will be less than perfect. BS 7373 is a useful guide to specifying requirements[6].

Due to unforeseen market forces or new legislation, design changes may be needed which impact on the plant capacity (which could affect quality) or directly influence product quality. It is therefore extremely important that the client and the contractor have in place a mutually agreed procedure for change control to meet this challenge. If a change policy is not formulated and agreed, differences will remain unresolved. Ultimately, differences must be reconciled to the satisfaction of all parties. The earlier differences are resolved, the less the cost impact on the project. If a minor problem is not resolved quickly it can escalate with the passage of time into a major dispute.

After contract review, which ensures that the contract basis (including such topics as price, delivery, payment terms — see ISO 9001) is correct, the design contractor and subcontractors can prepare the necessary quality plans based on the latest specification as issued by the client. These plans can be in the form of check-lists or method statements that define inspection hold points and acceptance criteria. These documents will, when completed, be evidence that the plant has been constructed, fabricated, installed and tested in accordance with the client's requirements. They prove to the relevant safety and other authorities that the installation conforms to the appropriate codes of practice and legislation.

Once the installation has been completed, commissioning can commence and the test results recorded. The results of the first production runs give the

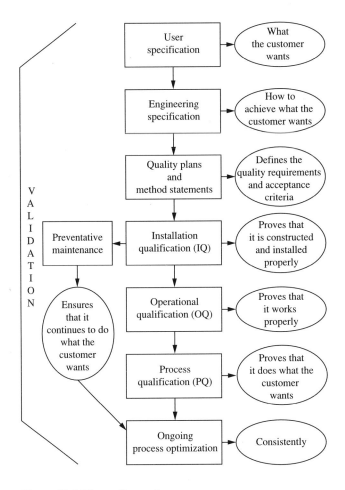

Figure 12.3 The quality cycle

plant performance which must match or exceed the requirements of the client's specification. This commissioning period may take time, but once complete, and providing the plant is operating in accordance with the terms of the contract, the plant may be formally handed over. This does not mean that the results should not be again examined, since with time the process can be further refined and optimized.

If the concepts of the quality cycle described here are applied in principle, then the process plant will, in itself, be a quality product. It can be shown to have been constructed at minimum cost to the required levels of quality and will manufacture the chemical product safely and reliably.

References in Chapter 12

1. Juran, J.M. (ed), 1988, *Quality Control Handbook*, 4th edition (McGraw-Hill).

2. ISO 8402: Quality Vocabulary, Part 1: International Terms, 1986 (equivalent to BS 4778, 1987).

3. ISO 9001: Quality Systems — Model for Quality Assurance in Design, Development Production, Installation and Servicing, 1994 (equivalent to BS 5750).

4. Owen, F. and Maidment, D. (eds), 1996, *Quality Assurance: A Guide to the Application of ISO 9001 to Process Plant Projects*, 2nd edition (Institution of Chemical Engineers).

5. BS 6143: Guide to the Determination and Use of Quality Related Costs, 1981.

6. BS 7373: Guide to the Preparation of Specifications, 1991.

Hazard studies

13

Philip Charsley, John Gillett
and Dinesh Fernando

Ideally, plant and systems should be designed to be inherently safe and free of health and environmental risks. Assessment of the potential hazards of proposed new plant and systems is now a legal obligation for employers in many countries, following the lead of the European Community and the United States. Hazard studies are now agreed as essential for designing and operating safe, healthy and environmentally acceptable processes and their control systems.

Hazard assessment

The steps required in a hazard assessment are:

- hazard identification;
- risk evaluation;
- elimination of hazards or, if not practicable, selection of suitable controls.

If risk evaluation shows that a risk is not significant, no further action is required except that the safety system should record that the hazard was identified and assessed[1].

Hazard studies

'Hazard and operability' (Hazop) studies were originally developed by ICI for checking the designs of large continuous chemical plants. They were extended to batch processes, and for some complex projects can now be applied in six stages covering the life cycle of a project[2]. Hazard studies now cover not only safety but also loss control. The technique is now probably the preferred method of process hazard identification and control worldwide.

The objectives of a hazard study are:

- to identify all potential causes of process upset scenarios which could lead to significant safety or operability risks;

- to decide whether the current design ensures that the risk from every identified scenario is suitably small and, if not, to recommend modifications which will reduce the risk to a suitably small amount, or specify a further study to investigate the problem with the objective of identifying a suitable solution.

Safety, health, environment, reliability and quality

Hazard studies should be performed on all projects to meet the needs of good manufacturing practice and legislation. This policy leads to more objectives, which may be the following:

- to maximize the value of the facilities to the company by reducing process-related risks to tolerable levels and to improve operating efficiency;
- to recommend cost-effective risk mitigation measures;
- to recommend cost-effective actions to improve the profitability of operations.

Hazard studies can provide assurance that systems are operable and meet safety standards. To do so needs an effective system for co-ordinating hazard studies, allocating trained study leaders to projects, forward planning of hazard study resources and hazard study training.

The first stage of a study may show that no further stages are needed. Or at worst it may show that the project should be reconsidered and perhaps aborted.

Hazard identification

Hazard identification can be carried out in two stages. The first uses engineering drawings or schematic diagrams which show all the proposed hardware and the related systems.

The second stage is often initiated through analysing tasks, by attention to those critical tasks in commissioning, start-up, normal operations, shutdown, preparation for maintenance and maintenance itself which have the potential for leading to significant hazards or losses.

The written procedure or work practice resulting from the analysis of critical tasks can then be subjected to a hazard study using appropriate guidewords. This type of study allows not only identification of potential causes of human error, but also anticipation of such errors so that opportunities to recover from them may be built in.

Use of guidewords

Guidewords are used to try to identify all significant problems. This technique is very powerful, but it is difficult to ensure that it is sufficiently rigorous not to miss any significant risk. One requirement is a capable, trained and large enough team. The other is a suitable set of 'prompts'.

PROMPTS SHOULD BE APPLIED TO ALL THE
IMPORTANT PARAMETERS OF THE PROCESS UNDER STUDY.

Hazard study methodology therefore uses a set of guidewords which are applied to all the important parameters (process variables such as flow, pressure, temperature, level, agitation, reaction speed and so on) of the process under study, to identify deviations from design intent which could raise risks. An example is the list shown in Table 13.1. The problem of completeness lies in the identification of the 'parameters of importance'. The method adopted by many proponents of the hazard study technique is first to ask the team to identify this set of parameters of importance, and then to apply to them the hazard guideword list to generate a much longer check-list of guidewords to be used as the prompts.

Table 13.1 Generic hazard guidewords for continuous chemical processes

NO FLOW	MORE TEMPERATURE	SAMPLING
REVERSE FLOW	LESS TEMPERATURE	CORROSION/EROSION
MORE FLOW	MORE VISCOSITY	SERVICE FAILURE
LESS FLOW	LESS VISCOSITY	ABNORMAL OPERATION
MORE LEVEL	COMPOSITION CHANGE	MAINTENANCE
LESS LEVEL	CONTAMINATION	IGNITION
MORE PRESSURE	RELIEF	SPARE EQUIPMENT
LESS PRESSURE	INSTRUMENTATION	SAFETY

155

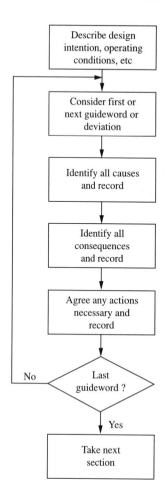

Figure 13.1 Scenario identification in a hazard study

The study leader should always check before using a list of guidewords that the team believes it to be sufficient. A special exercise is required to generate an appropriate guideword set if non-standard equipment is involved or if there is much involvement of operators in controlling a process. The use of a guideword set to identify scenarios is illustrated by the flowchart Figure 13.1.

The completeness and appropriateness of the set of guidewords is the key to the completeness of scenario identification. Attention to the choice of guidewords is therefore a mandatory step in hazard study procedure.

Work breakdown

The study leader divides the system to be studied into sections which are not so large or complex that the team may become confused when applying the guidewords and consequently miss some scenarios. In order to identify every potential cause of problems, all guidewords are applied to each section.

During this process the action of all safety systems is ignored. The identification process should assume the failure of safety systems. The reliability and effectiveness of these systems is considered later, when judging the seriousness and likelihood of each scenario (see Reference 3).

Completeness of the engineering information

A study may follow all the procedural recommendations given above but not identify all the potential hazards. This can occur if not all the piping and instrumentation diagrams (P&IDs) have been studied, or if not every section of the P&IDs is subjected to study. It is also possible if the P&IDs are out of date and do not incorporate recent changes. A statement of scope listing all relevant P&IDs must therefore be obtained. A good explanation should be required and agreed for not studying particular P&IDs.

The leader in the study of existing plant who is informed that a P&ID is not up to date must obtain an accurate replacement. Correction of a diagram by a team member is not acceptable: physical checking is essential.

For batch systems, it is also necessary to ensure that all sections are studied for every step in the process.

Six-stage hazard study process in a project life cycle

Figure 13.2 (page 158) shows a six-stage hazard study over the complete life - cycle of a project.

Hazard Study 1 is performed as early in the project life cycle as possible. The aim of this study is to identify and eliminate or minimize hazards, by reviewing all the safety, health and environment information relevant to the project. Previous incidents, authorizations required, materials hazards, and safety, health and environment standards and criteria are reviewed.

Hazard Study 2 is performed during project feasibility studies, once a preliminary process flowsheet is available. The aim is to identify significant hazards, and to eliminate or minimize and control them to meet the safety, health and environment standards and criteria. Environmental impact and occupational health statements are written for the complete project life cycle. Sometimes a quantified risk assessment may be performed to assist project decision-making on managing hazards identified.

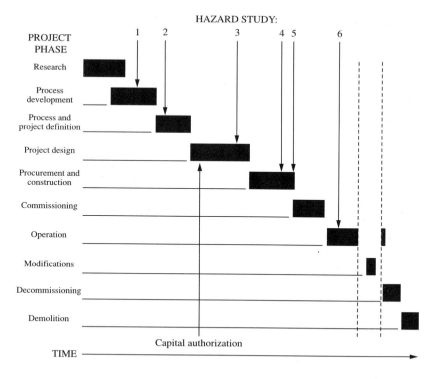

Figure 13.2 The six-stage hazard study methodology for a typical pharmaceutical project life cycle

Hazard Study 3 is a hazard and operability study of the design to identify any hazardous deviations and take action to remove them. This study was traditionally called 'Hazop' as it frequently identified potential operating problems and procedures. Hazard Study 3 is performed once sufficient definite design information is available.

Hazard Studies 4 and 5 are performed after construction but before process fluids are introduced. They are audits to check that all of the hazard study actions have been completed.

Hazard Study 6 is performed after a few months of beneficial production. It usually includes a report on the lessons learned during the project.

The composition of hazard study teams varies for different types of project, and stage by stage through a project. Specialist hazard study leaders should lead Studies 1, 2 and 3. They contribute to Studies 4, 5 and 6, but these are usually led by the commissioning manager or plant manager.

Hazard studies under ISO 9000[3]

A quality assurance procedure is applied to ensure that everything relevant to a project has been covered in the study and that all hazard study reports and supporting documents are filed in a single project safety, health and environment dossier.

The standards of documentation and audit must meet the requirements of external authorities and legislation internationally. This can best be achieved, maintained and developed by using staff who know the type of process and plant and by co-ordinating all hazard studies centrally.

Senior management and authorities in many countries are asking for hazard studies, but may have no idea whether the reports they receive are satisfactory. They now need an answer to the question, 'Has the team done a good enough job?'. ISO 9000 contains many aspects of value in answering this question. Application of ISO 9000 to hazard studies is not straightforward but can lead to establishing the following quality criteria:

- all potential scenarios leading to significant safety or operability issues are identified;
- decisions are made on the acceptability of the risk level from every one of these scenarios;
- if a risk is intolerable, recommendations for change are made which will bring it within tolerable limits;
- recommendations are implemented as rapidly as feasible, when justified against client company criteria;
- an authorized rejection notice is produced to explain the background to the rejection of any safety recommendation.

Achievement of these quality objectives needs attention to:
- team composition, and qualifications;
- methodology followed (that is, brainstorming method);
- guidewords used;
- completeness of coverage;
- judgement criteria applied;
- categorization of recommendations;
- testing of the recommendations against their objectives;
- decision-making and follow-up of recommendations;
- continuous improvement of the hazard study process.

Computer control and human error

Assessment of potential hazards must include specific attention to the computer-based systems used to control processes[4]. The same principles apply as described above, though different guidewords are appropriate. The term Chazop is sometimes used to describe what is required. The control system and the processes it is to control must be considered together, as well as the components of the control system.

Various methods for this have been developed. In one, two sets of guidewords are used, one for the hardware and logic of the system, and the other for the human factors. As with the hazard studies of the proposed plant, two or more stages of Chazop can be appropriate, as the system is being defined and developed. Essential at each stage are:

- an inter-disciplinary team;
- systematic questioning.

Computer system validation is a very powerful tool for making sure that the system is right. It is not possible to study all the potential deviations in the system. Validation is therefore necessary to set up a system which is inherently safe (see Reference 2).

Incident reporting

Every project should incorporate the lessons of past ones. Reports of near-misses on previous projects are a major contribution. For every accident that causes injury or damage there are hundreds of near-misses and minor accidents. Learning from these is an important step in reducing the risks of accidents and improving the performance of safety management systems[5]. Because of the larger sample size, near-miss data provide a more sensitive indicator of the performance of safety systems than lost-time accident statistics.

Near-misses are also important during the testing, pre-commissioning and commissioning work for a project. The information can draw attention to problems and help correct them before they lead to something more serious.

Reporting near-misses

Unless personnel report minor accidents and particularly near-misses, management has no certain way of finding out if safety precautions are being maintained, are deficient or are not in place.

Serious accidents usually are not freak events without precedent. If a serious accident does take place, then it is likely that some or all of its previous events have occurred before but, through luck or someone's quick thinking, a major loss didn't quite happen. These events can be referred to as hazards, near-misses or minor accidents, but whatever they are called, they should be a strong influence on assessing safety and the risk of major accidents.

Published reviews of accidents by Heinrich, Bird and Germain and others show that for each serious accident there are many lesser incidents and even more near-misses[6]. For example, Bird and Germain found that for each major injury there were 10 minor injuries, 80 property damage accidents and 600 incidents with no visible injury or damage. Figures from other studies do not agree exactly, but the principle illustrated in Figures 13.3 and 13.4 holds true throughout.

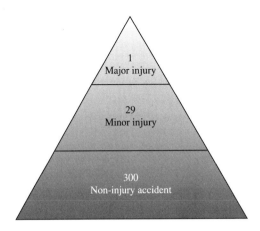

Figure 13.3 Heinrich's survey of accident rates

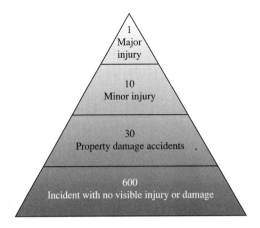

Figure 13.4 Bird's survey of accident ratios

Therefore a proactive policy for improving is for companies to pay attention to the bottom of the accident triangle and actively try to reduce the number of near-misses and hazardous situations.

Encouraging incident reporting

An important part of this process is encouraging personnel to report these events to management so a decision can be made on whether a major loss could have occurred, or the incident highlights a fault in the design or procedures. Ideally, when a near-miss occurs or a hazard is observed, it is reported and investigated almost as if an accident had actually happened.

The most important prerequisite for encouraging incident reporting is a blame-free company culture. Personnel should never feel that there will be recriminations for what they have reported, even if it initially looks as if they have made a mistake. In general, personnel want to work safely and are unlikely to do something that knowingly endangers themselves or the plant.

In fact the root causes of most incidents can eventually be traced back to faults in the management system and all incident reports should be regarded as valuable feedback.

The following points are important for getting near-misses and hazards reported:

- react in a positive way;
- give more attention to safety;
- recognize individual performance promptly;
- develop awareness of the value of accident information;
- follow up reported problems;
- publicize near-misses, on site;
- make personnel aware of the value of incident reporting — this is where training plays such an important role.

Near-misses, hazards and minor accidents are no-cost or low-cost signs that something is wrong with existing methods of work or procedures. Through an effective incident reporting system, companies can generate valuable feedback on the safety performance of the management system without necessarily suffering serious losses.

References in Chapter 13

1. Wallace, I.G., 1994, *Developing Effective Safety Systems* (Institution of Chemical Engineers).
    Kletz, T., 1992, *Hazop and Hazan*, 3rd edition (Institution of Chemical Engineers).

2. Gillett, J.E., 1996, *Hazard Study and Risk Assessment in the Pharmaceutical Industry* (Interpharm Press Inc).

3. Charsley, P. and Brown, W., 1993, Hazop studies under ISO 9000, *CCPS International Process Safety Management Conference and Workshop, San Francisco.* Charsley, P., 1996, Hazop and risk assessment, *Loss Prevention Bulletin,* 124: 16–19.

4. Grey, S., 1995, *Practical Risk Assessment for Project Management,* Wiley series in software engineering (John Wiley).
Jones, C., 1994, *Assessment and Control of Software Risks* (Prentice Hall).
Kletz, T., Chung, P., Broomfield, E. and Shen-Orr, C., 1995, *Computer Control and Human Error* (Institution of Chemical Engineers).
GAMP Guide, Validation of Automated Systems in Pharmaceutical Manufacture, Version 3.0 (ISPE).

5. Fernando, D., 1995, Incident reporting, *The Chemical Engineer,* 28 September, 13–14.

6. Heinrich, H.W., in Petersen, D. *et al* (eds), 1980, *Industrial Accident Prevention: A Safety Management Approach,* 5th edition (McGraw-Hill).
Bird, F.E. and Germain, G.L., 1966, *Damage Control* (American Management Association).

Further reading

Bird, F.E. and Germain, G.L., 1990, *Practical Loss Control Leadership,* revised edition (International Loss Control Institute).

Fletcher, J.A. and Douglas, H.M., 1971, *Total Loss Control …* (Associated Business Programmes).

Kletz, T., 1993, *Lessons from Disaster: How Organisations Have no Memory and Accidents Recur* (Institution of Chemical Engineers).

Wells, G., 1996, *Hazard Identification and Risk Assessment* (Institution of Chemical Engineers).

Hazard Spotting, 1998, multimedia safety training package (Institution of Chemical Engineers).

Incident Reporting, 1995, safety training package (Institution of Chemical Engineers).

Safety Auditing, 1998, safety training package (Institution of Chemical Engineers).

The Accident Database, 1997, CD-ROM (Institution of Chemical Engineers).

Risk analysis and risk management

Peter Thompson

Risk and uncertainty are inherent in all projects and contracts. Size can be one of the major causes of risk. So can changes in political or commercial planning. Other causes of risk are the complexity of a project, location, urgency, and familiarity with the type of work. Time and cost overruns can invalidate the economic case for a project, turning a potential profit into a loss.

Project risks

In project management terms, the most serious effects of risk can be summarized as follows:

- failure to achieve the required quality and operational requirements;
- failure to keep within the cost estimate;
- failure to achieve the required completion date.

The purpose of risk analysis and management is to help managers avoid failures. In order to proceed with the analysis and subsequent response the priority assigned to each of these objectives must first be agreed.

Not all risks are calamitous. Costs may be less than anticipated, the weather may be kind, revenues may exceed expectation. Uncertainty can sometimes be beneficial, if all parties are prepared.

Risk analysis and management are not intended to kill off worthwhile projects, nor to discourage capital investment. The aims are, firstly, to ensure that only those projects which are genuinely worthwhile are sanctioned and, secondly, to avoid problems.

Attitude of mind is important when applying the techniques of risk analysis and management. They should be viewed as a constructive process, and can be the most creative tasks of project management. They should generate realism, and so increase a commitment by all members of the team to control. Through encouraging problem-solving, they open the way to innovative solutions to getting a project completed.

NOT ALL RISKS ARE CALAMITOUS.
THE WEATHER MAY BE KIND.

The responsibility for identifying risks and setting a policy on who bears them rests with the client and the project manager.

Systematic risk analysis and risk management

Risk analysis and management are not easy. They are better done systematically in two stages:

- risk analysis;

followed by

- risk management.

Risk analysis can be qualitative and quantitative. Firstly, the sources of risk are identified. Secondly, their effects are assessed or analysed.

Risk management requires management responses and policies to reduce and control the main risks identified in the analysis.

Qualitative risk analysis

This process has two aims:

- risk identification;
- initial risk assessment.

The objective is to compile a list of the main risk sources and a description of their likely consequences, perhaps including a first approximation of their potential effect on estimates of cost and time.

Research has shown that a practicable target is to compile a list of between five and ten main risks for a project — or for each work package if the project is large or complex.

Three techniques are commonly used to identify risks:
- check-lists of risk compiled from previous experience;
- interviews with key project participants;
- brainstorming with the project team.

Many managers believe this initial qualitative analysis is essential and brings considerable benefits in terms of understanding the project and its potential problems. In some cases a project has been totally re-thought as a result of this analysis.

There is a second, but equally important, reason for the early identification of risk and uncertainty: it concentrates the attention of senior managers on the need for strategies for the control and allocation of risk — for example, through the choice of a contract strategy. It will also make obvious what further design, development work or other actions such as clarifying objectives are most needed.

The realism of estimates increases as a project proceeds but, of course, the most influential decisions are made early in the life of projects. So, despite the difficulties, a realistic estimate of the final cost and duration of the total project is required as early as possible. It is then that all the potential risk and uncertainties which can affect these estimates and act as constraints on the project should be identified.

Quantitative risk analysis

Quantitative analysis usually involves more sophisticated analysis techniques, often requiring computer programs. To some people this is the most formal aspect of the whole process requiring:
- estimates of uncertainty in predicting the cost and duration of activities;
- probabilistic combination of individual uncertainties.

Techniques can be applied with varying levels of effort and resources, ranging from a few days using relatively simple programs to several man-months, using different programs. Examples of the output from these analyses are given later in this chapter.

Mathematical models and analytical techniques can be useful indicators of trends and problems for attention. They should not be relied on as the sole guide to decisions. Their accuracy depends on the realism of assumptions, the skill of the model builder and the quality and amount of resources used to obtain data.

Risk management

This part of the process involves the formulation of management responses to the main risks. It may start during the qualitative analysis phase as the need to respond to some risks may be urgent and the solution fairly obvious. Interaction between the risk analysis and management phases is common.

The greater the uncertainties the more flexible the response must be. In the extreme, risks may have such serious consequences as to demand a reappraisal of a project or even its complete abandonment. It is more likely that risk identification and analysis will reveal a need for re-design, more detailed design, further site investigation or market surveys, a different packaging of the work content, the use of alternative contract strategies or different methods of construction.

Risk management can involve:

- identifying preventive measures to avoid a risk or reduce its effects;
- proceeding with a project stage by stage, initiating further investigation to reduce uncertainty through better information;
- considering risk transfer in contract and subcontract strategy, with attention to the motivational effects and the control of risk allocation;
- considering risk transfer to insurers;
- setting and managing risk allowances in cost estimates, programmes and specifications;
- establishing contingency plans to deal with risks if they occur.

Risk management will not remove all risk from projects and contracts. It can ensure that risks are managed most efficiently. Whether or not contractors are employed to design and supply part or all of a project, the client and the project manager must recognize that certain risks will remain to be carried by the client. This 'residual risk' must be allowed for in the client's estimate of time and cost.

Effective management of risky projects demands rapid and realistic predictions of alternative courses of action and positive decision-making. It requires flexible attitudes and procedures.

Risks can be transferred to contractors, but the client should expect to pay for this. Responsibility for adopting this risk response must therefore lie with the client, who should ensure it is in its own best interests to transfer the risk. Similarly with a contractor employing a subcontractor. It demands analysis of the contractor's own and the other parties' objectives, the relative abilities of the parties to assume the risk and their extent of control over the situation.

Clearly, risk management has major benefits for any enterprise. It is more than just a way of helping to get projects completed on time and to budget. For example, it can:

- enable decision-making to be more systematic and less subjective;
- allow the robustness of projects to specific uncertainties to be compared;
- make the relative importance of each risk immediately apparent;
- give an improved understanding of the project through identifying the risks and thinking through response scenarios;
- demonstrate company responsibility to customers;
- have a powerful impact on management by forcing a realization that there is a range of possible outcomes for a project;
- improve corporate experience and communication.

When to apply risk management

At the start of every project

The greatest uncertainty is encountered early in the life of a new project. Consequently, decisions taken during the earliest stages of a project can have a very large impact on its final cost and duration. Attention to risks is thus most valuable early in a project proposal while there is still the flexibility in design and planning to consider how the serious risks may be avoided. Not all can be avoided — for instance, changes in the predictions of the demand for the service or product — and the risks can change. Risk management should therefore be continued throughout the life of a project. It influences commitment by the client:

- in deciding the project 'master plan' or brief resulting from the evaluation of various schemes in the project appraisal stage;
- in preparing the final proposal for sanction (funding);
- in deciding the contract strategy and basis for awarding contracts.

Market, competition and other causes of later changes are an unavoidable feature of many projects. Their likely extent and effects are frequently underestimated during these early phases.

Applying risk management at the project appraisal stage gives the client a much clearer idea of the project, and enables decisions to be made with far more confidence. It is an essential part of cost-benefit analysis which should span the entire envisaged life cycle of the investment.

Risks are specific to a project, are interactive, sometimes cumulative. They all affect cost and benefit. They may be grouped in several general categories, for example:

- political;
- institutional;
- environmental;

- physical hazards;
- technical and functional;
- delay;
- markets;
- performance during implementation and operation of the facility.

Political and environmental risks frequently result in compromise following comparison of cost with benefit. They are likely to have a significant influence on the conceptual design and the response should therefore be agreed prior to sanction.

Resources are not usually expended in defining a project in detail before appraisal has shown whether it is worth proceeding with. Appraisal therefore cannot be accurate. The available effort at this stage is therefore concentrated on:

- seeking solutions which avoid or at least reduce risk;
- considering whether the extent or nature of the major risks are such that the normal ways of transferring the risk to other parties may be impossible or particularly expensive;
- outlining any special strategies for risk transfer, for instance by insurance or unconventional contractual arrangements.

Risk in funding decisions

This stage, commonly known as 'sanction' by clients, is of critical importance in the life of a project as it leads to the major expenditure on design, procurement and construction.

Traditionally, a sanction proposal includes a cost estimate, project programme and technical specification. The cost estimate and programme identify and include allowances for risk.

There should also be an extra component in the proposal — namely, a plan for risk management which concentrates on contract strategy but may include other proposals such as insurance. The choice of contract strategy ought to be based on consideration of the responsibilities for the risks of design, construction and services, their interfaces, the division of work packages, the number and type of contracts, and methods of selecting the contractor.

The importance of time

Many risks are associated with specific time constraints imposed on the project. The preparation of an outline programme is therefore an essential early requirement of any approach to risk identification. Risk management can then be

1	Define	OBJECTIVES	
2	Identify	CONSTRAINTS	
3	Compile	PLAN	Time forecast List assumptions Cost forecast
4		RISK MANAGEMENT Identify risks arising from uncertainty/constraints/assumptions Analyse implications Plan response	
	Seek	OPPORTUNITIES to reduce risk and to improve performance	
5	Determine	CONTINGENCIES and how they are to be MANAGED	

Figure 14.1 Risk management in the project planning cycle

considered as an essential part of the continuous and structured project planning cycle — as illustrated in Figure 14.1. It presents an opportunity to review critically all aspects of the plan, as it is revised and contingencies are allocated to accommodate change.

Risk during project implementation

Risk in contracts

Risk cannot be eliminated through the drafting and placing of contracts, but the strategy chosen or assumed for dealing with risk in contracts can greatly influence how risks are managed. The contractual arrangements and terms have a significant influence on the risk carried by each party and on the clarity with which they are perceived, and therefore on the cost, quality and duration of the project.

The main decisions where the client can gain from risk management are:
- in formulating contract terms, particularly in choosing an equitable risk allocation;
- in assessing the opportunities for risk management made possible by different types of contractual arrangements;

- in choosing terms ('conditions') of contract which define the risks and their allocation and provide incentives for the efficient management of risks as they occur during construction.

These choices are discussed in Chapter 18.

Before tenders for a contract are invited, the client or its advisers should prepare an up-to-date estimate of the expected tender price based on the information contained in the tender documents. This is used to:

- assess the consequences of risk allocation;
- check the adequacy of the information in the documents;
- provide criteria for assessing contractors' tenders, particularly in judging how risks will affect the relationship between final contract price and tender amount and between final completion date and the tendered programme;
- strengthen the client's position in contract negotiation and in subsequent contract management.

The same applies to subcontracting decisions.

Institutional risk

Amongst the client's staff and advisers some if not all the risks relevant to a project are usually known, but each risk may be known to only some of them. If recognized, a risk also tends to be seen differently by engineering, financial, commercial and legal departments, by the eventual users of the completed facility, and by general managers and their advisers. The attitudes, experience and careers of individuals may cause genuine differences of understanding of objectives, and so affect their evaluations and perceptions of risk. These 'institutional' risks can seriously affect the initial identification and subsequent management of potential risks crucial to project success.

To remedy this the client organization must achieve real teamwork to obtain and apply the experience of users, all levels of staff and outsiders. The value of doing so is commonly acknowledged by managers. It is not so often achieved. What it demands is bringing people together, and maintaining this from the stage of preparing the proposals for sanction through to the handing over of the facility for operation. The most important data is likely to be known by those with recent experience of completing other projects. To draw on this requires senior managers to consult down to this level, and to do so directly in order to avoid the bureaucratic problem of intermediaries shaping information to suit what they think the seniors want to hear. For major projects, establishing an empowered broad-based steering group or project board may be advisable.

The institutional risks may influence other parties, as it is the client who can take action to identify, anticipate and avoid their potential effects. All others are limited by what the client agrees needs attention. Every contractor clearly should also have a co-ordinated policy on risk management, but unless the client recognizes a risk the other parties to a project will tend to give attention to it only as far as they think it wise to protect their own interests.

Joint ventures

Joint ventures, alliance partnerships and consortia (JVCs) are attractive to project clients and contractors for undertaking some projects, but also may incur risks unfamiliar to their members or to others.

Cases indicate that the reasons for entering into a JVC vary. They include a wish to combine resources and spread the risks of a project. They are most typically formed for temporary or selective co-operation for the purpose of carrying out one project. Some are continuing arrangements for development work, a series of related projects or for the operation of completed facilities, but they are selective in that the members continue with their other business activities independently, sometimes in competition.

The special risks to the members of a JVC are in foreseeing and agreeing what relationships and commitments between them are needed to control and carry out their external commitments to others. The main risks to the client and other parties are that the internal structure does not support the completion of its external obligations. The two lessons are therefore that from the start the members of a JVC should agree on an organizational structure suitable for completing their intended projects, and that the structure should be designed to minimize interdependence between the members.

The style and system of management appropriate for co-operative concentration on one project at a time are likely to be different to the styles and systems used in the members' organizations for their normal business. A JVC is a means of sharing risk, but to do so it demands sharing control.

Project size and design flexibility

Ideally design should be complete and final and a plan for project execution agreed before the decision to sanction a project. In practice this is not often achieved because of uncertainties in market, political or physical conditions. The flexibility for these uncertainties can tempt the client and engineers to make avoidable changes, particularly if using contract and internal procedures evolved to order variations.

The lessons of successful projects provide the following answers:
• consider design options before project sanctioning. Even under pressures to limit expenditure, this is the time to consider alternatives and preferences, so as to know how to proceed when the decision is made whether to go ahead with the project;

- involve and commit all downstream parties to the decisions taken, motivating them to feel that they own the project and are personally responsible for the results;
- decide all novel and uncertain design in detail before project sanctioning, so as to have a basis for assessing the risks and also the effects of changes if proposed later;
- plan the project execution to the same extent of detail, so as to incorporate space and other margins for the likely needs of construction, commissioning and operation;
- after project sanctioning consider no design changes except those imposed by law or which promise at least double the financial rate of return or other base criterion for the sanctioning of the project;
- maintain continuity of the senior staff, particularly those responsible for the engineering decisions;
- if the project is novel, design in stages and concentrate expenditure in the first stage on work which reduces the uncertainties of whether and how to proceed with the project;
- if the project is urgent, make final design decisions before starting construction. Overlapping design and construction can cause greater delays than it promises to save.

Design freezing

Some experienced clients and engineers state that the recurrent lesson of their projects is that design should be complete and 'frozen' at the stage of approving a project. Some describe design freezing as 'essential'. Clearly it is not essential, as many projects are achieved satisfactorily without doing it. If design is frozen in a rigid way, the concept and the phrase can mislead people on a project into thinking that they do not need to allow for irresistible forces for revision such as markets, mistakes or new data having specific effects on safety. Freezing in detail at the start is the policy to follow only if no reasons whatever will be accepted for changing decisions previously made — for instance, on an emergency project where speed is the overriding basis for decisions.

The practical lesson of industrial and public projects is that design flexibility and spare capacity are needed because of uncertainties of project construction, operation and maintenance, but to use them successfully there must be:

- a system that controls how and when they are used;
- a contract strategy appropriate for the expected extent of variations.

Flexibility and spare capacity without control to discipline how they are used can become a cover for poor initial decisions.

To minimize the risks of expensive later changes or drastic rebuilding, the client should give attention to how decisions on the size or capacity of a project are to be made, as well as their content. A range of size, capacity and margins should be, and usually is, considered. The detailed implications of size are studied before project sanctioning. Design work itself is relatively cheap, so that attention to detail can cost much less than it saves by avoiding later problems, delays and rework.

Quantitative techniques for project risk analysis

A simple method for considering project risks would be to analyse any risk independently of others, with no attempt to estimate the probability of occurrence of that risk. The estimated effects of each risk could then be accumulated to provide maximum and minimum project outcome values.

Though more complex, greater realism and confidence can be achieved by applying probabilities to the risks and considering the interdependencies between the risks. The two most useful techniques for doing so are sensitivity analysis and probability analysis, as discussed briefly in this section.

The choice of risk analysis technique to be used depends upon many factors, principally:

- the type and size of project;
- the information available;
- the cost of the analysis and the time available to carry it out;
- the experience and expertise of the analysts.

The application of any risk analysis technique requires that the uncertain data can be given a range of different values. For example, if the duration and costs for specific activities are uncertain, use a range of values within which the decision-maker believes they are likely to lie.

An interdisciplinary team is usually needed combining engineers with appropriate experience and suitable risk analysis training, together with computer software and specialist advice. A single, fairly simple study may take two analysts six weeks, plus other staff time for input and review, depending on the objectives of the analysis. Much less work may be adequate if only a few risks are known to be significant, and the analysis much quicker if staff are familiar with using the techniques. A large complex project of long duration may require several updated studies at different points through its life.

Sensitivity analysis

Sensitivity analysis is a technique used to consider the effect on the whole project of changes in the value of each variable which is considered to be a potentially serious risk to the project.

The analysis involves repetitive calculation of the effects on the project outcome of a range of values of the variables. Project outcome is usually considered in terms of speed of construction, final costs or an economic criterion such as net present value (NPV) or internal rate of return (IRR). As an example, assume that one of the risks in a project is the cost of energy and there is a risk that this cost could increase by 5%, 10%, 15% or 20%. In this analysis the project outcome is recalculated for each of these changes in the cost of energy, and the results can then be represented graphically by plotting the percentage change in the variable against the percentage change in the economic parameter.

The results of a sensitivity analysis can be shown on a 'spider diagram' as in Figure 14.2 (page 176). This example is based upon analysing the possible costs to the client of risks in investing in a manufacturing facility. The spider diagram shows the results of calculating the sensitivity of the cost to changes in each risk which could affect productivity on site. For instance, it indicates that a decrease in output when grouting can have a significant effect on the overall cost to the contractor.

The technique is very useful because often the effect of a small change in one variable (a cost or a duration, for example) produces a marked difference in the project outcome. When several risks are being assessed in this way, a 'spider diagram' provides a dramatic way of showing the most sensitive or critical risks towards which management must direct its attention.

A sensitivity analysis should be performed for all the risks and uncertainties which may affect a project in order to identify those which have a large impact on the economic return, cost, time, or whatever are the objectives. It can be used to identify the variables which need to be considered for carrying out a probability analysis.

A limitation of sensitivity analysis is that each risk is considered independently with no attempt made to quantify their probabilities of occurrence. This technique is also limited because in reality a variable would not change without other project factors changing and this is not reflected in the analysis. With experience, the number of risks to consider can be reduced since those having a large impact on a certain type of project tend to become easily recognizable.

Note also that single variables are likely to embrace different causes. For example, delay in completion can arise from numerous delays to different elements in the implementation phase — design, fabrication, supply of plant units and so on. The effect is the same — to delay completion and start of use of the facility.

Analysis normally predicts the *effect* of uncertainty: response has to be applied to the cause(s).

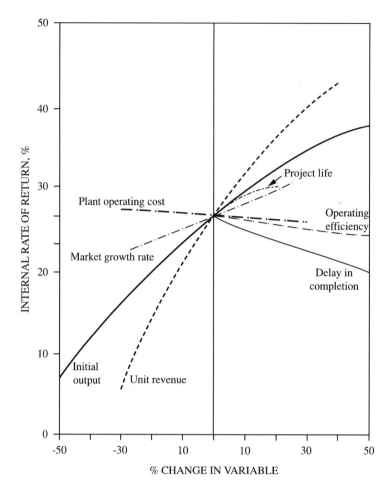

Figure 14.2 Manufacturing plant — sensitivity analysis of uncertainties of cost and benefit. A 10% decrease in the market price (unit revenue) for the product reduces the predicted return by 5%.

Probability analysis

Probability analysis overcomes many of the limitations of sensitivity analysis by specifying a probability distribution for each risk, and then considering the effects on the risks in combination. The result of the analysis is a range of values in which the final outcome could lie. An essential step in this type of risk analysis is estimating the range of probabilities within which the possible outcomes of a given process may occur.

Random ('Monte Carlo') sampling is used where calculation of data inserted into an equation would be difficult or impossible. It is used in a probability analysis in the following way:

• the range of values for the risks being considered are estimated and a suitable probability distribution of each risk is chosen;

• a value for each risk within its specified range is selected; this value is randomly chosen within the estimated probability distribution;

• the outcome of the project is calculated combining the values selected for each risk;

• the calculation is repeated a number of times to obtain the probability distribution of the project outcome; the number of cycles depends on the degree of confidence required, but 1000 is usually sufficient to make the sampling bias insignificant.

The range and probability of the final outcome of the project can be represented graphically, as in Figure 14.3, where it has been calculated for the internal rate of return from a project.

When the main objective of the project is to achieve a specified completion date, a probabilistic time analysis can be performed. A similar approach can be adopted to ascertain a likely range of project cost.

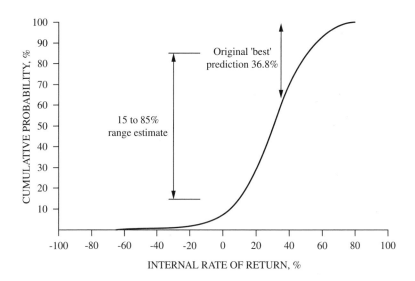

Figure 14.3 Manufacturing plant — project base case — cumulative frequency.
The original deterministic prediction of 36.8% is seen to be optimistic, as there is 60% probability that the return will be less than this value.

Risk management

By identifying risks at an early stage of planning a project or a tender, and assessing their relative importance, project management can be adapted to reduce the risks and allocate them to the parties best able to control them or absorb them should they occur. Studies should be carried out early in the life of a project, well before decisions are made to proceed.

Further reading

Association for Project Management, 1997, *Project Risk and Management Guide, 'PRAM'* (APM Group).

Kähkönen, K. and Arto, K.A. (eds), 1997, *Managing Risks in Projects* (Spon).

Pitblado, R. and Turney, R., 1996, *Risk Assessment in the Process Industries* (Institution of Chemical Engineers).

Thompson, P.A., 1996, The contribution of teamwork to project risk management, *Proceedings, International Project Management Association Congress, Paris*.

Thompson, P.A. and Norris, C., 1993, The perception, analysis and management of risks in engineering projects, *Proceedings of the Institution of Civil Engineers*, 97 (1): 42–47.

Thompson, P.A. and Perry, J.G. (eds), 1992, *Engineering Construction Risks* (Thomas Telford Publications) (reprinted with revisions 1998).

Ward, S.C. and Chapman, C.B., 1997, *Project Risk Management — Processes, Techniques and Insights* (John Wiley & Sons).

Wearne, S.H., 1997, Institutional risks in project management, in Kähkönen, K. and Arto, K.A. (eds), *Managing Risks in Projects* (Spon).

Wearne, S.H. and Wright, D., 1996, Organisational risks of joint ventures, consortia and alliance partnerships, *International Journal of Project and Business Risk Management*, 2 (1): 45–58.

Cost estimating

Graham Wilkinson

15

Estimates of cost are usually required to guide the selection, definition and control of projects large and small. Increasing accuracy and different estimating methods are therefore required stage by stage through a project. The accuracy attainable depends on the amount of engineering information available.

Stages of a project

Figure 15.1 shows three stages of work for a project. Each stage requires estimates of expected cost, but for different decisions and therefore different accuracy. In Figure 15.1 'sanctioning' means approval of the project for execution.

The conception stage

The conception stage of a possible project is sometimes known as the feasibility study. As discussed in Chapter 2, its purpose is to provide sufficient information for a management decision on whether the project may be financially attractive. The cost estimate for this stage is normally based upon only a small proportion of the engineering work which would be required over all three

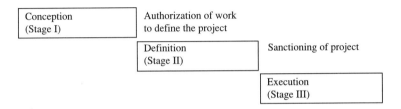

Figure 15.1 Project stages and management decisions

project stages. In some instances the conception stage may not be needed — for example, small projects, or the replacement of equipment or systems.

The cost estimate for this stage includes an evaluation of possible alternative designs and perhaps locations. For this purpose 'study estimates' accurate to ±20% are usually adequate, as comparative costs are more important than accuracy.

To achieve this accuracy requires spending 1 to 2% of the total cost of the engineering work which would be required to complete the project, in order to be able to define:

- plant type (batch system, revamp, etc);
- provisional list of equipment;
- process flow diagram (basic data).

After the comparison of alternatives, questions which are still essential for evaluating the concept are studied and a more accurate cost estimate — the 'definition estimate' — prepared as a basis on which to request authorization to proceed to project definition. The accuracy required for definition estimates is typically ±15%. To achieve this accuracy requires spending 3 to 6% of the total cost of the engineering work required to complete the project in order to decide:

- plant type (batch system, revamp, etc);
- equipment list;
- process flow diagram (basic data and essential instrument equipment and wiring control loops);
- civil and structural engineering layouts and general site specifications (reclaimed land, piled foundations required, etc).

Definition stage

The accuracy required for approval estimates is typically ±10%. To achieve this accuracy requires spending 10 to 20% of the total cost of the engineering work required to complete the project in order to decide:

- plant type (batch system, revamp, etc);
- equipment list;
- process flow diagram (basic data and all instrument loops);
- plot plan;
- civil and structural work details (type and size);
- equipment and plant layout (including piping);
- motor list;
- electrical power supply and special instrument equipment.

The result is a detailed cost estimate drawn up to serve as a basis for requesting project sanctioning.

Execution stage

Once the project is approved a budget is required as a basis for monitoring costs through to completion of the project. It should be up to date and in more detail than the approval estimate. A projection of all costs is therefore usually prepared, based on estimates of quantities of material (known as material 'take-offs'), vendor prices and engineering man-hours.

A PROJECTION OF ALL COSTS IS USUALLY PREPARED,
BASED ON MATERIAL 'TAKE-OFFS'.

Figure 15.2 (page 182) illustrates the dependence of the accuracy of the estimating on the amount of engineering data used.

Estimating techniques

The type of estimating technique used depends upon the data available when the estimate is required.

Capacity methods

Capacity methods are based on the production capacity or throughput of the proposed plant, average costs of functional units or 'step counting' methods — that is, using published correlations to estimate the costs of the essential steps within the process under evaluation, such as the following proposed by Wilson[1]:

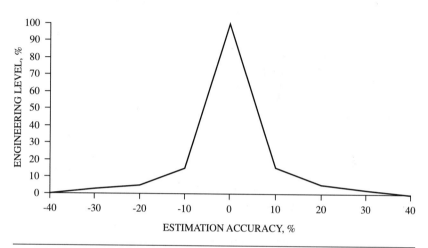

If data available	Resulting potential accuracy of estimate		
	±40%	±20%	±10%
Equipment list	Yes	Yes	Yes
Plant type and size	Yes	Yes	Yes
Process flow diagram	Yes	Yes	Yes
Civil and structural layouts, etc		Yes	Yes
Plant layout with elevation		Yes	Yes
Layout of off-site plant, etc		Yes	Yes
Schedule of piping			Yes
Piping layout			Yes
Piping isometrics			Yes
Electrical cable schedule			Yes
Instrument loop drawings			Yes
Electrical control drawings			Yes
Foundation detail drawings			Yes
Buildings, outline drawings			Yes
Suppliers' quotations, equipment			Yes

Figure 15.2 Estimation accuracy as function of engineering data available

$$C = fN(AUC)F_P F_T F_M$$

in which:

C = capital cost of plant, £(sterling);

f = investment factor, which is based on Lang factor (see later) and AUC;

N = number of main plant items except pumps;

AUC = average unit cost of main plant items, where V = flow capacity (tonnes per year)

= $21 V^{0.675}$ £(sterling);

F_P = factor for design pressure;

F_T = factor for design temperature;

F_M = factor for materials of construction.

Structural methods

In 'structural' estimating a project is divided into its principal items (major process equipment) and subsidiary items (civil and structural work, piping, electrical and instrumentation). The costs of the major equipment are determined individually, and those for subsidiary items using multiplying factors. If the costs of subsidiary items are based upon a continuous process plant, then modification factors may be required for different types of plant. Tables 15.4 and 15.5 on pages 195 and 196 give illustrations of subsidiary costs derived from factors.

Methods based on specific data

The costs for subsidiary items are determined using characteristic data which describe the scope of plant equipment and specific costs.

Calculation methods

The costs of the main plant items are estimated from manufacturers' quotations. The costs for subsidiary items are calculated in detail on the basis of quantities of materials.

Requirements for successful estimating

Estimating accuracy

Despite all the research carried out over the years, estimating remains inexact and liable to error because it is dependent on the quality and reliability of the process and engineering data available. Both the quality and reliability of the data for estimating is dependent on the time expended on the engineering work for a project. This is illustrated in Figure 15.2.

In Figure 15.2 and subsequent discussion, 'Engineering level' means the percentage of the total cost of the engineering work expended at that stage of a project.

An appropriate period must therefore be allowed at each stage of a project for the engineering work needed to provide the basis for the accuracy required in cost estimates.

Estimates with an accuracy of ±10% can be achieved at engineering levels between 10 and 20%. Above engineering levels ±20% the accuracy of estimating can only be significantly increased with much greater expenditure. There is normally little value in investing in work to achieve this greater accuracy, as market data to predict sales volumes and profits, which are as important to project viability, are normally less certain.

The system for estimating costs of small projects is basically similar to that for medium to large projects. The attainable accuracy varies with size of project. For projects of capital size below approximately £200,000 the attainable accuracy of estimation for the same planning levels is less. Accuracy increases with capital project sizes above approximately £10 million.

Structure of an estimating system

The methods of estimating for each stage should be selected to take into account the accuracy required and the project data available. Table 15.1 shows a typical estimating system.

Table 15.1 Structure of a typical estimating system

Project stage	Estimating stage	Estimating accuracy, %	Engineering level, %	Methods of estimating
	Order-of-cost	±40	Approx 0	Capacity methods
Conception	Study estimate	±20	2 to 3	Individual factors
	Definition estimate	±15	3 to 6	Cost structure of similar plants
Definition	Approval estimate	±10	10 to 20	Cost structure of similar plants and specific data
Execution	Projection	±5	Approx 80	Calculation

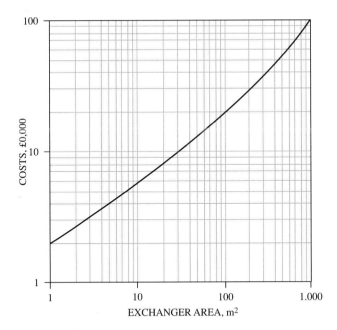

Figure 15.3 Regression curve for the costs of a shell-and-tube heat exchanger.
Material: CS/CS, Pressure: 25.00 bar, Basis: 1995

Methods of estimating

Among the methods of estimating for projects, particular importance is attached to those which are used for cost estimates on which the decisions to continue a project are based. These are, primarily:

- structural methods;
- methods based on specific data.

The major equipment has the greatest influence on the total cost of most process plant projects. Its cost should be individually estimated on the basis of the data in the equipment list.

Actual costs of previous orders are valuable as basic data[2]. Those costs should have been recorded on a database, adjusted to a uniform price basis, and evaluated in each case for the individual types of major equipment using regression analysis. The regression curves provide estimated values, via an indexing program, for any desired cost basis.

Figure 15.3 shows an example of a regression curve for a shell-and-tube heat exchanger. The actuating variable in this example is the exchanger area, with construction materials and pressure as further variables. The costs of the subsidiary items are estimated using cost structures and specific data.

Overall factors

Analysis by Lang[3] of the costs of many completed projects in the late 1940s showed that relatively constant relationships exist between the costs of major equipment and total plant costs. From the author's experience small chemical plants costing up to £2 million, typically comprising either a complete batch plant or a revamp of existing units, have an average overall factor of 4.0 — that is, the direct plant costs for a small chemical plant project are four times the major equipment costs. These direct costs exclude engineering costs as these are dependent on whether the engineering is completed by the company's own engineering department or by a contractor. A contingency factor is also added to cover unforeseen errors or omissions.

Table 15.2 gives an example of a typical accounting system structure with factors.

Individual factors

Individual factors, like overall factors, can be obtained as a function of the average equipment value by evaluating the costs of completed projects for the individual subsidiary items, using regression analysis. A precondition of applying this technique is that a standardized accounting and work breakdown structure must be used. The factors shown in Table 15.2 are typical only, and it must be emphasized that those proposing to use this method must develop their own factors.

Estimating engineering costs

Estimates of project costs at the conception stage can exclude engineering costs if the primary role of the estimate is to compare different design options. This is normally acceptable, as the anticipated engineering content will be very similar for the different options. If these costs are not included, then the estimate should clearly state that engineering costs are excluded. In the later stages the aim is to produce a cost estimate as near as possible to the final project cost and should include all the associated costs.

Engineering costs may be better estimated at the later stages, because of the advances in the engineering and planning of the project. Since firm details of the process and engineering flow diagrams and other engineering documents are available, an accurate estimate should be possible of the man-hours required for each discipline.

From the author's experience, engineering costs depend on the type and size of project. Typical engineering costs as a percentage of the total installed cost

186

Table 15.2 Structure of a typical accounting system (basis UK 1995 £sterling)

Group	Description	Factor	Percentage
A	Civil and structural work (material and labour): • Pipe bridges, sewers, rail tracks, roads • Buildings, steel, construction	0.59	16
B	Auxiliary construction work (material and labour): • Foundations, platforms, excavation work • Insulation • Painting • Heating, ventilation, installation • Fire protection	0.32	8
D–G	Major equipment	1.00	25
H	Piping within battery limits	0.30	7
I	Piping outside battery limits	0.02	1
K	Electrical (material): • Electrical energy — supply • Electrical equipment	0.21	5
L	Instrumentation (material): • Process control • Instrument equipment	0.58	14
M	Installation	0.98	24
	Total direct costs	**4.00**	**100**

(1996 basis) for a project are:

Small projects, total installed cost up to approx	£40,000	28%
Medium sized projects, total installed cost up to approx	£200,000	20%
Large projects, total installed cost up to approx	£10,000,000	10%

These percentages can be used as a guide when estimating urgent projects.

Contingency

'Contingency' is often mistaken as an allowance to cover for inaccuracies in the estimate.

The true definition of the contingency allowance is to cover the costs of work which is required to complete the project because of either insufficient information or at the time its scope is unspecified. For example, if a project estimate was required quickly, it could have quite a high contingency allowance, as the reduced time period to estimate means that sections of the project work may not have sufficient details to estimate accurately, and there may be difficulties in obtaining actual quotations within the allocated time, or there may be gaps in the project scope.

Work breakdown structure

Estimates of project costs at the conception stage can exclude engineering costs if the primary role of the estimate is to compare different design options. This is normally acceptable, as the anticipated engineering content will be very similar for the different options. If these costs are not included, then the estimate should clearly state that engineering costs are excluded. In contrast, in the later stages the aim is to produce a cost estimate as near as possible to the final project cost.

Larger projects are too complex to plan, estimate, monitor and control effectively unless they are first divided into more manageable packages. A work breakdown system divides the project into a number of packages each with a defined scope and 'deliverables' — that is, distinct end products. Once such a work breakdown exists, each item can be treated as a package of work and the account codes structured ('nested') so that their costs can be added together ('rolled up') to ascertain the total project cost whenever required.

Very large projects are first split into smaller sub-projects, and these sub-projects are further split into a hierarchy of smaller work packages. Figure

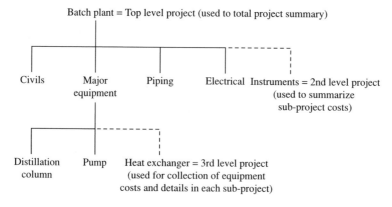

Figure 15.4 Simplified work breakdown structure for a batch type chemical plant

15.4 illustrates such a work breakdown structure. In reality how far the practice of work breakdown is continued is very much dependent on a company's project strategy (as also discussed in Chapter 18).

The work breakdown must achieve three main objectives:

(1) Every part of the project must be clearly and simply identified.

(2) The relationship of each part to all other parts within the project must be clearly shown.

(3) Every part of the total project must be included, with no part missing, or the total summary cost will be untrue.

The second objective is achieved by the logical sequential build-up of the work breakdown. The first objective can be achieved by assigning an identification number to each piece of the work breakdown. By devising a suitable coding system the location and relationship of a piece of equipment is easily ascertained. The third part is the most difficult and relies on the experience of the estimating engineer, but by the careful use of estimating check-lists vital omissions can be minimized.

The cost coding of a project should be related to the other information systems in a company, so that cost data are recorded on a common basis and can be exchanged. A cost code system for a project is therefore normally based upon the company's accounting codes.

The functions of the code are:

• each code number acts as a unique name that identifies that part of the project;

• the code is arranged so that it categorizes and qualifies, by itself or by the addition of sub-codes, that part of the project it identifies.

The example in Figure 15.5 shows the previous work breakdown of a batch type chemical plant with a coding system applied. The top level consists of a

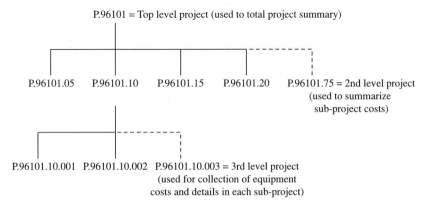

Figure 15.5 A three-tier work breakdown with cost coding structure

six-digit code. The first digit in this project might be a 'P', indicating it is a project. This level is for summarizing data about the total project and should be related to a project description, name of project manager, etc.

The middle level consists of a two-digit number that could be based on the company's existing code of accounts — for example, 05 = civil engineering, 10 = major equipment, 15 = piping, 20 = electrical, and so on. This level relates to descriptive information on each sub-project.

The bottom level code number consists of a three-digit sequential number allocated to the pieces of equipment in each sub-project. This level is used for recording the estimates and actual costs of individual pieces of equipment, services and other defined packages of work.

The major benefits of applying a cost coding system are:
- all parts are uniquely identified and their associated costs allocated correctly;
- rapid and efficient search, retrieval and analysis of information, especially with computer relational database systems;
- standard company project cost and progress reports can be generated;
- statistical analysis of previous projects to aid in comparative estimating, monitoring estimating consistency, identifying common design data (including drawings, purchase order information and specifications) for use in future projects — that is, retained engineering know-how.

Estimating check-list

The main aim of an estimating check-list is to help identify all the tasks for a project. It includes all factors, technical, commercial, statutory and environmental, and any specific needs of the company. Every company can develop its own estimating check-list, but if sufficient estimating experience or information is not available, then one of the commercial lists can be used. A typical example can be found in *A Guide to Capital Cost Estimating*, published by the Institution of Chemical Engineers and the Association of Cost Engineers[4].

Whether the estimate is prepared by the company to evaluate possible project alternatives or by a contractor bidding for a project, the objective is to avoid omissions as someone will have to pay for them (client or contractor, depending upon the terms of the contract).

Estimating consistency

Costs are more likely to be underestimated than overestimated. This can normally be attributed to:
- incomplete definition of the scope of the project;
- additions to the original scope of the project;

- optimism from the estimator or the people involved in completing tasks within the project;
- optimistic forecasts of the accuracy of estimates — commonly occurring when the estimator is required to produce definition type estimates from insufficient project information.

Costs can be overestimated because of:

- inexperience of people preparing an estimate;
- insufficient workscope details, which require high provisional sums and contingency allowances;
- playing safe, adding a 'feel-good' cushion or suffering from a spare funds syndrome, normally the result of lack of confidence in previous estimates.

COSTS CAN BE OVERESTIMATED BECAUSE
OF ADDING A 'FEEL-GOOD' CUSHION.

Neither of these situations should be tolerated. The experienced project manager learns to add or subtract amounts from such estimates.

The risks to a project from incorrect cost estimates are great. If the project cost is underestimated, when excess costs arise the project team or a contractor may not be able to pay and can be tempted to reduce standards or omit work essential to performance and safety. If the project cost is overestimated then the project may not appear to be a viable proposition to proceed. If a contractor overstates the cost estimate while tendering for a project then he runs the risk of losing the project to competition. Therefore all cost estimating must be realistic to safeguard the interests of every party involved.

The computer as a tool in estimating

Cost estimating is not an exact science and relies heavily on experience and judgement. Many of the techniques used in cost estimating can be computerized and gain the benefits of efficient storage, retrieval and analysis of cost data, speed of calculation, consistency and 'what-if' scenarios. The computer is only a tool. The accuracy of estimates is dependent on the data available, not the power of the computer processor.

Commercially available systems look attractive to help cope with increasing engineering workloads and the trend of reducing available personnel. Altering a software package can take much time and resources to be effective and reliable. Doing so is a project in itself, to be sanctioned only if it is certain to be cost-beneficial.

Most commercial computer-based estimating systems force their users towards a near complete project definition and hence are more suited to the second stage of a project. Every system requires the prices to be calibrated so that they reflect the costs that the company operating the system expects from its purchasing power, labour costs, overheads and so on.

Example of the structural approach to cost estimating

This example shows how a cost estimate can be produced with relatively little engineering effort and still achieve an accuracy of approximately ±20%.

The process is a plant type batch system, producing approximately 1200 tonnes of product per year. Figure 15.6 is the process flow diagram; Table 15.3 (page 194) gives equipment data. The main equipment costs could be derived from historical company cost data or from manufacturers' quotations. The equipment is to be sited outdoors, within existing plant battery limits. All foundations are to be steel-reinforced concrete, except the column, which requires piling.

Tables 15.4 and 15.5 (pages 195 and 196) give cost group factors and subsidiary costs derived from factors. Generally, equipment costs stored are adjusted to a uniform design and price basis. That is, the design is based upon on operation in a continuous process and the price is fixed to a period in time. To estimate for a batch system, which normally requires an increased number of lines of a higher complexity (more fittings), then the main and subsidiary items would require additional multiplying factors.

Modification factors are additional factors to convert costs based upon general continuous process plant to other types of operating conditions — for example, batch, liquid solid handling, etc.

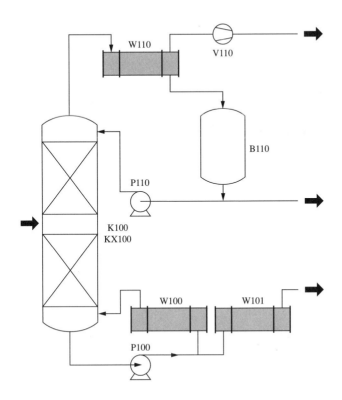

Figure 15.6 Process flow diagram

Table 15.6 (page 197) gives the project cost estimate summary, while Table 15.7 (pages 198–199) shows an estimate for the same project produced using a more traditional and time-consuming method relying on a vast database of costs.

References in Chapter 15

1. Wilson, G.T., 1971, Capital investment for chemical plant, *British Chemical Engineering*, 16: 931–934.

2. Miller, P.F., 1988, *Project Cost Databanks* (Butterworth).

3. Lang, H.J., 1947, Engineering approach to preliminary cost estimating, *Chemical Engineering*, 54: 130–133.

4. Institution of Chemical Engineers and Association of Cost Engineers, 1988, *A Guide to Capital Cost Estimating*, 3rd edition, 125–127.

Table 15.3 Equipment data

Equipment number	No. off	Type description	Description			
B100	1	Vessel	Not insulated			
		Carbon steel		D–G:	£3000	
		Pressure:	6 bar	A–M:	£36,000	
		Volume:	2 m^3	Factor %:	1200	
K100	1	Column	Outdoors			
		Carbon steel		D–G:	£18,000	
		Pressure:	6 bar	A–M:	£97,000	
		Diameter:	1 m	Factor %:	539	
		Height:	10 m			
KX100	2	Column internals	BX			
		304L		D–G:	£64,000	
		Pressure:	1 bar	A–M:	£64,000	
		Diameter:	1 m	Factor %:	100	
		Height:	10 m			
P100	1	Pump	Centrifugal			
		Cast steel		D–G:	£3000	
		Pressure:	25 bar	A–M:	£22,000	
		Flow:	25 m^3/hr	Factor %:	732	
		Head:	50 m			
P110	1	Pump	Centrifugal			
		Cast steel		D–G:	£2000	
		Pressure:	25 bar	A–M:	£20,000	
		Flow:	5 m^3/hr	Factor %:	1000	
		Head:	50 m			
V110	1	Vacuum system	Two-stage			
		Cast steel		D–G:	£6000	
		Pressure:	5 Mbar	A–M:	£37,000	
		Flow:	50 m^3/hr	Factor %:	618	
W100.W110	2	Heat exchanger	Shell and tube			
		CS/CS		D–G:	£28,000	
		Pressure:	25 bar	A–M:	£118,000	
		Area:	100 m^2	Factor %:	421	
W101	1	Heat exchanger	Shell and tube			
		CS/CS		D–G:	£4000	
		Pressure:	25 bar	A–M:	£31,000	
		Area:	10 m^2	Factor %:	775	

Table 15.4 Cost group factors

Equipment		A	B	$\sum$D–G	H	K	L	M	Factor %
				Cost groups, factor %					
B110	Vessel	267	33	100	67	33	433	267	1200
K100	Column	0	133	100	28	11	156	111	539
KX100	Column internals	0	0	100	0	0	0	0	100
P100	Pump	233	33	100	33	67	33	233	732
P110	Pump	300	50	100	50	100	50	350	1000
V110	Vacuum system	100	17	100	17	50	167	167	618
W100	Heat exchanger	107	36	100	21	7	64	86	421
W110	Heat exchanger	107	36	100	21	7	64	86	421
W101	Heat exchanger	150	75	100	50	25	200	175	775
Modification factors for batch system		1.0	1.24	1.0	1.22	1.0	1.0	1.3	

Table 15.5 Subsidiary costs using factors
(the example has deliberately been kept simple to outline the process)

Equipment		Cost groups, £000							Factor %
		A	B	$\sum$D–G	H	K	L	M	
B110	Vessel	8	1	3	2	1	13	8	1200
K100	Column	0	24	18	5	2	28	20	539
KX100	Column internals	0	0	64	0	0	0	0	100
P100	Pump	7	1	3	1	2	1	7	732
P110	Pump	6	1	2	1	2	1	7	1000
V110	Vacuum system	6	1	6	1	3	10	10	618
W100	Heat exchanger	15	5	14	3	1	9	12	421
W110	Heat exchanger	15	5	14	3	1	9	2	421
W101	Heat exchanger	6	3	4	2	1	8	7	775
Basic plant total		63	41	128	18	13	79	73	
Modification factors for batch system		1.0	1.24	1.0	1.22	1.0	1.0	1.3	
Total, £000		63	51	128	22	13	79	95	

Table 15.6 Example of a project cost estimate summary

Group	Description	Cost
A	Civil and structural work (material and labour): • Pipe bridges, sewers, rail tracks, roads • Buildings, steel, construction	£63,000
B	Auxiliary construction work (material and labour): • Foundations, platforms, excavation work • Insulation • Painting • Heating, ventilation, installation • Fire protection	£51,000
D–G	Major equipment	£128,000
H	Piping within battery limits	£22,000
I	Piping outside battery limits	
K	Electrical (material): • Electrical energy — supply • Electrical equipment	£13,000
L	Instrumentation (material): • Process control • Instrument equipment	£79,000
M	Installation	£95,000
	Total direct costs	**£451,000**
N	Engineering	£90,000
U	Contingency	£59,000
	Total project cost	**£600,000**

Table 15.7 Traditional manual method of project cost estimating

Group	Description		Cost
A	Civil and structural work (material and labour): $£79/m^3 \times 700\ m^3$	£55,300	
	Staircase £1500/m × 9 m	£13,500	£68,800
B	Auxiliary construction work (material and labour):		
	8% of A	£5500	
	• Foundations, platforms, excavation work	£48,960	
	• Insulation (£68 × 720 m)		
	• Painting		
	• Heating, ventilation, installation		
	• Fire protection	£1800	£56,260
D–G	Major equipment		£128,000
H	Piping within battery limits		
	8 pieces of equipment assumes 6 pipes/equipment × average 15 m length		
	720 m of 80 mm dia @ £21/m	£15,120	
	70 valves @ £206	£14,420	
	Installation 720 m × 4 hrs × £21 = £60,480		
	for group M		£29,540
I	Piping outside battery limits	£0	£0
K	Electrical (material):		
	Motors 4 kW (£1000) and 2 kW (£600)	£1600	
	Lights, controls: motor cost × 1.5	£2400	
	Cable: motor cost × 2	£3200	
	Area lighting: $£21/m^2 \times 100\ m^2$	£2100	
	Earth protection 8 pieces equipment × £500	£4000	
	(DIFFICULT GROUP TO ESTIMATE —		
	could be ×2 estimate)		£13,300
L	Instrumentation (material):		
	Instrument equipment 6 major pieces of equipment		
	× £15,000		£90,000
			Continued opposite

Table 15.7 (cont'd)   Traditional manual method of project cost estimating

Group	Description		Cost
M	Installation		
	10% of A and B groups	£12,506	
	See group H	£60,480	
	70% of K	£9310	
	25% of L	£22,500	£104,796
N	10% of D–G	£12,800	
	Same as M for H	£60,480	
	75% of K	£9975	
	25% of L	£22,500	
	10% of M	£10,480	£116,235
	Total project cost		**£606,931**

Further reading

Dinatall, J., 1978, Conceptual estimating requirements and conditions that have an impact on construction costs and time frame, *5th International Cost Engineering Congress, Utrecht.*

Kharbanda, O.P. and Stallworthy, E., 1978, *Capital Cost Estimating for the Process Industries* (Butterworth Scientific).

Modern Cost Engineering: Methods and Data, Volume II, Chemical Engineering, 1984 (McGraw-Hill).

Reynolds, T., 1997, Costing from cradle to grave, *The Chemical Engineer*, Issue 637, 22–23.

Smith, N.J. (ed), 1995, *Project Cost Estimating* (Thomas Telford Publications).

Sweeting, J., 1997, *Project Cost Estimating — Principles and Practice* (Institution of Chemical Engineers).

Project planning

Harry Moody

The success or failure of a project is usually judged by whether it achieves specific objectives in time, cost and performance. Project time-scales are always being squeezed by management and there is rarely enough time to complete project work, so it is important to make the best possible use of the available time. Project objectives are achieved by co-ordinating the efforts of a range of people who invariably have different levels of knowledge and experience.

The purpose of planning

The purpose of planning is to manage the future utilization of time and resources on a project. Remember that because of the nature of project work, changes to the plan are almost certainly going to occur at some stage. Therefore, the procedures used for planning must be chosen carefully to ensure that the plan can be updated quickly, so that it remains a realistic guide to the most efficient way of completing the project and achieving the objectives.

Small projects involving no more than familiar activities may be planned simply, but the plan should be agreed to avoid the risk of failing to meet start and completion dates for key activities. More complex projects involving a diversity of people and organizations necessitate formal procedures and systems for planning.

Effective planning entails:
- setting out a desirable course of events to achieve specific objectives;
- establishing the prerequisites (such as obtaining information, materials, contractors) for the chosen course to be realized;
- considering how to deal with foreseeable happenings that will change the initial chosen plan.

Why plan?

There are many reasons including:
- project management entails interaction between people and therefore needs a disciplined approach if objectives and targets are to be achieved;

- the complexities involved in a typical project mean that no one person can have a full working knowledge of every activity required to be undertaken, and therefore some means of sorting out interrelationships, priorities and so on is needed;
- if meaningful targets are set, actual performance can be measured and corrective action taken if performance is not satisfactory;
- productivity can be improved by setting tighter targets/exploring new methods of working;
- 'fire-fighting' and 'crisis management' should be avoided.

Objectives of effective project planning

The principal objectives of project planning are to:

- provide a means of expressing complex projects in a logical sequence of activities;
- provide an estimate of the time and effort involved in each of the activities which constitute a plan;
- identify the risks involved and make allowances to cover uncertainties;
- improve co-ordination and communication;
- determine priorities;
- reduce project duration and improve time control;
- make better use of resources;
- provide better and more timely data for decision-making;
- provide a means of ensuring performance takes place in line with plans.

Some benefits of effective project planning

Effective project planning gives the following benefits:

- improved definition of work to be carried out;
- better work schedules based on knowledge of resources required and resources available;
- identification of the best way of applying resources to achieve project objectives and conform with operating policies;
- establishment of more realistic budgets for performing the work;
- ability to monitor progress and detect those points where delays will jeopardize the attainment of the project objectives in time to permit corrective action to be taken;
- more realistic prediction of final project costs and completion date;
- alternative strategies can be explored;
- the need for contingency planning is highlighted.

Project planning strategy

The planning of a project commences when deciding the project strategy, as discussed in Chapter 3. Some of the key points include:

- involve all appropriate parties in order to get agreed data and commitment to the resulting plan;
- decide the level of planning to be undertaken — break the project down into discrete work packages, stopping at the appropriate managerial level given the current state of the project;
- present levels of plan — for different levels of users;
- use the plan as a communication aid to persuade people to perform tasks before delaying the work of others — so ensure the methodology adopted for presenting the plan is kept simple;
- make the plan sufficiently flexible to permit some room for manoeuvre;
- list and publish any assumptions made during the preparation of the plan;
- issue the plan before work commences.

Planning the plan

Before rushing into the application of planning technique(s), allocate time for consideration of a number of questions including:

- exactly what has to be achieved? Why? Are the objectives clearly established?
- how is it proposed to achieve the end result? Are there different strategies available? Are existing procedures relevant?
- where is the work to be carried out?
- who is going to do the work? Are internal and/or external resources going to be used?
- when has the work to be done? Do restraints exist?
- how important is the work in terms of achieving organizational goals? What importance will be given to the work?
- who has the ultimate authority in relation to the work? What are the lines of responsibility? Who does the project manager report to?
- how is performance (success/failure) going to be set? What are the standards which will be used for assessing performance?

Sources of planning data

Every project is a unique undertaking. Some of the work will bear similarities to previous projects, however, and some will be completely novel.

For work which has been undertaken previously, the sources of planning data may include:

- in-house labour — time sheet analysis system;
- equipment and materials — bid analysis sheets, supplier performance files, stock control records;

- contractors — quantity surveyor reports;
- workshop/maintenance operations — job cards, clearance notes;
- standard sub-networks — often included in project management procedural documentation and/or held on computer file;
- published data — standard man-hours and durations for construction activities.

For work which is novel, a system of 'three duration' estimating can be used. The three duration estimates comprise:

t_O optimistic duration;
t_M most likely duration;
t_P pessimistic duration.

The three duration estimates can be combined to produce a forecast of the expected duration (t_E) using the formula:

$$t_E = \frac{t_O + 4t_M + t_P}{6}$$

Planning techniques

The targets set for the project are invariably time related. If the time-scale is extremely short — for example, up to three months — then the plan may be prepared using the day as the basic time unit. Longer duration projects may use the week as the basic unit, or even the month if the project is going to take several years.

The choice of time unit depends on a number of factors including:

- organizational procedures;
- degree of control to be exerted over the project;
- the level of planning being undertaken;
- frequency of review meetings.

Activities

Compiling a list of the activities of work for a project is often the most difficult part of the planning process. It is a little easier if the project objectives and scope are clearly defined. The main emphasis is on identifying *what* has to be done within the scope of the project to achieve the objectives. Activities can be derived as follows:

- evaluating performance on recently completed projects;

- discussing the project with project team members and other specialists involved;
- brainstorming;
- accessing published check-lists and databases.

Bar charting

Henry L Gantt developed a production planning and control system (Gantt charts) for use on flow assembly lines in factories. Gantt charts are constructed using horizontal bars to represent activities against the time-scale. This graphical technique is widely used today and is usually referred to as bar charting.

Bar charts are the most commonly used format to present plans. They are a simplistic presentation of activities associated with a project. Activities represented in a bar chart indicate intentions. While other planning techniques help in the analysis of project performance, bar charts really only present the best results. Bar charts are useful for indicating targets — that is, milestone dates — and therefore are appropriate for formal statements of intention such as contractual programmes.

Activities are drawn in the form of horizontal bars. The bars are positioned relative to a time-scale. The time-scale can be either in calendar format or in day/week numbers.

It is normal practice to list the activities by earliest scheduled start and to have one activity per horizontal line. Important constraints or milestone dates can be shown by either drawing a vertical line or using triangles.

Figure 16.1 is an example of a bar chart.

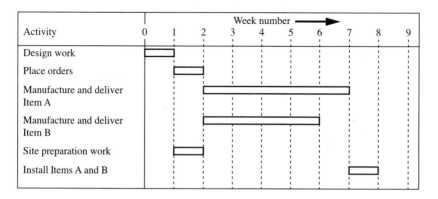

Figure 16.1 An example of a bar chart

The advantages of using bar charts are self-evident. The disadvantages of using bar charts are:

- they do not show logic;
- they do not indicate the degree of criticality of activities;
- they are difficult to update;
- there are limitations on size;
- there are limitations on resource scheduling.

Linked bar charting

The bar chart shown in Figure 16.1 assumes that all activities will start at the earliest logical point in time. In other words it is an optimistic programme. Note that no attempt has so far been made to show the interdependence between the various activities in a programme. Linked bar charts do show the links between one activity and those preceding activities which have to be completed before a particular activity can start. Similarly, links are shown between the activity and succeeding activities which are dependent on the activity being completed. The visual presentation of dependencies between activities has the advantage of highlighting the effect of delays in any one activity.

Activities which can, if desired, be delayed without extending the overall project completion date are said to have 'float'. This concept of float is used extensively in project planning.

A bar chart is constructed for the various activities associated with the project. All activities are shown on their earliest possible start dates. The example shown in Figure 16.1 will be used to demonstrate the technique. The links are now added to the bar chart as indicated on Figure 16.2.

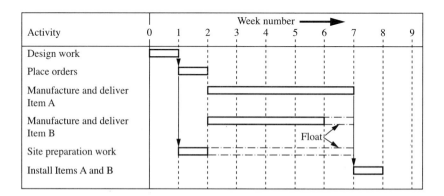

Figure 16.2 An example of a linked bar chart

The linked bar chart is interpreted as follows:
- as soon as the design work has been completed orders can be placed for Items A and B and also the preparation of the site can commence — thus there are two vertical links shown at the end of the design activity;
- the next activity which can now logically start is the manufacture and delivery of both Items A and B — two vertical links can be drawn from the completion of the order-placing process to the start of the two manufacturing activities;
- the installation of Items A and B can only occur when all the items are delivered to site and the site preparation has been completed — a vertical link is drawn from the completion of the delivery of Item A to the start of the installation activity;
- the only restraint on the delivery of Item B and the preparation of the site is that they must be completed before installation commences. This means that the start of manufacture of Item B could be delayed by up to one week and the preparation of the site by up to five weeks. Float is shown on the linked bar chart by means of broken horizontal lines;
- activities which do not have float are described as critical. They must start and finish during the weeks shown. The critical path follows the critical activities through the links on the bar chart — the critical path involves design work, placing orders, manufacturing and delivering Item A and the installation work. The importance of the critical path can be highlighted by redrawing the bar chart as shown in Figure 16.3.

In dealing with short duration projects, linked bar charts provide an excellent means of preparing and presenting plans.

Activity	Float (weeks)	Week number → 0 1 2 3 4 5 6 7 8 9
Design work	0	
Place orders	0	
Manufacture and deliver Item A	0	
Install Items A and B	0	
Manufacture and deliver Item B	1	
Site preparation work	5	

Figure 16.3 Bar chart with activities arranged in ascending order of float

Network analysis techniques

The use of planning networks, with their associated analyses, offers an integrated management control system which is particularly suited to complex projects and situations involving risk and uncertainty. The combined diagrammatic and analytical approach to the problems of planning and control eliminates ambiguity and reduces misunderstanding between groups and/or people involved in a project. In particular, it helps in the following operations:

- determining and studying the critical path;
- studying how non-critical activities can become critical if delayed or if their work content is changed;
- exploring the impact of alternative strategies for achieving project objectives;
- finalizing the work to be carried out and hence the scope of the project;
- improving the production of work schedules by optimizing the resources required against those available at any moment;
- deciding the best way of applying resources to achieve project objectives and conform with operating policies;
- monitoring and reviewing progress against the agreed time-scale.

Precedence diagramming

Each activity/work package is contained within a box-shaped node. Information relating to an activity is located in particular sectors of the box-shaped node as shown in Figure 16.4.

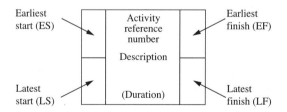

Figure 16.4 Information contained in the box-shaped node

Earliest start + Duration = Earliest finish

Latest start + Duration = Latest finish

Total float (TF)   = Latest start − Earliest start

= Latest finish − Earliest finish

If Total float = 0 then activity is critical

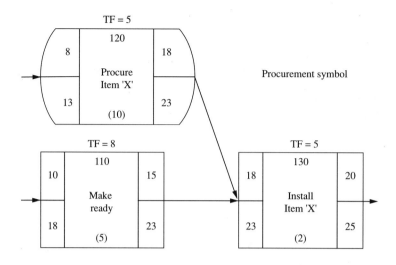

Figure 16.5 Finish-to-start relationship

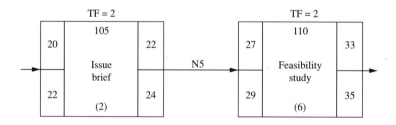

Figure 16.6 Nominal delay between activities
Note: N5 indicates that activity 110 cannot start until 5 time units have elapsed after the completion of activity 105

The logic diagram is constructed using some (or all) of the relationships demonstrated in Figures 16.5 to 16.12 (pages 208–211).

Finish-to-start relationships are the most commonly used relationship between activities.

Circumstances do arise when recognized delays will occur between consecutive activities in a network. For example, 'Issue drawing for comments' and 'Analyse comments'. The extent of the nominal ('N') delay is indicated on the dependency link between the activities. It is quite acceptable to add additional activities in the network to explain the reason for delays occurring. The current approach to using network analysis is to avoid producing extra large networks at the early stages of project planning.

There are occasions when an activity can start at the same time as another activity, but not before. They are represented on the precedence diagram by adding an 'S' to the appropriate dependency links. Situations where an activity can start at a defined time interval after a preceding activity are indicated by adding a time value to the 'S' symbol.

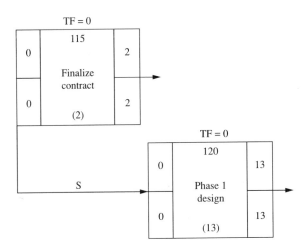

Figure 16.7 Start-to-start relationships

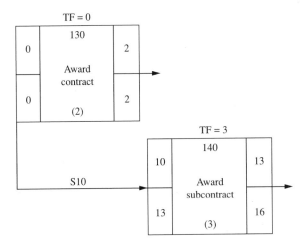

Figure 16.8 Start-to-start relationship with time value
Note: S10 indicates that activity 140 can start 10 time units after activity 130 has commenced

Situations arise whereby an activity cannot be fully completed until another activity has been finished. For example, 'Complete design of plant items' and 'All capital spares on order'. This scenario is represented on the precedence diagram by adding an 'F' to the appropriate dependency link. A situation in which an activity cannot be completed until a specified time after the completion of another activity is shown on the precedence diagram by adding the appropriate time value to the 'F' symbol.

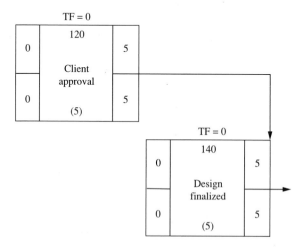

Figure 16.9 Finish-to-finish relationships

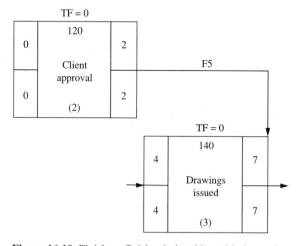

Figure 16.10 Finish-to-finish relationships with time value
Note: F5 indicates that activity 140 cannot be completed until 5 time units have elapsed after the completion of activity 120

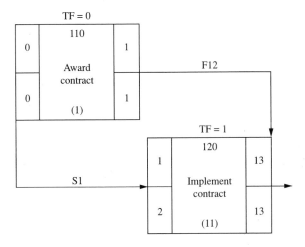

Figure 16.11 Start-to-start and finish-to-finish relationships
Note: The total float for activity 120 is derived from the formula:
TF = LF − ES − Duration = 13 − 1 − 11 = 1 week

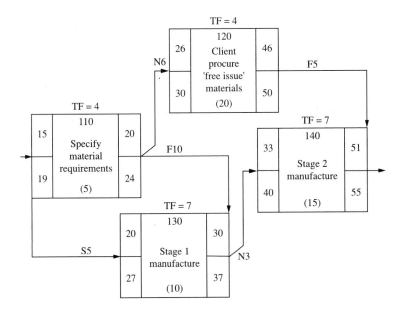

Figure 16.12 Typical precedence diagram
Note: durations are in days

Activity reference	Description	Float (days)	Day number ──► 15 20 25 30 35 40 45 50 55 60
110	Specify material requirements	4	
120	Client procure 'free issue' materials	4	
140	Stage 2 manufacture	7	
130	Stage 1 manufacture	7	

Figure 16.13 Bar chart representation of precedence diagram

Lag start and finish relationships involve a combination of start-to-start and finish-to-finish relationships. In Figure 16.11 work on the contract will not start (in earnest) until one week after the formal signing of the contract documents. The contract has to be completed in 12 working weeks from the date when the contract is awarded.

Figure 16.12 shows a section of a typical precedence diagram and Figure 16.13 a bar chart based on the network.

Activity-on-arrow networking

There are a number of methods which can be used for drawing logic diagrams for critical path analysis. One of the major alternative systems is activity-on-arrow networking. In this system the arrows represent activities and the nodes represent events (see Figure 16.14). The examples used to illustrate precedence diagramming are repeated in Figures 16.15 to 16.20 (pages 213–215).

Event numbers are used to denote the activity reference. For example, in Figure 16.15 activity 10–30 is 'Procure item X'.

Broken arrows, referred to as dummies, are used to represent relationships between events (often referred as lead-lag).

Activity-on-arrow networks are generally considered to be more difficult to read than precedence diagrams. The use of dummies and the activity numbering system can sometimes lead to confusion.

Precedence diagrams are relatively easy to follow and are widely used in conjunction with work packages. Complex logic scenarios can result in dependency links criss-crossing and this can lead to confusion.

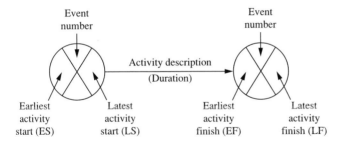

Figure 16.14 Activity-on-arrow system
Total float (TF) = (Latest finish − Earliest start) − Duration

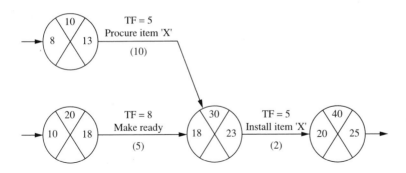

Figure 16.15 Finish-to-start relationship

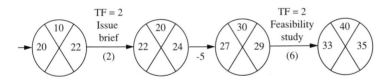

Figure 16.16 Nominal delay between activities

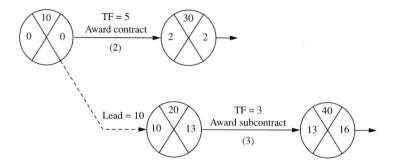

Figure 16.17 Start-to-start relationships

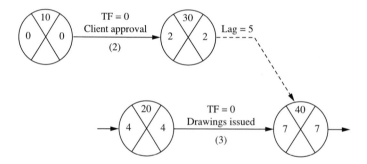

Figure 16.18 Finish-to-finish relationships

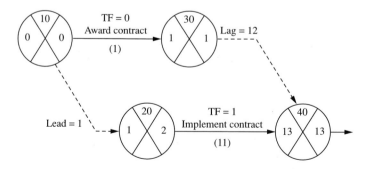

Figure 16.19 Lead-lag relationships

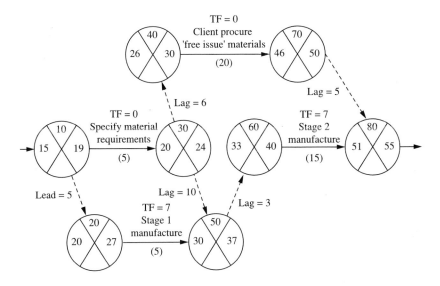

Figure 16.20 Typical activity-on-arrow network

Computer software packages

All of the above planning techniques are readily available on a wide range of software packages and can be used on either desktop or larger computer systems.

Case study – Project 'X'

A process unit requires to be refurbished and upgraded. The project plan commences at sanction and it is proposed that much of the work will be carried out by contractors. It is assumed that the client has completed all of the definition work.

Figure 16.21 (pages 216–217) represents a part of the embryonic precedence diagram. Figure 16.22 (page 218) is a summary master bar chart and shows milestone dates.

There is no one unique method for planning a project. The same project can be planned in many varying degrees of detail and this can affect the accuracy of the logic diagram. Nearly all plans omit something. In this particular case there must be queries. For example:

• why is there no reference to the casting of floor(s)?
• why is there no interface with the existing overall production process control system?

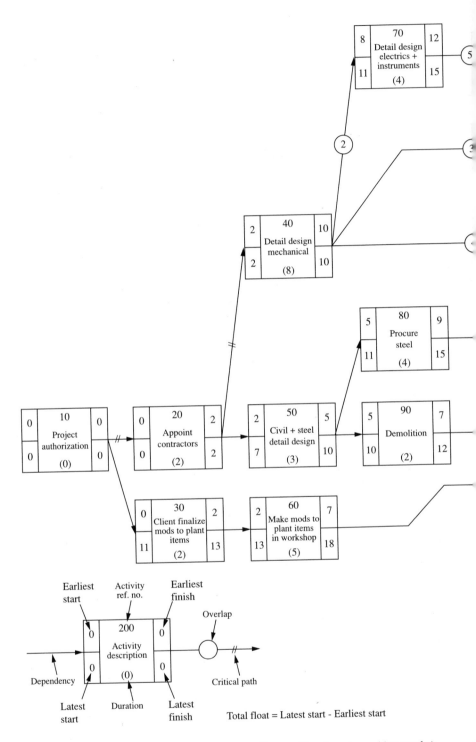

Figure 16.21 Project 'X' embryonic precedence diagram (durations in working weeks)

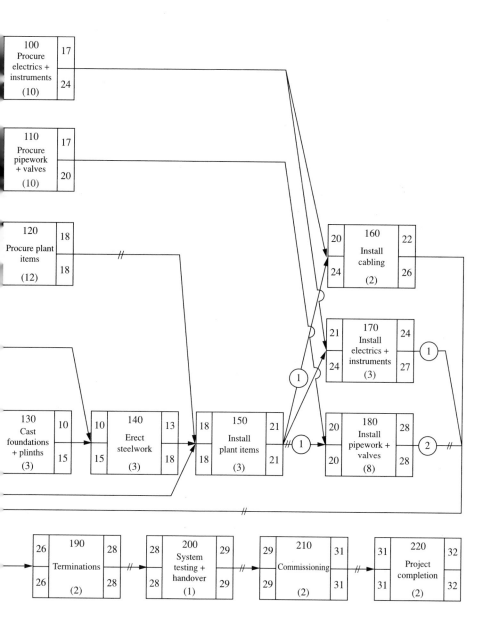

- why is there no reference to interfacing with the existing process and engineering services?
- why is there no reference to updating operating procedures, training of staff and so on?
- why is there no reference to design reviews, safety and quality audits?

A risk assessment of the plan should embrace all these queries but in addition address the following:

- the current and recent performance of the contractor(s) who will be involved during project implementation;
- the procurement of the new plant items (activity 120). How has the estimated duration of 12 weeks been derived? How have the suppliers performed in terms of achieving agreed lead times?

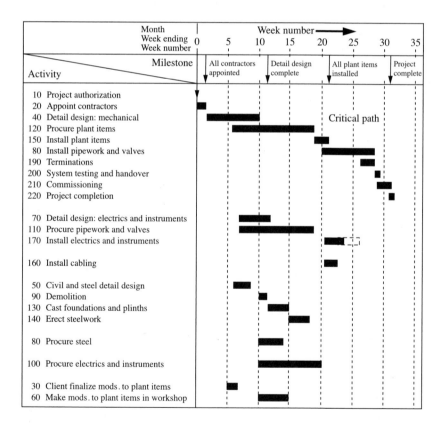

Figure 16.22 Project programme

- the client is going to refurbish some workshop items and 'free issue' to the contractor for installation. It is difficult to imagine that the total float of 11 weeks is realistic;
- the labour-intensive parts of the installation — activities 160, 170 and 180 — are shown as occurring concurrently. How is the work to be controlled? A 'free-for-all' would only lead to inefficiency and an extension to the project duration;
- is the combined duration for activities 200 and 210 practicable? It is frequently the case that insufficient time is allocated for commissioning and customer acceptance;
- what is the likelihood of significant changes of intent occurring? This type of project often generates a procession of ongoing changes.

Work breakdown structure (WBS) – Project 'X'

Some of the problems relating to the planning of a large project such as Project 'X' can be overcome by using work breakdown structure (WBS).

WBS is a formal and systematic way of defining and identifying what the component parts of a project are, breaking down the work to be planned, structuring and integrating the project organization and the control and information systems. WBS is a practical tool which is particularly useful for managing a project as a set of sub-projects and defining packages of work for contractors — as discussed in Chapter 18.

Figure 16.23 (page 220) shows the sequence of steps in developing and applying WBS.

The initial stages involve the application of WBS to identify meaningful packages of work. A work package is a discrete task, activity or job, which has an observable start and finish, and an end product of some form which is of value to the 'customer'. The best way to picture a work package is to think of a mini-project wholly contained within the main project.

The overriding purpose of WBS is to provide answers to two questions:
- what has to be accomplished to achieve the project objective(s)?
- what is the necessary hierarchical relationship of the work effort?

In addition, the application of WBS to a project also provides information on:
- the complete list of work tasks to be carried out during project implementation;
- responsibilities, allocation of personnel, costs, durations, risk and the sequence of carrying out work.

The derivation of the work packages at each level can be facilitated through the use of a matrix of responsibility as shown in Table 16.1 (page 220). Some of the key points to note include:

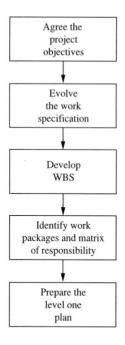

Figure 16.23 Stages in implementing work breakdown structure

Table 16.1 Matrix of responsibility

Work package	Specification	Man-hours	Cost estimate, £	Person with internal responsibility	Customer contact
A	100/3A	200	30,000	Joe Bloggs	Tom White
B	210/6/C	85	20,000	Jean Smith	Joe Green
C	75/Q/Z12	30	8000	Bill Reynolds	Ann Brown
D	1854/92W	?	?	Fred Wells	Mark Mann

• the principal lines of communication are identified by naming the people concerned;

• the work package specification sheet should be cross-referenced so that the timing of the work, what has to be done, how it is to be done and who is delegating the work can be clearly identified;

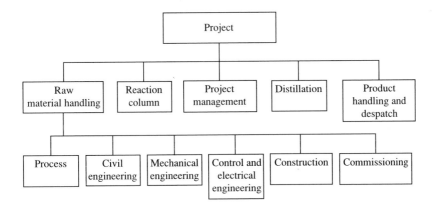

Figure 16.24 WBS by zone of project plus project functions

• work should not start on Package 'D' until a man-hour estimate and a cost estimate are prepared and approved.

For many projects the WBS can be on the basis of zones of a site and project/contract function. Figure 16.24 shows an example.

Specification for a work package

Figure 16.25 (page 222) shows a pro forma for developing the specification for a work package. The specification should include:

• formal description (title) for the package;
• clear definition of the scope of the package — for example, marked-up drawing showing geographical boundaries and so on;
• the methodology which will be used to produce drawings, calculations, sizes, schedules and so on;
• clear definition of the information required to start actual work on the package;
• clear definition of the start activity for the package;
• definition of the information which will be produced by the package (the 'deliverables');
• clear definition of the finish activity of the package;
• identification of the person with prime responsibility for the package;
• identification of the person(s) who will assist in undertaking the package — that is, establish formal accountability;
• an indication as to the degree of confidence that can be placed on the whole specification.

Project title:	Location:
Work package title:	Date:
Work package number:	Revision:
Project manager:	
Work package nominee:	

Specification of customer requirements:

Technical description of the work to be undertaken:

Deliverables:
1.

2.

Estimated lead time for each deliverable	Working weeks	Preceding work package number(s)	Succeeding work package number(s)
1. 2.			

Personnel involved:
1.

2.

Review meetings:
1. Frequency:

2. Dates:

Reporting schedule:

Figure 16.25 Work package specification sheet

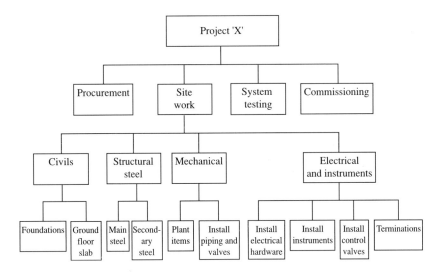

Figure 16.26 WBS for Project 'X'

Application of WBS to case study – Project 'X'

Figure 16.26 shows the embryonic work breakdown. The level of detail depends on:

- the current state of knowledge relating to the project;
- identification of 'mini-project' managers/supervisors;
- the organizational structure;
- the extent to which the work is proceduralized.

Every effort should be made at this stage to put some detail against each of the principal work hierarchical sub-divisions. For example, under the heading 'Procurement' there could be a breakdown relating to plant items, piping materials, electrical materials and instruments.

On most projects it is advisable to include a general heading of 'Project management' and break it down into work packages involving planning, costing, contractor liaison, performance reviews, reporting and so on. Each package requires effort and therefore the man-hours have to be included in the total man-hour budget.

The level one precedence diagram can now be prepared using the work packages from Figure 16.26. The work packages are taken from the WBS at the maximum level of detail:

- appointing contractor(s);
- plant item design;

- rack piping design;
- branch piping design;
- design for bobbin pieces;
- electrical hardware design;
- main steel design;
- modifications to existing items;
- casting ground floor slab;
- etc.

Resource levelling

The availability of resources is an integral factor in formulating plans and establishing work schedules.

The first step in analysing resource requirements is to estimate the man-hours for activities/work packages. Figure 16.27 shows the outline procedure. Evolving and using meaningful 'norms of performance' is an essential element of effective resource planning. Norms can be derived from detailed analysis of time sheets — provided personnel book to the job number, work package number and the key task being undertaken.

The second step in resource analysis is to consider the total demand for key resources. The definition of key resources is likely to differ for different types of project. In particular, consider those resources which are scarce and/or costly to employ.

When considering the project as a whole, there will be competition between activities and the demand may either exceed the planned availability of resources or produce a fluctuating pattern for their use. Float is used to adjust the timing of activities so that the resource imposed limits are not exceeded. In some cases it will not be possible to satisfy both these restraints and the previously calculated completion date — the duration of the project is then extended.

It is clear that the adjustment, or levelling, of one resource will have an effect on the usage of others. Generally resource levelling is only applied to a few key resources. The use of an appropriate computer program can allow a greater degree of sophistication.

Once the key resources have been adjusted a new completion date results. If this is not acceptable, the resource limits must be adjusted and the process repeated.

When resource levelling has produced a satisfactory solution, the start and finish dates for each activity are said to be at their 'scheduled' values. It is probable that only a few scheduled activities will have residual float — that is, most activities will now be critical.

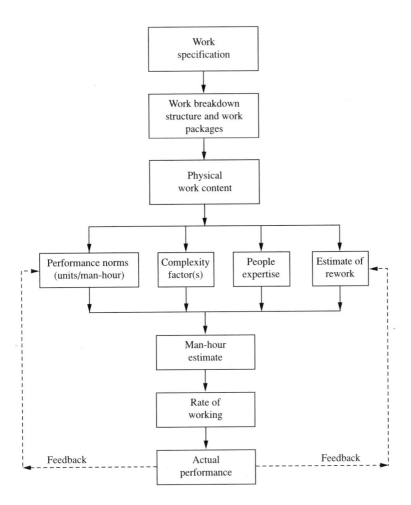

Figure 16.27 Man-hour estimating model

Resource scheduling techniques

The technique for retaining the project completion date and identifying the minimum level of resource requirement possible is demonstrated using the design work package for Project 'X'. It is assumed that the design work will be carried out by general purpose draughtspersons.

Figure 16.28 (page 226) shows the initial plan for the design work in bar chart format. All activities are on their earliest starts. The entries under the heading 'Total standard man-hours' have been derived from assessing the total quantity of work to be carried out and dividing by the appropriate norm of

Activity	Total standard man-hours	Uniform rate man-hours/ week	Week number (1–11)
General			
GA drawings	100	50	
Line diagrams	120	40	
Plant items			
Heat exchangers	50	25	
Tanks and hoppers	100	25	
Other	80	20	
Piping			
Piping GAs	60	20	
Isometrics	1000	250	
Material and valve schedules	60	20	
Electrical			
Hardware	60	20	
Cabling	100	25	
Instruments			
Control data sheets	90	30	
Instrument schedules	80	20	
Cabling	100	25	
Material schedules	60	20	
Civils			
Foundations	40	20	
Floors and plinths	600	150	
Material schedules	120	30	
Steelwork			
Main steel	90	30	
Secondary steel	100	50	

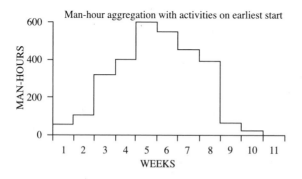

Figure 16.28 Initial plan for design work with man-hour aggregation

performance. For example, if the total quantity of piping is 5000 metres and the norm is 5 metres per man-hour then 1000 standard man-hours are required. The total standard man-hours for each activity has been spread uniformly across each bar on the bar chart and the summation of the man-hours required to be inputted per week is indicated by the histogram.

The histogram indicates that the peak demand for drafting effort will occur during Week 5. If the work package completion has not to be extended beyond 10 weeks and the maximum input of man-hours has not to exceed 500 in any one week then the options available include changing:

• the sequence of doing the work;
• rate of working on designated activities;
• daily hours worked;
• the working week;
• continuity of work by splitting activities.

Figure 16.29 (page 228) shows the actions taken to reduce the peak demand for man-hours:

• the specification of instrument requirements and schedules commences one week later, as does the design of main steelwork;
• the rate of working on activities involving the production of isometrics and the design of floors and plinths has been reduced and the appropriate adjustment has been made to the durations.

The resultant histogram does reduce the original peak demand from 620 man-hours down to 500 man-hours. Before this solution is accepted and implemented the associated risks need to be properly assessed. For example:

• does the design organization regularly achieve the norms of performance?
• what degree of confidence exists in the estimate of physical quantities? Could the metres of pipework increase from 5000 to 6000 or more?
• the delay in the start of two key activities could readily lead to a situation whereby the continuity of site work is not guaranteed. Pipework installation is on the critical path and material shortages must be avoided.

Use of S-curves

Figure 16.30 (page 229) shows an S-curve for the overall cumulative man-hours. S-curves can be extremely useful for monitoring performance and determining overall productive efficiency. In addition to man-hours they can be used for monitoring planned versus actual performance for other resources:

• money (commitments plus expenditure);
• preparation and issue of drawings;
• fabrication and erection of pipework;
• procurement (placing purchase orders through to delivery to stores).

Activity	Total standard man-hours	Uniform rate man-hours/ week	Week number (1–11)
General			
GA drawings	100	50	weeks 1–2
Line diagrams	120	40	weeks 2–4
Plant items			
Heat exchangers	50	25	weeks 3–4
Tanks and hoppers	100	25	weeks 2–5
Other	80	20	weeks 3–6
Piping			
Piping GAs	60	20	weeks 4–6
Isometrics	1000	200	weeks 5–9
Material and valve schedules	60	20	weeks 7–9
Electrical			
Hardware	60	20	weeks 4–6
Cabling	100	25	weeks 5–8
Instruments			
Control data sheets	90	30	weeks 3–5
Instrument schedules	80	20	weeks 5–8
Cabling	100	25	weeks 7–9
Material schedules	60	20	weeks 9–11
Civils			
Foundations	40	20	weeks 3–4
Floors and plinths	600	120	weeks 3–7
Material schedules	120	30	weeks 6–9
Steelwork			
Main steel	90	30	weeks 7–9
Secondary steel	100	50	weeks 7–9

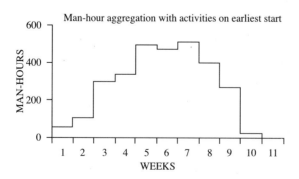

Man-hour aggregation with activities on earliest start

Figure 16.29 Resource levelling with activities on scheduled starts

Activity	Total standard man-hours	Cumulative man-hours	1	2	3	4	5	6	7	8	9	10	11
						Week number ⟶							
General		3000											
GA drawings	100		50	50									
Line diagrams	120			40	40	40							
Plant items													
Heat exchangers	50			25	25								
Tanks and hoppers	100	2500		25	25	25	25						
Other	80			20	20	20	20						
Piping													
Piping GAs	60			20	20	20							
Isometrics	1000						200	200	200	200	200		
Material and valve schedules	60	2000							20	20	20		
Electrical													
Hardware	60					20	20	20					
Cabling	100	1500				25	25	25	25				
Instruments													
Control data sheets	90				30	30	30						
Instrument schedules	80						20	20	20	20			
Cabling	100	1000						25	25	25	25		
Material schedules	80								20	20	20		
Civils													
Foundations	40				20	20							
Floors and plinths	600				120	120	120	120	120				
Material schedules	120	500					30	30	30	30			
Steelwork													
Main steel	90							30	30	30			
Secondary steel	100								50	50			
		0											

		1	2	3	4	5	6	7	8	9	10	11
Weekly total man-hours		50	115	300	345	510	490	520	395	265	20	–
Cumulative man-hours		50	165	465	810	1320	1810	2330	2725	2990	3010	–

Figure 16.30 S-curve of cumulative man-hours

Further reading

Lockyer, K.G. and Gordon, J., 1995, *Project Management and Project Network Techniques*, 6th edition (Pitman Publishing).

Open University, 1990, *Software Project Planning*, M355, Block IV, Unit 13 (Open University).

Smith, N.J. (ed), 1995, *Engineering Project Management*, Chapter 10 (Blackwell Science).

Williams, T., 1993, What is critical?, *International Journal of Project Management*, 11 (4): 197–200.

British Standard BS 6046: Use of Network Techniques in Project Management, Part 1, 1984, and Part 2, 1992.

Project monitoring and control

Harry Moody

The project plan and budgets should contain some flexibility and sufficient man-hours and money to enable a project to be implemented within the framework set by the objectives. It is extremely naïve to assume that changes will not occur during the life of a project. It is therefore essential to establish systems and procedures to deal with unexpected difficulties which will arise from time to time. The project plan and the man-hour budgets are then revised or updated to produce the new optimum solution corresponding to the changed requirements. Changes are identified by monitoring and progressing at regular intervals — that is, per shift/daily/weekly.

The principles of control

The sequence of operations generally described as 'control' involve:

- setting standards;
- measuring performance against standards;
- evaluating the effect of deviations;
- evolving alternative strategies for taking corrective action;
- deciding the corrective action to be taken;
- assessing the success/failure of the corrective action;
- reporting performance.

To maintain effective control some fundamental principles must be complied with:

- controls must be set according to tasks performed — there are many techniques available which may or may not apply, depending on the nature of the task;
- deviations must be reported immediately — most control systems fail because their monitoring process provides information too late to be of immediate use;
- controls must conform to organizational procedures — if the organization is well defined and responsibility for work done is clear then it is much simpler to identify those responsibilities for deviations;

- controls should focus attention at selected key points;
- controls should be flexible and economical to operate;
- controls should be simple to use and must indicate where corrective action is required.

The 80/20 rule

It is often the case that it is physically impossible to measure accurately and assess all of the work on a sanctioned project. Therefore some methodology is needed for selecting the key areas upon which to concentrate. The 'key areas' can be identified by using Pareto analysis (the 80/20 rule) which states that a few items in any group constitute the significant proportion.

It is usually interpreted to mean that 20% of the items in a group will have an 80% impact on the final outcome. In terms of controlling time, man-hours and money the 20% of items can be identified in several ways:

- work packages with high value (man-hours/money);
- work packages on the critical path;
- work packages which have been designated as high risk.

Figure 17.1 is a graphical representation of the 80/20 rule.

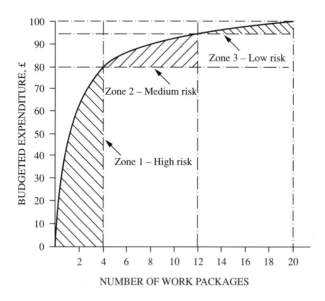

Figure 17.1 The 80/20 rule

Control procedures for the various zones might entail:
- Zone 1 — tight control with frequent progress and review meetings. Formal change control system in operation;
- Zone 2 — control checks backed up by regular progress and review meetings;
- Zone 3 — well-defined specifications and procedures. Spot checks required to ensure adequate progress is being made.

The rolling wave concept

Control during project implementation starts with the authorization to work on the first wave of work packages. This is followed by authorizing work on subsequent waves of work packages. It is the job of those responsible for managing projects to ensure that the necessary information is available to enable a good productive start to each work package.

Figure 17.2 demonstrates waves occurring between adjacent sets of milestone dates.

Most projects, because of time and budgetary constraints, require packages of work to be undertaken concurrently. If the concurrent work packages include those that are deemed to be extra high risk, then the project manager has to devote sufficient time and energy to ensure 'all is well'.

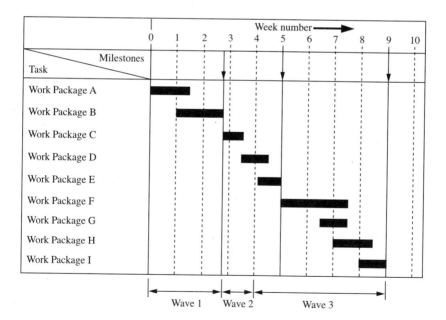

Figure 17.2 The rolling wave

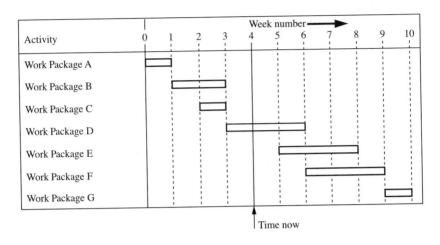

Figure 17.3 Bar chart with cursor at 'Time now'

Some project organizations treat each work package as a subcontract. Subcontracts can be awarded both internally and externally. Cost control is initiated by awarding fixed price contracts. This approach may be acceptable for certain types of work packages but it is essential to ensure that the type of contract to be used does take account of requirements for flexibility, risk, incentive and so on.

Techniques for the control of time

Bar charts
In its simplest form a bar chart can be used for assessing performance by adding a cursor line through 'Time now'. Figure 17.3 shows the methodology. According to the schedule, Work Packages A, B and C should be complete and Work Package D should have started. The people responsible for the activities should be questioned to ascertain:
- has the activity started?
- has the activity finished?
- if the activity has started, when will it finish?

The responses can be used to update the bar chart as indicated in Figure 17.4.

The programme is going to be extended by 1½ time units unless action is taken now — for example, employing more resources, working longer hours, reducing the scope of work.

234

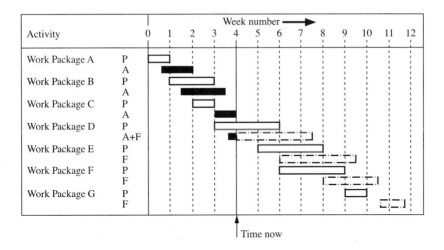

Activity		0	1	2	3	4	5	6	7	8	9	10	11	12

Week number ──▶

Work Package A P A
Work Package B P A
Work Package C P A
Work Package D P A+F
Work Package E P F
Work Package F P F
Work Package G P F

Time now

Figure 17.4 Bar chart with updated time information
P = Planned, A = Actual, F = Forecast

The problem with this example is that it concentrates on managing time (on a subjective basis) and ignores the man-hours consumed and the physical work to be done.

Bar chart showing progress and planned versus actual man-hours
Programme and progress bar charts are used to show the addition of quantifiable data (planned versus actual). A typical series of presentations is shown in Figures 17.5, 17.6 and 17.7 (pages 236 and 237).

Effective monitoring
Monitoring is the precursor to effective control and must therefore be used in time to influence future work. Monitoring has to provide interim data on the progress of activities and infer from these data whether the activities will be completed satisfactorily. Data are therefore required on:
• deviations — the difference between planned and actual rate of progress;
• rate of change of deviations — the trend of differences between planned and actual rates of progress;
• accumulated deviation — the integrated results of progress up to the moment of obtaining data compared to the planned amount.

All three sets of control data are needed for critical and crucial activities. If deviations alone are considered, a serious trend may be missed. Or there may be over-reaction to trivial deviations or inaccurate data.

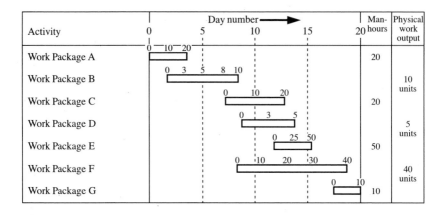

Figure 17.5 Programme and progress chart — Stage 1

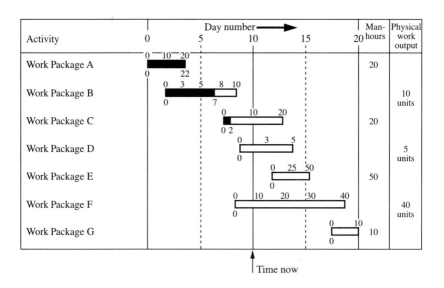

Figure 17.6 Programme and progress chart — Stage 2

236

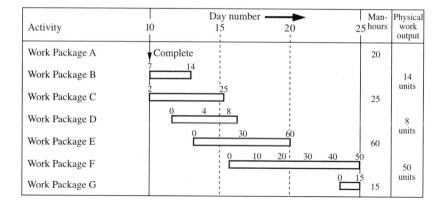

Figure 17.7 Programme and progress chart — Stage 3

At Day 10 the units to be produced and the man-hours are increased. This may be sufficient justification for reissuing the updated bar chart. However, it may still be possible to complete all of the work in 20 days by:
- making an immediate start on Work Packages D and F; and
- increasing the rate of progress on all outstanding Work Packages.

As far as possible, data should be obtained on the 'primary' resources essential for the progress of work. For instance, if the planning of the project has indicated that the number of qualified welders available is critical for an activity, the monitoring should obtain data on how many are actually at work, not just data on the output being achieved on the job.

Data on output achieved is important. If progress is poorer than expected, attention to output is needed to indicate what may be limits to the recovery possible by applying extra resources.

Actual performance should also be analysed in a form suitable for improving the data bank for planning future projects.

The same principles apply to monitoring cost variances and their trends to predict out-turn cost.

Network analysis

Updating a precedence diagram at 'Time now' to reflect the current state of progress and to give a forecast of the likely completion date for a project is relatively straightforward.

Information is required on the status of activities at 'Time now':
- those which have been completed;
- those which are started but not complete ('live' activities);

- forecast of the likely completion date for all live activities;
- details relating to changes which have to be made to the logic in the current plan;
- details of any significant change(s) to the scope of work.

The technique for updating is best explained by reference to an example. Figure 17.8 shows the original network against which progress is to be assessed. Monitoring performance at end Week 3 reveals the following information:

- Activity A is complete;
- Activity B requires a further six weeks to complete;
- Activity C requires a further five weeks to complete;
- Activities D and E — no change;
- Activity X — to be added to reflect a change of scope.

The updated network in Figure 17.9 indicates that the project time-scale has extended by one week. If it is essential to bring the completion back to Week 18, corrective action should be focused on reducing the duration of one or more of the activities on the 'new' critical path (Activities B, D and E).

S-curves

S-curves are used for monitoring the performance of a particular resource (manpower, materials, money) throughout the duration of a project.

Figure 17.10 demonstrates one of the simplest uses of S-curves. The planned cumulative requirement for a resource is plotted by putting all activities on their earliest and latest starts and adding the actual recorded performance.

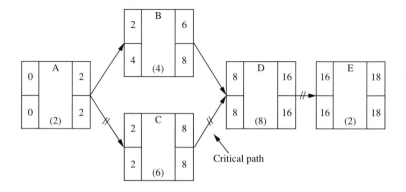

Figure 17.8 Original network

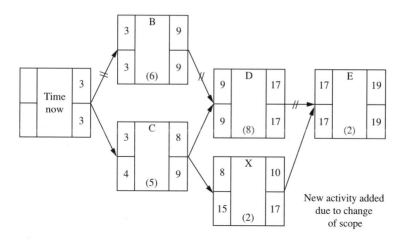

Figure 17.9 Updated network

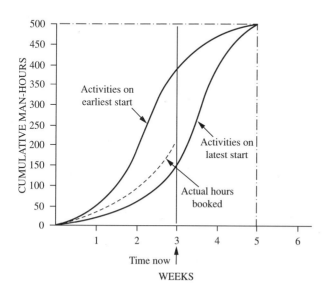

Figure 17.10 Cumulative man-hour S-curve

239

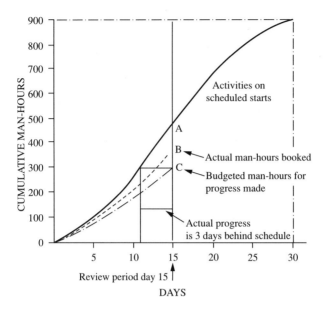

Figure 17.11 Using an S-curve to assess progress

Performance is considered to be satisfactory if the actual resource usage keeps within the envelope.

The S-curve shown in Figure 17.11 indicates the planned man-hours by scheduled start. The achieved performance can be evaluated at a particular point in time by:

- identifying the planned man-hours — 460 — point A;
- quantifying the actual hours booked to the project — 390 — point B;
- assessing the state of the job — the physical performance to date. If it is assumed the project is three days behind on actual progress then the corrected forecast of man-hours to do this amount of work is that originally estimated for Day 15, that is, 280 — point C. Ordinate B–C is therefore an indication of the performance of the labour force.

The assessment of physical performance for a project, contract, group of work packages or an individual work package often presents difficulties. One approach is to agree with the parties responsible for doing the work (prior to the commencement of the work) a percentage physical completion for each stage of the work. An example involving design, procurement, off-site fabrication, construction and testing follows:

	Percent complete
General layout drawings completed	30
Design of major pipework supports completed	35
Isometrics/manufacturing drawings prepared	85
Material schedules (including lagging) prepared	90
Drawings and schedules checked	95
Corrections made, checked and drawings issued for fabrication	100

	Percent complete
Materials ordered from suppliers	20
Materials delivered to shop floor	25
Piping cut and bent, etc	40
Piping flanged and welded	70
Piping assembled, checked, tested and approved	85
Finished pipework packed and delivered to site	100

	Percent complete
Pipework transported to place of installation	5
Pipework *in situ* and properly supported	40
Valves and other special fittings installed	60
Closure pipework fabricated and installed	75
Lagging (subcontract) completed	85
Systems testing completed	95
Acceptance by customer	100

This approach to assessing physical performance is normally used as part of cost control on larger projects. It is based on the concept of 'added value' as used by accountants — see the section on earned value on page 249. The actual percentage breakdown is often derived from analysing similar contracts and/or work packages using the services of a quantity surveyor.

The system can be scaled down for the smaller project as demonstrated in Figure 17.6, Work Package B (page 236). At 'Time now' only seven units (drawings, purchase orders, manufactured items, installed items) have been produced out of a total requirement of 10 so the percentage physical completion is 70.

Techniques for the control of cost

Personnel with responsibility for committing and spending money within the budget need to know their level of authority and the limits within which they are to operate. Projects with a short time-scale are extremely difficult to control in terms of costs. Accessing good quality information which is up to date is of paramount importance. Lines of communication with senior management need to be clearly defined and requirements on reporting cost performance should be established *before* work commences.

There may be occasions when money has to be spent and it is unclear where the money has to come from within the budget. This should be resolved (without any undue delay) by the appropriate personnel.

A contingency may arise on the work being undertaken and special permission may have to be sought to provide the necessary funds. This raises the key issue of whether or not a separate contingency fund should be used. In terms of effective cost control it is wrong to spread a blanket contingency allowance from the cost estimate across every item in the budget. The person responsible for the budget should vet every request for the expenditure of contingency monies. This is the essence of risk management.

Perhaps the biggest problem with booking money out of a budget arises when quite simply there is no money in the budget to cover the situation which has arisen. In this case a scope change system needs to be invoked. A scope change system exists to register adequately any changes which have occurred since the work was authorized. These are recorded in order to build up justification for further supplements if required or reallocation of elements within the budget. Decisions must be taken as to whether they were or were not covered in the existing sanction funds.

Traditional cost control using accruals

The official project accounts include a record of the actual expenditure of monies at a specific point in time. It is almost impossible to keep the accounts completely up to date so accruals are used to signify sums of money which are known to be 'missing' from the expenditure. Examples include:

- goods received (and accepted) but not yet invoiced;
- invoices received and either waiting for checking or payment;
- time sheets and stores requisitions which have been checked and cleared but have still to be debited from the project budget;
- the value of measured work performed by contractors but not yet invoiced or paid;
- retention monies (money held back for remedying defects or for performance guarantees).

Note that on smaller projects it is not possible to wait for the official project accounts to be issued. The project manager has to use the assessment of accruals as a means to cost control.

Cost control can be effective using the authorized budget as the master planning document if the following procedure is adopted:

- establish what has been spent/committed for each major item (work package, contract, purchase order, works order, cost code);
- estimate up to date how much more work has been done and how much is outstanding;
- establish what resources have been used up to date and what resources will be required to complete;
- estimate the approximate cost of the work to date (actual expenditure and accruals) and the cost of the known outstanding work. The combined figure gives the anticipated final cost (AFC);
- compare the AFC with the budget and determine areas of (significant) deviation;
- decide if any corrective action is required and take steps to carry it out;
- identify items where corrective action is needed but it is impossible to reduce/contain costs. Consider:

— establishing who will ultimately pay;

— raising a formal scope change/variation order;

— requesting some form of supplementary expenditure.

This procedure is time-consuming and, even if followed, cannot give an absolute guarantee of success. It will be easier to implement if the communication channels are clearly established and at the outset the message is conveyed that, 'Nobody, but nobody, has the right to spend money on a project without the authorization of the budget holder'.

An example of traditional cost control follows.

The master cost plan

Figure 17.12 (page 244) shows the breakdown of the authorized budget. On some high risk projects it may be advisable to hold a sum of money in reserve (a risk allowance budget).

The cost plan is based on estimating when money will be spent against each major item of work. So the summary bar chart for the project is used and the estimate of actual expenditure is based upon:

- the internal procedure used by the accountancy function for debiting internal charges — time sheets, stores requisitions, machine time in workshops, overheads;
- terms of payment agreed with suppliers for direct purchase orders;
- terms of payment agreed with contractors for their direct services and those of their subcontractors/suppliers.

Work Package	Budget, £x10,000	4	8	12	16	20	24	28	32
Detail design by client	2.25	1.00	1.25						
Modify existing plant items	4.54			2.80	1.74				
Client: commissioning	2.25							2.25	
Other client (itemized) costs	9.10	1.40	1.40	1.40	1.40	1.40	1.40	0.70	
Detail design by contractor(s)	9.10	3.60	4.50	1.00					
Procurement – new plant items	56.70					10.30	15.40	21.00	10.00
Procurement - civil materials and steelwork	11.34				5.00	5.80	0.54		
Procurement – electrics and instruments	11.34				2.00	7.00	2.34		
Demolition	1.13				1.13				
Cast foundations and plinths	1.13					1.13			
Erect steelwork	3.40					2.80	0.60		
Install plant items	3.40						3.40		
Install piping and ductwork	2.27						1.90	0.37	
Install cabling	1.13						1.13		
Install electrics and instruments	1.13						0.23	0.90	
Terminations	1.13							1.13	
Contractors: general site costs	5.66				1.10	2.00	2.00	0.56	
Totals	127.00	6.00	7.15	5.20	12.37	30.43	28.94	26.91	10.00

Figure 17.12 Budget and master cost plan

Notes:

(1) Assume a four-week working month. The total actual payments to external parties made during the course of a month are shown at the end of the month.

(2) Internal charges are assumed to be made by the accountancy function at month-end. They comprise direct charges — for example, cashing-up time sheets — and indirect charges through the apportionment of overheads.

Note that the planned expenditure after Week 12 rapidly increases and raises the question, 'On this type of project can this high expenditure rate occur and, if it can, how exactly is it to be controlled?'. It is the cost of the new plant items which gives rise to the high rate of expenditure. Exerting tight control during procurement involves:

- obtaining competitive quotes from a range of potential suppliers;
- awarding the orders to suppliers who have a good track record on costs and lead times;
- ensuring that purchase orders are placed at the agreed time and in the agreed sequence;

- making sure that no amendments are made to the purchase orders;
- maintaining regular communication links with the suppliers;
- paying by results.

  Use a worksheet similar to that shown in Figure 17.13.

Monitoring actual expenditure

Figure 17.14 (page 246) shows the situation at end Week 20. Actual expenditure is well down on what was planned and clearly demonstrates the 'knock-on' effect on costs when poor performance occurs at the early stages of project implementation. The problems on plant item design delayed the placing of purchase orders which in turn held up the manufacture of the plant items.

The actual expenditure figures quoted are derived from two sources:

- for activities completed some time previously, the project accounts should provide an accurate record;
- for recently completed/'live' activities accruals will have to be included.

Project number: Date:						Sheet number:	
Work package number	Supplier	Order number	Order value, £	Value of amendments, £	Value of invoices received, £	Value of invoices cleared for payment, £	Value of payments made to date, £

Figure 17.13 Cost details for material purchases

Work Package	Budget, £x10,000		0	4	8	12	16	20	24	28	32
Detail design by client	2.25	P		1.00	1.25						
		A		0.80	1.50	0.50					
Modify existing plant items	4.54	P				2.80	1.74				
		A				1.80	3.00	1.00			
Other client (itemized) costs	9.10	P		1.40	1.40	1.40	1.40	1.40			
		A		1.00	1.10	0.80	1.20	0.60			
Detail design by contractor(s)	9.10	P		3.60	4.50	1.00					
		A		1.80	5.00	3.00	1.00				
Procurement – new plant items	56.70	P						10.30			
		A					2.50	3.70			
Procurement – civil materials and steelwork	11.34	P					5.00	5.80			
		A					3.50	7.50			
Procurement – electrics and instruments	11.34	P					2.00	7.00			
		A						4.00			
Demolition	1.13	P					1.13				
		A						1.10			
Cast foundations and plinths	1.13	P						1.13			
		A						0.20			
Erect steelwork	3.40	P						2.80			
		A									
Contractors: general site costs	5.66	P					1.10	2.00			
		A						1.80			
Totals		P		6.00	7.15	5.20	12.37	30.43			
		A		3.60	7.60	6.10	11.20	19.90			

Time now

Figure 17.14 Monitoring expenditure using the master cost plan

Notes:

(1) P = Planned expenditure and A = Actual expenditure.

(2) Only completed/ 'live' activities are shown.

246

Work Package	Budget, £x10,000	Estimated expenditure at end Week 20			Estimate to complete known physical work	AFC	Variance, %
		From formal accounts	Accruals	Total			
Detail design by client	2.25	2.80		2.80		2.80	+24.4
Modify existing plant items	4.54	4.80	1.00	5.80		5.80	+27.8
Client: commissioning	2.25				2.25	2.25	
Other client (itemized) costs	9.10	3.90	0.80	4.70	5.00	9.70	+6.5
Detail design by contractor(s)	9.10	10.80		10.80		10.80	+18.7
Procurement – new plant items	56.70	1.90	4.30	6.20	55.80	62.00	+9.3
Procurement – electrics and instruments	11.34	4.20	6.80	11.00		11.00	-3.0
Procurement – civil materials and steelwork	11.34		4.00	4.00	11.00	15.00	+32.3
Demolition	1.13	1.10		1.10		1.10	-2.7
Cast foundations and plinths	1.13		0.20	0.20	1.30	1.50	+32.7
Erect steelwork	3.40				3.00	3.00	-11.8
Install plant items	3.40				4.00	4.00	+17.6
Install piping and ductwork	2.27				3.00	3.00	+32.2
Install cabling	1.13				1.50	1.50	+32.7
Install electrics and instruments	1.13				2.00	2.00	+76.9
Terminations	1.13				1.00	1.00	-11.5
Contractors: general site costs	5.66		1.80	1.80	5.00	6.80	+20.1
Totals	127.00	29.50	18.90	48.40	94.85	143.25	+12.8

Figure 17.15 Anticipated final cost
The variance $(+/-)$ is derived by comparing the anticipated final cost (AFC)
with the budget.

Assessing the amount of accruals is vital. The overriding purpose is to ensure that there is a clear up-to-date picture of the amount of money remaining in the budget.

Anticipated final cost

Figure 17.15 shows the preparation of the anticipated final cost based on recorded expenditure, accruals and the variances calculated against the budget. In overall terms a predicted overspend of only 12.8% at Week 20 of a 26-week programme may be a cause for celebration. However, the most difficult stages of the project may yet have to start — for example, construction work and commissioning.

Already AFCs in excess of the budget are being forecast for site work which has not yet started. Again, it is highly unlikely that this project will finish in Week 26 (see Figure 17.14), and the adage that time is money will surely apply.

Also a backlog of claims from the design contractor and suppliers could be about to surface … !

Graphical representation

Figure 17.16 shows the current state of the project in graphical format. It dramatically confirms that all is not well. It is time to 'stop' and reappraise performance to date.

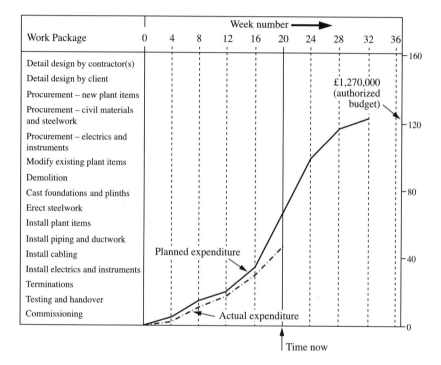

Figure 17.16 S-curve of cumulative expenditure

Notes:

(1) At the end of Week 20, the procurement of the new plant items is 60% complete, the procurement of electrics and instruments is 70% complete and the installation of plant items has yet to start.

(2) The actual expenditure (£295,000) lags behind the planned expenditure (£611,500) by £465,000. This indicates that the project is running approximately eight weeks behind programme and this is confirmed by the delay to the start of plant item installation.

Use of definitive/control estimates

A definitive or control estimate is prepared after a project is sanctioned. The basic idea is to re-estimate the project cost after completion of each major stage in the project life-cycle — that is, detail design, procurement, letting of site contracts, completion of construction. The definitive estimate has no official status in accountancy terms but it does serve a useful purpose because it:

- checks the validity of the original estimate;
- generates the need to measure and cost all known outstanding work;
- provides a measure of the impact of changes and generates the need to raise major scope change forms;
- gives a much more reliable forecast of the final outcome (AFC);
- checks the quality of the work associated with risk assessment and allowances;
- helps determine how the contingency and risk funds are being utilized;
- generates productivity data for comparisons with company standards;
- highlights the need to improve the quality of (cost) data used for estimating purposes.

Definitive estimates are of particular interest at three stages during project implementation:

- at the bottom of the S-curve just before it starts to get steep;
- halfway up the steep part of the S-curve of planned expenditure to ensure rate of spend is in line (and will continue to be in line) with the cost plan;
- at the top of the steep part of the S-curve just before it starts to ease off.

Figure 17.17 (page 250) illustrates this concept.

Definitive estimating is time-consuming because it must be done in detail and should fully involve the personnel who helped compile the original estimate(s).

Project monitoring using earned value analysis

By and large, project personnel are paid to produce physical assets which are of benefit to the organization — that is, help achieve corporate objectives. It is recognized that most technical work does involve the use of labour, materials, machines; what the sponsor of a project wants to see, in return for the provision of funds, is assets in full working order.

Control of work for a project is therefore based upon monitoring the earned value of the work done. This goes beyond using purely monetary measures. Instead it concentrates on equating actual physical performance to what was originally planned and then puts a monetary value on what has still to be achieved to give the AFC.

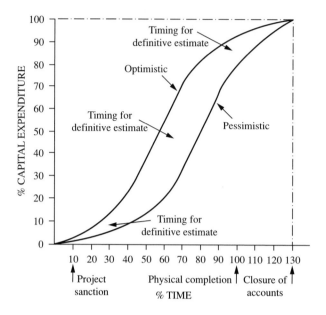

Figure 17.17 Timing of definitive estimates

Example

- Figure 17.18 shows the agreed work schedule for the production of eight general arrangement drawings which comprise a work package.
- Figure 17.19 shows the planned S-curve for the man-hours and indicates the hours booked via time sheets up to the end of Week 3. The achieved performance is apparently behind programme (by approximately one week).
- The 'earned value of work done' approach attempts to establish what physical progress has been made with the man-hours so far booked to the job. This is done by going back to the original approved bar chart and ascertaining how many of the design tasks are complete in line with the programme at the end of each week. Table 17.1 (page 252) indicates the planned versus actual recorded performance for Weeks 1 to 3.
- Figure 17.20 (page 252) shows the earned value up to the end of Week 3.
- The productive efficiency can now be determined by comparing the earned value of work done with the actual man-hours booked — that is, $330/400 \times 100 = 82.5\%$.
- The likely total man-hours which will be expended to complete the job is $810/0.825 = 982$. If this work is being undertaken by a contractor then the client may only agree to pay for 810 man-hours, leaving the contractor to stand the cost of the additional 182 man-hours.

250

Work Package	Duration, weeks	Planned man-hours	Weeks						
			1	2	3	4	5	6	7
A	1	80	80						
B	2	200	100	100					
C	1	50		50					
D	2	100		50	50				
E	3	90		30	30	30			
F	2	100			50	50			
G	1	40				40			
H	3	150				50	50	50	
Total man-hours			180	230	130	170	50	50	–
Cumulative man-hours			180	410	540	710	760	810	–

Figure 17.18 Planning for rewarding by results

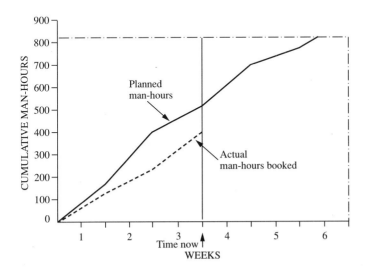

Figure 17.19 Man-hour performance: planned versus actual

251

Table 17.1 Calculating the earned value					
Week number	Planned man-hours per week	Actual man-hours per week	Drawings planned to be completed per week	Drawings actually completed per week	Earned value man-hours per week
1	180	120	A	A	80
2	230	130	B+C	—	—
3	130	150	D	B+C	250
Cumulative totals	540	400	A,B,C,D	A,B,C	330

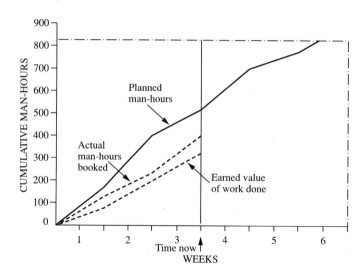

Figure 17.20 Man-hour performance: showing earned value

• The situation may not be quite as bad as portrayed. Activity D could have commenced and, although not finished, might be 75% complete and therefore of value to the client. So some system is required for rewarding intermediate progress. If the progress on Activity D merited a 50% credit then the productive efficiency becomes (330+50)/400 = 95%. Figure 17.21 illustrates the methodology of rewarding for partial completion of work.

Drawing reference	Planned to be completed	Progress to date	Physical % complete	Man-hours		Earned value work done, %
				Budget	% weighting	
A	Yes	Issued	100	80	9.9	9.9
B	Yes	Issued	100	200	24.7	24.7
C	Yes	Issued	100	50	6.2	6.2
D	Yes	Final check	90	100	12.3	11.1
E	No	Schematic	30	90	11.1	3.3
F	No	Not started	–	100	12.3	–
G	No	Not started	–	40	5.0	–
H	No	Not started	–	150	18.5	–
			Totals	810	100.0	55.2

Figure 17.21 Earned value for partial completion

Agreed sequence for earning value:

(1) 30% for completing schematic

(2) 60% for completing dimensioning

(3) 90% if final check complete

(4) 100% for final issue and full acceptance

Note that the use of a detailed system for the award of partial completion of work can involve a great deal of administrative effort and therefore requires justification. At the outset it is vital to ensure that the work package is critical and the success of the project depends on its completion to time. Even if the overall work package is critical there will be activities within the package which have float and so a system of rewarding for earned value could be weighted differentially.

Cost and schedule analysis

Earned value can be used to assess performance throughout the project life cycle. The method of analysis uses three basic terms:

- BCWS — the budgeted cost for work scheduled;
- BCWP — the budgeted cost for work performed;
- ACWP — the actual cost of work performed to date.

Example

The production of the eight general arrangement drawings referred to in Figure 17.18 is used to illustrate the principles. It is assumed that the going rate for

Drawing reference	Duration, weeks	Planned man-hours	Weeks →					
			1	2	3	4	5	6
A	1	80	1600					
B	2	200	2000	2000				
C	1	50		1000				
D	2	100		1000	1000			
E	3	90		600	600	600		
F	2	100			1000	1000		
G	1	40				800		
H	3	150				1000	1000	1000
Total cost, £			3600	4600	2600	3400	1000	1000
BCWS = cumulative cost, £			3600	8200	10800	14200	15200	16200

Figure 17.22 The budgeted cost of work scheduled

design work is £20.00 per man-hour. Therefore the budgeted cost of work scheduled (BCWS) is as shown in Figure 17.22.

Two further basic terms can be determined from the chart:
• BAC (budget at completion) — the total budgeted cost for the work (£16,200);
• TAC (time at completion) — the planned duration for the work (six weeks).

'Time now' is the end of Week 4 and the recorded progress to date is:

Week 1 — Drawing A completed and issued;

Week 2 — Drawing B completed and issued;

Week 3 — Drawing C completed and issued.

Week 4 — Drawings D and F completed and issued.

The BCWP and the ACWP per week and cumulatively are tabulated in Figure 17.23.

Variance analysis

Two significant variances can be measured:
• the cost variance (CV) is the difference between the BCWP and the ACWP. If the difference is positive then the project is under budget and if it is negative the project is over budget;
• the schedule variance (SV) is the difference between the BCWP and the BCWS. Note that the schedule variance is assessed in financial terms. If the difference is negative then the project is behind schedule and the amount of money indicates what it will cost to catch up.

Figure 17.24 shows the calculation to determine the cost and schedule variances.

Item	Weeks →					
	1	2	3	4	5	6
1. Budgeted cost of work performed						
Drawings issued	A	B	C	D, F		
Credited man-hours	80	200	50	200		
BCWP per week, £	1600	4000	1000	4000		
BCWP cumulative, £	1600	5600	6600	10600		
2. Actual cost of work performed						
Man-hours from time sheets	60	100	250	250		
ACWP per week, £	1200	2000	5000	5000		
ACWP cumulative, £	1200	3200	8200	13200		

Figure 17.23 The budgeted and actual cost of work performed

Item	Weeks →					
	1	2	3	4	5	6
1. Key information						
BCWS per week	3600	4600	2600	3400		
BCWS cumulative	3600	8200	10800	14200		
BCWP per week, £	1600	4000	1000	4000		
BCWP cumulative, £	1600	5600	6600	10600		
ACWP per week	1200	2000	5000	5000		
ACWP cumulative	1200	3200	8200	13200		
2. Cost variance, £						
(BCWP-ACWP) per week	-400	-2000	-4000	-1000		
Cumulative CV	-400	-2400	-1600	-2600		
3. Schedule variance, £						
(BCWP-BCWS) per week	-2000	-600	-1600	+600		
Cumulative SV	-2000	-2600	-4200	-3600		

Figure 17.24 Cost and schedule variance

Estimation of AFC and work package duration

The anticipated final cost (AFC) is calculated using the formula:

$$AFC = \frac{ACWP}{BCWP} \times BAC. \text{ At end Week 4} \qquad AFC = £20,174.$$

The estimated time at completion (ETC) is calculated using the formula:

$$ETC = \frac{BCWS}{BCWP} \times TAC. \text{ At end Week 4} \qquad ETC = 8 \text{ weeks.}$$

Figure 17.25 is a graphical representation of the state of the design work package at the end of Week 4.

Trend analysis

A summary of the data arising from the cost and schedule analysis is shown in Figure 17.26. The data plotted as Figures 17.27, 17.28 and 17.29 enables adverse trends to be detected and corrective action taken where appropriate.

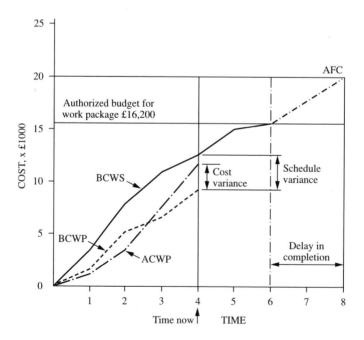

Figure 17.25 Cost and schedule analysis

Item	Weeks ➝					
	1	2	3	4	5	6
Cost variance, £	+400	+2400	-1600	-2600		
Schedule variance, £	-2000	-2600	-4200	-3600		
Anticipated final cost, £	12,150	9257	20,127	20,174		
Estimated completion, weeks	13.5	9	10	8		

Figure 17.26 Trend analysis data

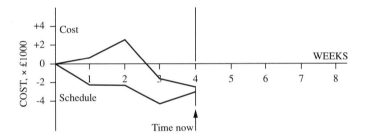

Figure 17.27 Weekly cost and schedule variance trends

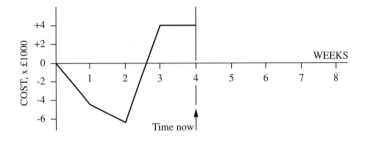

Figure 17.28 Weekly forecast of anticipated final cost (compared to budget)

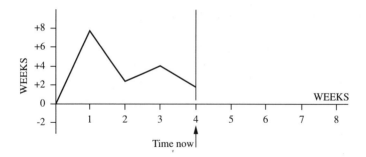

Figure 17.29 Weekly forecast of completion

In the early stages, the CV and AFC trend charts both indicated that the work package would be completed for less than £16,200. However, from Week 1, the SV and the forecasted completion trends consistently show that the work package will be late finishing. The trends during the last two weeks are not encouraging and the ongoing forecast of a late completion coupled with over-expenditure necessitates an immediate performance review of the work package. But the situation may not be quite as bad as portrayed, for work could be proceeding on Drawings E, G and H. The quicker the facts are established, the better.

Managing change

It is exceedingly naïve to assume that a project will be implemented exactly in line with the authorized project programme and budget. Deviations occur for all manner of reasons including:

- customer changes;
- funding changes;
- omissions from technical scope, programme and budget;
- environmental, health and safety regulations;
- operational changes;
- over-optimistic estimating;
- inadequate risk identification and assessment;
- programme changes;
- contract changes;
- supplier performance.

This list highlights the need to make the management of change one of the most important tasks during the implementation stage of a project. If formal procedures are not used then there is a real risk that the project could rapidly go out of control. Procedures must:

- identify changes from the original project/work package scope;
- forecast cost/effect on other work/time required to implement;
- include proper managerial analysis prior to authorizing/rejecting a change, including assessment of environmental health, safety and operational effects;
- ensure proper records are kept of actual costs and so on;
- specify a system to assist in the resolution of disputes between the various parties with a vested interest in the project;
- include a follow-up system to ensure that changes are implemented satisfactorily.

Figure 17.30 (page 260) illustrates the type of form that can be used as part of the overall procedures for managing change. Nobody likes to spend time filling in forms, particularly if the project provides a real technical challenge, but in this case it is essential if effective control is to be exerted. It is a salutary exercise to examine minutes of meetings, identify proposed changes and record how long it takes to complete the relevant documentation and receive formal approval.

Keep in mind that once work has been authorized on a change, to all intents and purposes it becomes an integral part of the total work load. Regular cost reports produced throughout the life of the project should include the original scope of the project plus the changes authorized to date.

Further reading

Barnes, N.M.L. (ed), 1990, *Financial Control* (Thomas Telford Publications).

Bower, D.A., 1996, Evaluating the indirect cost of change, *Proceedings, International Project Management Association Congress, Paris*.

Clark, F.D. and Lorenzoni, A.B., 1985, *Applied Cost Engineering* (Marcel Dekker).

Harrison, F.L., 1992, *Advanced Project Management*, 3rd edition (Gower Publishing Co).

Kharbanda, O.P. *et al*, 1987, *Project Cost Control in Action*, 2nd edition (Gower Publishing Co).

Wearne, S.H. (ed), 1989, *Control of Engineering Projects* (Thomas Telford Publications).

British Standard BS 6046: Use of Network Techniques in Project Management, Part 4, 1992.

Description of change:	
Project title:	Revision number:
Job number:	Date issued:
1. Justification for change	
2. Work package(s) affected	
3. Scope of work	
4. Effort required	
5. Estimated cost of implementation	
6. Effect on project plan and time-scale	
7. Supporting documentation	

Revision number 1	Originated by: Date: Approved by: Date:	Accepted by: Date: Approved by: Date:
Revision number 2	Originated by: Date: Approved by: Date:	Accepted by: Date: Approved by: Date:

Figure 17.30 Change authorization form

Contracts for goods and services

18

Stephen Wearne

This chapter reviews choices in the number and terms of contracts for the supply of goods and services for projects, and the lessons of the successful planning and management of contracts.

Definitions

What is a contract?

A contract is an agreement between two or more parties that is enforceable at law. The rules for contracts established by law vary from country to country. Under English law an agreement to buy goods or services is a contract if:

- intention — the parties genuinely intend to enter into a legally enforceable relationship;
- offer and acceptance — the terms of the contract are offered by one party and accepted by the other(s);
- possibility and legality — the terms require performance of activities which are possible and legal;
- consideration — the terms include payment in money or kind in return for performance;
- capacity — the parties have the legal capacity to enter into the contract.

The single word 'contract' is used here to mean all such agreements, whether known within a company as a contract, order, purchase order or subcontract and whether for a small purchase of a service or materials or large-scale physical work such as construction.

Scope of a contract

The terms of a contract should define:

- **who is to be responsible for what?** — who is to be responsible for defining objectives and priorities, financing, innovations, design, quality, operating decisions, safety studies, approvals, scheduling, procurement, software, construction, equipment installation, inspection, testing, commissioning and managing each of these;

- **who bears which risks?** — who is to bear the risks of investing in the project, defining it, specifying performance, design risks, selecting subcontractors, subcontractors' defaults, site productivity, delays, mistakes and insurance;
- **what are the terms of payment?** — for design, development, equipment, software, demolition, construction, management and other services.

These choices are reviewed later in this chapter.

Parties to a contract

The parties to contracts are in practice variously called:

- client, customer, purchaser or employer; and
- contractor, vendor or supplier.

In this book 'client' and 'contractor' are used to mean the two parties to a contract.

The parties to a subcontract are usually called:

- main contractor and subcontractor.

Words used in contracts

Most contracts for major engineering and construction work include a list of definitions of some of the words used in them. This is wise and helpful, but unfortunately the definitions vary from contract to contract and so there are no standard meanings used consistently. As far as possible the most typical meanings are used in this book.

Planning a contract

Objectives

To be successful a contract needs to be designed to suit its objectives. The client usually designs a contract. The client may have several objectives — for instance:

- to utilize the skills and expertise of contractors' managers, engineers, craftsmen, buyers and so on for the limited duration of a project;
- to have the benefit of contractors' resources such as proven products, licensed processes, materials in stock, and so on;
- to get work started quicker than would be possible by recruiting and training direct employees;
- to get contractors to take some of the cost risks of a project, usually the risks of planning to use people, plant, materials and subcontractors economically;

- to get contractors to obtain the financial resources for a project, and perhaps also for operating it;
- to be free as clients to concentrate on the objectives of the project, their subsequent use, and other interests;
- to encourage the development of successful contractors.

A client may want to achieve several of these objectives. For a contract to contribute to the success of a project, one objective must have priority in designing the contract, and the others given lesser or no importance. Whichever has priority governs the decision on the work breakdown into one or more contracts (see also Chapters 15 and 16) and the decisions on the scope, type and terms of contracts.

The same principles apply to decisions by a main contractor to employ subcontractors.

Number of contracts

One of the objectives listed in the previous section may be appropriate to only a part of a project. If so, an option for the client is to employ one contractor for that part and one or more others for the remainder. Or a project might be so large that more than one contractor is appropriate to share the risks. For the equipment required for a new factory one contractor might be employed to install equipment supplied by others.

A series of contractors can be employed in turn — for instance, one to start to manufacture a long-lead item, another for demolition work, another for new foundations, the superstructure and building work, and others for designing systems, developing software, supplying equipment, installing it and systems and services, testing and commissioning for replacing part of a factory — each under different terms of contract. Different contractors could be employed separately for the structural, finishing and services work for a building project, instead of one main contractor subletting these specialist tasks. Or a joint venture or consortium could be employed together as one organization.

Choice of types of contract

The obvious principle is to choose contract terms which are likely to meet every party's objectives and therefore avoid conflict. Experience shows that this demands attention to the choice of number, risks and terms of payment of main contracts and subcontracts for a project. The ideal choice of contract terms varies from project to project, depending upon a client's priorities between quality, economy, speed and flexibility, public policies, the contractors willing and able to do the work, and the ability of all to operate the preferred contract arrangement.

One comprehensive contract (known severally as turnkey, engineer-procure-install-construct, all-in, package deal, design+build contracts)

A comprehensive contract which makes one contractor responsible for all the work for a project has the following potential advantages to clients:

- the client has only one contractor to deal with, so the project team can be relatively simple in organization and smaller than required for other types of contracts;
- the client's staff can concentrate on project objectives. Their minimum involvement in design choices may result in fewer design changes;
- the contractor has to manage all the relationships between design, procurement, subcontractors and so on;
- contractors have the greatest scope for being efficient and therefore economical and profitable;
- contractors are able to plan all the work as a whole and so offer shorter programmes;
- it encourages the development of larger contractors;

But a comprehensive contract has the following potential disadvantages compared to other types of contract:

- the process of assessing and pre-qualifying contractors, drafting contract documents, obtaining contractors' comments, getting tenders, negotiating, and assessing competing designs before agreeing a contract may take longer and add to costs;
- the overall management of relationships between design, fabrication and so on remains the same. It is shifted to the contractor and away from the client's control;
- much of the work is usually subcontracted, so the client has limited or only indirect ability to assess and influence whether it will be completed correctly and on time;
- few contractors may have the financial strength or be able and willing to manage all of a large project, so that the choice of contractor may be limited;
- all the project is in the hands of one contractor, unless it is a joint venture;
- contractually the client's control of the contractor's performance depends upon the effect of their contract, so that the client formally has only indirect influence through legal rights to order remedial actions, threaten termination and exact damages for failures of performance rather than direct managerial power to control the resources being used;
- many specialist companies prefer to work directly for the ultimate user of their products and services. If employed as subcontractors they may not be so well motivated to perform, and formally they can be controlled only through the main contractor;

- it is possible that the lengthier the span of a contract the greater the risk that client and contractor will concentrate their attention on the initial work and underestimate the time and resources needed for completion. But in some instances long-term risks get greater attention.

The extent that advantage is taken of physical possibilities to employ only one contractor for the work for a project therefore depends upon:
- the capacity, know-how, quality and motivation of contractors;
- the number of suitable contractors;
- the relative importance of quality, safety, time and cost;
- the ability of the client to manage a comprehensive contract.

One comprehensive contract can therefore be appropriate for a 'stand-alone' project not interdependent with other installations or services, and with the risks shared between client and contractor.

If one contractor is to have 'performance' responsibilities — that is, to undertake to design and supply a complete project or systems to meet a specification which states the client's requirements — the client logically has to at least agree the performance, life-cycle economy, standards, approvals and all else that matters in design before agreeing such a contract. If the client may want to make changes to the specification or the contractor's design after concluding the agreement, the contract needs to include provisions for ordering and agreeing these changes, but only to a limited extent.

Stage-by-stage contracts

The potential advantages to a client of proceeding in a sequence of two or more contracts stage by stage through the design and then the implementation of a project are:
- starting with a contract for design only makes it possible for most uncertainties and alternatives to be settled before they affect implementation;
- the design decisions which most affect project cost are separated from contractors' influence;
- a newly-formed client's team has time to prepare to enter into the later, more expensive contract;
- a contractor can be chosen as best for one particular stage of work;
- if a design contractor is not also a contractor for the subsequent work, the design contractor's staff can be employed as supervisors or advisers for other stages;
- the end of each stage is an opportunity to review new information and change, confirm or stop the project;
- the client can vary the speed of continuing with the project.

But a sequence of contracts has the following potential disadvantages:

- the client has to plan and manage the interactions between design, procurement and all stages, particularly the sequence of contracts and the risks of errors by one contractor causing claims on the client from one or more other contractors;
- the client has no firm indication of the final cost of the project until the final contracts have been agreed;
- no party can plan far ahead;
- to achieve some of the potential advantages the client needs to take care that the design from a design contractor can be used to invite other contractors to tender for the subsequent contract;
- time needed at each stage to select a contractor, start a new contract and establish procedures between all parties could delay completion of the project;
- client's and contractor's staff tend to concentrate on their stage of work and may not be directly responsible for meeting the final objectives of the project;
- all parties may get only limited feedback of the ultimate results of their contribution.

IN A SEQUENCE OF CONTRACTS NO PARTY
CAN PLAN FAR AHEAD.

The most common example of stage-by-stage contracts is a design contract between a client and a consultant or design contractor, and then a contract between the client and a 'main' contractor.

Stage-by-stage contracts are logical if limiting the client's commitments and risks such as cost has a greater priority than early completion. Detailed and final design can be completed and priced before the client is committed to the major costs of proceeding with the rest of the project.

Parallel contracts

The potential advantages of dividing work amongst contractors in parallel are:
- a contractor can be chosen as best in expertise or resources for one particular type of work;
- confidential information is limited to the client and the contractors involved.

The potential disadvantage is:
- that the client (or another organization on the client's behalf) has to plan and manage the work overall, and particularly the interactions between the parallel contracts and the risks of actions by one contractor causing claims from the other contractors.

Separating responsibilities for stages and types of work is logical if design requirements are uncertain at the start, the project team is newly formed or contractors have limited capabilities or know-how relative to the size or type of work needed for a project.

Parallel contracts and direct management by clients of the detail is logical for work which is urgent or is interdependent with the operation of existing installations, because of the financial importance to them of maintaining services and production.

Traditional contract responsibilities

In what are often called 'traditional contracts' in the process industries a main contractor is responsible for the design, procurement and installation work for a project. In building and civil engineering, 'traditional contract' means that a main contractor is responsible for construction to a design provided by the client or its consultants.

Subcontracts

In nearly all engineering and construction the main contractors employ subcontractors and suppliers of equipment, materials and services in parallel.

A common principle is that in a main contract a contractor is responsible to the client for the performance of its subcontractors. Practice varies in whether a main contractor is free to decide the terms of subcontracts or has to match their terms 'back-to-back' with the main contract, choose the subcontractors, accept their work and decide when to pay them. It also varies in whether and when a client may bypass a main contractor and take over a subcontract.

The potential advantages and disadvantages of the choices for clients in employing a contractor apply in turn to a contractor in planning the employment of a subcontractor.

The potential advantages of being a subcontractor are:
• being able to concentrate on providing a specialized or local service for many clients and main contractors, each of whom may have only an occasional project or uneven programmes of work;
• interfaces with others are the main contractor's risk;
• avoiding investment in common services which may be provided more economically by the client or main contractor.

The potential disadvantages are:
• the inability to plan far ahead;
• speed is needed in agreeing most subcontracts and in establishing relationships with the main contractor;
• payment may be very delayed in the chain from the client, long after incurring the cost of purchases and work, even though pay-when-paid practices are to be avoided;
• formal communications with clients are indirect.

Main contractors usually employ many subcontractors in parallel, to use their expertise and resources when required, but in turn the subcontractors employ others to supply materials and for specific work in a project. This hierarchy of contracting can form a long chain of procurement, starting with agreeing the main contract, then subcontracts, and then sub-subcontracts. The last are sometimes the source of information or materials which are needed first for a project. The procurement chain is therefore critical in many project programmes. The chain of payment operates in reverse, from the client through the main contractor, and then to subcontractors and onwards.

Parallel direct contracts between a client and each specialist contractor are an alternative to one main contract favoured by clients, for the reasons listed earlier, but in turn the specialist contractors are likely to employ subcontractors. In planning the use of contractors a client should therefore consider the effects of a hierarchy of contracts on critical activities and on motivation of subcontractors to perform.

Risks

Project risks

The major risks of any contract are the client's, in deciding to proceed with a project, and then stating or agreeing scope and specification, choosing the contract strategy, and selecting a contractor.

Some risks can be due to a client's uncertainty at the start in specifying what is wanted. For instance, the contract may be for the design and supply of equipment that is to be part of a system which will be defined by discussions during the contract. Another example is where the initial prediction of the purpose of a project may have to be varied during the work in order to meet changes in predictions of the demand for the goods or services that it is to produce when completed.

Risk allocation

As discussed in Chapter 14, the options available to a client in allocating the remaining risks are:

• avoid it — by changing project design or timing, or reducing dependence upon contractors and others;

• transfer it — to a main contractor, vendors or design contractors, or partial transfer in a joint venture;

• reduce it — by a combination of any of the above and insurance;

• absorb it — by allowing for extra costs, delay or reduced performance.

Clients in developed countries rarely invite tenders on the basis that a contractor is to be committed to complete work regardless of these risks. If they did, contractors would have to cover themselves by high prices in excess of the most probable direct and indirect costs they might incur. Governments and other clients in countries with less engineering expertise at times ask tenderers to carry more risks, but the trend in industrial countries since early this century has been that a risk should be the responsibility of whichever party is best able to manage it to suit the objectives of a project.

Ideally the allocation of risks between the parties to a contract is therefore based on:

• managerial principles that planning and supervision to get work completed satisfactorily are of more value than guarantees and rights to damages for default;

• commercial principles that a risk should be taken by whichever party is able to control it, insure or manage its consequences most economically;

• legal principles that unfair contract terms and penalties may not be enforceable;

- the implied terms of contracts under law, especially the duties of all parties on health, safety, welfare and the environment.

Any party to a project may therefore be at risk to some extent whatever the contracts between them, for instance that work may be frustrated by forces beyond their control. If so, the time lost and all or some of their consequent costs may not be recoverable.

The choice of terms of contract can motivate those who design, write software, manufacture equipment and so on, to be economical, quick or whatever are the client's objectives for a project. Contracts which place more than these risks on contractors are likely to be uneconomical and fail to achieve their objectives. The best contractors may be unwilling to tender for them.

Liquidated damages terms in contracts

A familiar but not necessarily satisfactory instance of transferring a risk is the inclusion in a contract of 'liquidated damages' terms which make the contractor liable to pay a specified sum for a specified breach in performance, such as lateness in delivery. This is an alternative to the contractor being at risk for damages at large, and can be positively reinforced by also offering to pay 'bonus' amounts for completion on time or for recovery after delay.

The intention of these terms in contracts is to encourage contractors to avoid being late. In practice, their effectiveness may be limited because a contractor, aware that he may be late, can calculate whether it is cheaper to lose the sum specified rather than employ extra resources to recover lost time — especially as the latter often requires using resources uneconomically. Such contractual liabilities may also be mitigated or unenforceable because the contractor can show that the work has been affected by the client, third parties or risks excepted from the contractor's liabilities.

The more detailed the protectionary terms in a contract, the greater the potential scope for disputes, and the greater the need for experienced project management by client and contractor to anticipate and avoid all such problems. Elaborate contractual terms are no substitute for detailed attention to risks, planning and supervision by both parties to get work completed satisfactorily.

Terms of payment

Cost is the primary measure used by clients when selecting projects, assessing risks, comparing prospective contractors' tenders, and reviewing the immediate and the longer-term results. Value for money over the life of the project is thus the concern of clients and, in effect, money for value over the life of a contract the concern of contractors.

In planning a contract to purchase a major structure, materials, design or other services a client should therefore consider what terms of payment are likely to motivate contractors to try to achieve the objectives of the project. The same applies to a contractor when planning to purchase from subcontractors, so that all the following comments may be equally relevant to subcontracts.

Fixed price payment

Fixed price terms of payment are preferred by many clients who place performance contracts — that is, when a contractor is responsible for design, supply of equipment or fabrication work to a price, and the client does not expect to have to specify further detail or changes.

Fixed price contracts have these potential advantages to a client:
- the contractor takes the risk that his actual costs may be greater than the contract price;
- being paid for performance should also be an incentive to the contractor to avoid delays to the works, and the contractor's price includes the financing costs of the work;
- it provides the simplest basis for competitive tenders.

Fixed price terms of payment are appropriate for projects which are fully specified before prospective contractors are invited to tender. Also completion of the chosen contractor's work on time or ahead of programme is more valuable to the client than second thoughts on design or changes to any terms of what has been agreed.

The potential disadvantages to a client are:
- time and man-hours should be devoted to exploring design choices and risks to decide a final and full specification before inviting tenders;
- any subsequent changes by the client could lead to a claim from the contractor for extra time and payment for affecting the planned use of resources. This might have the indirect advantage to a client that the risk of such claims could deter the client's staff or advisers from proposing changes.

Lump sum payment

The words 'lump sum' are often used in engineering and construction to mean that a contractor is paid on completing a major stage of work — for instance, on handing over a section of a project. In practice 'lump sum' is also used to mean that the amount to be paid is fixed, based on the tender price but perhaps subject to change to compensate for inflationary effects on contractors' costs.

Firm or fixed price payment

The words firm and fixed usually mean that the tender price is to be the final

271

contract price. They may also mean that there is no term in the contract for the client or client's representative to order variations.

Like other words used in contract management, 'fixed price' has no fixed meaning and 'firm price' no firm meaning. What matters in each contract are the terms of payment in that contract and what the governing law permits.

Down payment or payment for preliminaries

These terms are intended to induce a contractor to make a quick start to his activities because of the incentive of being paid the costs soon after incurring them.

A potential risk to the client is that the value of early payments may be lost if the contractor subsequently fails to complete his contractual obligations.

Protection against this can be arranged by requiring the contractor to provide a performance bond before receiving the payment.

Milestone and planned progress payment systems

Payment to a contractor can be in stages, in a series of payments for achieving defined 'milestones' of progress. The word 'milestone' usually means that payment is based upon progress in completing what the client wants. Payment for achieving defined percentages of a contractor's programme is known as a 'planned payment system'.

Compared to paying a lump sum after the completion of all work, these terms of payment have the potential advantage to a client that:
• the contractor has an incentive to proceed with work because payment is made sooner after incurring the costs. The incentive can be increased by the achievement of a milestone earning a contractor a 'bonus' payment.

A potential advantage to both parties is that the contractor's risks and financing costs should be less. The client has to meet the extra financing cost instead.

The potential disadvantages are:
• the milestones or equivalents have to be defined and their achievement proved. To avoid doubts and disputes they need to be defined precisely;
• the contract and its management are more complex than payment of one lump sum on completion.

The contract should state whether payment is due when a stage is achieved ahead of programme, and what payment is due if one stage is missed but the next is achieved.

Unit rates basis of payment

Unit rate terms of payment provide a basis for paying a contractor in proportion to the amount of work completed. For many UK building and civil engineering contracts the predicted quantities of each type of work are listed in a 'bill of quantities' or 'schedule of measured work'. When tendering, contractors enter their 'rates' (unit prices). Payment for work done is based upon the rates. The total contract price is thus based upon fixed rates but changes if the quantities change.

In some contracts what is called a 'schedule of rates' is similar to a bill of quantities in form and purpose, as contractors when tendering are asked to offer rates on the basis of indications of possible total quantities of each item of work in a defined period or within a limit of say ±15% change in any quantity. In other cases the rates are to be the basis of payment for any quantity of work which the client requires at any time.

The potential advantages to a client of basing payment to a contractor on unit rates are:

- unit rate payment systems provide a flexible basis for changing quantities of work based upon competitive prices from tenderers, provided there are agreed limits to the variations in quantities;

- the tendered rates from competing contractors can be compared to assess whether the contractors have understood the work and how they have allowed for risks;

- a contract can be agreed using approximate quantities and therefore before design is complete, and payment is made only for actual quantities of work done;

- payment depends upon progress, in detail, and should therefore motivate a contractor to complete work.

- if large changes are made in the quantity of an item, a new rate can be based upon the tender rate adjusted for the effects of the change in quantity;

- design changes can be planned using the unit rates to estimate their costs and to choose the cheapest of alternative ways of making proposed changes.

The potential disadvantages are:

- listing all the work in detail for unit pricing (usually in a bill of quantities or schedule of rates) is complex to prepare and measure. Its preparation and administration take time and resources, particularly the services of quantity surveyors or other experts in measuring quantities;

- complexity in defining and measuring items provides a basis for uncertainty and disputes;

- the tenders for contracts under which payment will be based upon unit rates and remeasurement need to be checked to see if prospective contractors have inserted relatively high rates for the items of work they expect may increase in quantity, and lower rates for those that may decrease;

- logically a rate cannot apply to any quantity at any time during a contract, as costs depend not only upon quantities of materials but also upon how economically people and equipment are employed by continuous work;
- unit rates provide a facility for the client to make changes which are avoidable, and so allows design and other decisions which could be final before inviting tenders to be made only provisionally or postponed;
- it does not totally avoid the problem that design and other changes imposed on a contractor can lead to disputes about their effects on costs.

Schedules of rates for units of completed work have the potential advantage of establishing a basis for payment when types of work but not quantities or continuity can be certain, but at the risk to clients that tenderers will state rates that allow for very uneconomic use of resources.

Dividing the work to be done for a project into separate items for pricing and payment purposes should therefore be no more detailed than is cost-effective for achieving the accuracy of payment control required by the client.

Contract price adjustment for escalation (CPA)

Inclusion of terms for compensating contractors for escalation of their costs due to inflation has potential advantages. They are that contractors do not have to price high enough to be safe if inflation is above predicted rates, and that clients have to pay only for the real costs so far as these are measured by the method chosen for calculating the effect on contract price. A disadvantage for clients is that they cannot be sure in advance what the extra costs will be. Directly and indirectly they also have to pay their own and the contractor's costs of calculating and handling the extra payments.

If a contract does not include such terms, the tender prices from contractors are likely to be higher in times of inflation, but the client knows that the total contract price due to be paid will be independent of inflation. The client may also expect that contractors will have the incentive to complete their work more rapidly if inflation is likely to cause their costs to rise. The extreme risk here is that a contractor may lose so much money it goes out of business before completing the works.

Cost-reimbursable and dayworks payment / Time and materials

All these are price-based terms of payment. In contrast to these are cost-based terms of payment.

The simplest form of cost-reimbursable contract is one under which a client pays ('reimburses') all a contractor's actual costs of all the employees on the contract ('payroll burden') and of materials, equipment and payments to subcontractors, plus usually a fixed sum or percentage for financing, overheads and profit. More complicated is a contract under which the costs-plus of achieving all satisfactory or acceptable work are reimbursed, but none or only some of the costs of rejected work.

Contractors can be invited to bid competitively for these contracts by being asked to state their rates per hour or per day for categories of people, equipment and other services. This is also a unit rate system, but different from those mentioned earlier in that payment is for costs rather than performance. In the UK construction industry it is known as 'dayworks'.

The potential advantages to a client of cost-reimbursable contracts are:

- speed. Work can be started as soon as it is defined;
- flexibility. Changes can be made by the client or work repeated without any basis for disputes that a contractor will incur costs not covered by payment.

Potential disadvantages to a client are:

- the contractor is not responsible for cost control and the productive use of resources;
- to achieve speed the contractor may need an incentive.

Under all such contracts the client in effect employs a contractor as an extension of the client's own organization. To control the cost of cost-reimbursable work the client's project team must direct the contractor's use of resources. The contractor's risks are limited, but so is the prospective profit.

These contracts are appropriate if the categories of people and other resources likely to be needed can be predicted but what they are to do will remain uncertain until near the time for doing it.

Target-incentive contracts

A development of the reimbursable type of contract is for a client and a contractor to agree at the start a probable cost for a then uncertain scope of work but also agree that the contractor will share savings in cost against target but be reimbursed less than costs-plus if the target is exceeded.

Compared to simple reimbursable terms of payment, the potential advantage to a client of target-based terms is that both parties have an incentive to limit the costs, and to a contractor that at least the costs will be reimbursed.

Problems may arise if the basis of the target is not precise or is changed, as the parties may then dispute whether work found to be needed was to be expected to be included or is to alter the target.

Convertible terms of payment

The potential advantage of starting a contract on reimbursable or target-cost terms of payment is that the contractor can mobilize resources and begin work before much design has been decided. A convertible contract is one that includes agreement that it will become fixed price or unit rate based when major uncertainties are resolved. This has the potential advantage of limiting the contract price after the conversion, but the potential disadvantages of little or no opportunity for competitive tendering. Alternatively, progress is likely to be delayed at that stage if the client takes an option in the convertible contract to invite other contractors to tender to take over the work.

Retention money

Most larger contracts for construction work include a term that a percentage of payments due to the contractor as fixed price, milestone achievement or quantities of work completed will be retained by the client for a specified period (up to one year is usual) and the 'retention' amount then paid ('released') if the contractor has completed obligations such as rectifying defective work.

The potential advantage of 'retention' to a client is that a contractor may be motivated to complete work correctly first time, in order to be paid the retained amount as early as possible.

The potential disadvantages are:
- tender prices may be higher, to allow for the extra financing cost to the contractor;
- there may be more disputes about whether work is satisfactory;
- the contractor can calculate whether it is more profitable to leave rectifying faulty work until resources become available.

Indicative prices

Prices obtained from potential contractors for the purpose of compiling an estimate of the cost of a proposed project (what is often called 'shopping around') are not contractual if at the time of obtaining the prices there was no intent to enter into a contract.

Alternatives in contract strategy

Management contracting, 'construction management'

The past 25 years have seen many innovations in construction procurement in North America and the UK away from employing one main or lead contractor to engineer, procure the equipment and construct a project complete.

The alternative role known as 'construction management contractor' usually means that a contractor is employed to bring contracting experience into the client's team, to provide construction advice to design and to place the sub-contracts jointly with or on behalf of the client at limited risk to the management contractor. (The 'subcontracts' are then more accurately called 'works contracts'.) The works contracts can be planned in a series — for instance, when design information or funds are available. This arrangement can be of advantage to the client if:

- the project is urgent and design depends upon innovation;
- uncertainty of the market, funding, public approval, site conditions or other reasons may affect proceeding with the project;
- the management contractor's experience is valuable early in design and planning;
- placing a series of works contracts only when sections of design are final avoids disputes between client and contractor about design delays or changes;
- incentive payments linked to project outcome motivate the management contractor to anticipate construction problems rather than exploit them for contractual advantage.

Concession contracts

Design-finance-build-operate (DFBO), build-own-operate-transfer (BOOT) and other forms of concession contracts to contractors are linked in recent history with privatization of what were public services. In principle they are separate.

Often in such contracts the contractor is a consortium of construction, finance and other parties and an employer of an architect/engineer organization. This body is the promoter of the project and either legally or effectively the owner until the concession period has matured. Once given the concession, the contractor has in turn to choose a strategy for procurement of design and construction.

The essence of the concession is the liability to finance not only design and construction but also operation and maintenance, again until the concession period has matured.

A concession contract could be of advantage to a client to:

- buy all possible services by contract rather than employ its own project and operational staff;
- minimize capital investment;
- contract out all possible risks;
- break away from established habits and their perceived disadvantages.

Needs of project management

The New Engineering Contract system (NEC) separates the role of client's Project Manager from the roles of designer, construction supervisor and disputes adjudicator traditionally all the role of 'the Engineer' in engineering and construction contracts. The NEC has been designed to provide a basis for project management and to establish a compatible set of contracts for many engineering projects and for design, project management and other services.

Partnering and alliances

Partnering between client and contractor to manage their contract relationships co-operatively has been the subject of experiments, study and discussion over the past ten years in the USA and more recently in the UK. It now extends to major subcontractors. The potential advantages to clients are in:

- establishing understanding of all parties' needs, practices and problems over a programme of work, especially for more than one project;
- anticipating problems and avoiding contractual disputes;
- improving competitive advantage through improved cost, quality and schedule;
- benefiting from reduced overhead costs.

If applied for a series of projects or packages of work, client and contractor can benefit from the continuity of knowledge of practices and people, scope for continuous improvement and savings in tendering costs and time.

Clients who have changed from their normal practice by trying management contracting, partnering or alternatives may have found them to have been effective because they altered responsibilities and made better use of expertise in ways suitable for the nature and risks of the projects and the abilities and resources of the players. The alternatives may have been effective because the clients who chose to try them wanted improvements in performance and therefore gave more attention to their procurement policies and subsequent contract management. The co-operation which partnering should establish has probably always been a recipe for success whatever may be the terms of a contract.

Contract documents

For a small project it is usually sufficient for a contract to consist of a drawing and an exchange of letters. The drawing can show the location and amount of work. The materials can be specified on it. Or these and the completion date, price and other terms that matter to the parties can be stated in a letter. If the agreement is the result of a series of letters and replies — what is known as offer and counter-offers — one final letter should state all that has been agreed and replace all previous communications so as to leave no doubt about what has been offered and accepted.

To avoid these doubts on all but small projects the practice has evolved of stating the various terms of a contract in a set of documents. These can be lengthy, but some can be the same for many contracts and so do not have to be prepared anew each time. The set of documents traditionally used in UK engineering contracts is:

- drawings;
- specification;
- conditions of contract;
- agreement;
- payment schedule, schedule of rates or bill of quantities.

The drawing and specification should establish the type and nature of all the work and tests, the location of a site, access and services. In a specification the work to be done by a contractor should be defined in terms of its use for a purpose.

Usually the client or a design contractor produces the first drawings showing at least an outline scheme. Development of the design and alternatives can be by competing contractors or one chosen to implement the project, but usually with submission for comment to the client.

What are often called 'conditions of contract' are sets of terms which state the general responsibilities, risks and liabilities of the parties and establish procedures between them. The proposed conditions are usually stated by a client when inviting tenders for a contract. Model and standard sets of conditions of contract are used by companies. The major UK and international models are listed at the end of this chapter.

Signature of an 'agreement' establishes that a large or complex contract has been agreed. It states the terms of the contract, particularly if alternatives have been exchanged in a process of offers and counter-offers and negotiations of differences. An exchange of letters or a printed form accepted by the parties is sufficient for most smaller contracts. An oral agreement is sufficient to establish commitment under English law but can lead to arguments about what was agreed.

International practice

The ruling law, legal systems and legal attitudes vary from country to country, even between England and Scotland. These differences, as well as cultural and business practices, can complicate contracts with parties in other countries. A contract between parties in more than one country should therefore state which country's law applies, which language will rule, and where disputes are to be settled.

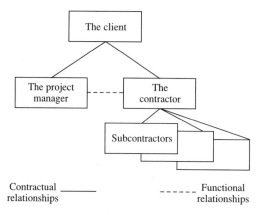

Figure 18.1 Formal relationships between client, contractor and 'the project manager'

'The Project Manager' or 'the Engineer'

In the model conditions published by the UK engineering institutions and by FIDIC (see Appendix to this chapter), a person to be named under a contract as 'the Project Manager' or 'the Engineer' has powers and duties to instruct and supervise a contractor. Figure 18.1 shows the formal relationships between this person and the parties during the contract.

The powers and duties of the role vary from contract to contract. Typically this person has the power in a contract to approve the contractor's proposed programme, control the choice of subcontractors, instruct the contractor to vary the work, grant extra time and authorize payment. Each contract should be studied to ascertain the powers and duties of the role and to consider their effects on the relationships between the parties.

Note that the initial capital letters in the words Project Manager or Engineer are used to indicate the particular person named.

Conclusion – the lessons of contracts

Contract preparation

- Be clear what you want. Say what you mean. Eschew obfuscation.
- Plan how it will end before you start.
- Specify only what you can test.
- Be aware of how a contract is created and how it can be discharged.

- Decide what terms of payment are effective.
- Define the obligations and rights of every party.
- Anticipate what can go wrong, applying risk management.
- Choose the terms of contract logically, depending upon the nature of the work, its certainty, its urgency, the motivation of all parties and other factors such as the relationship between an investment in new plant and systems already in use.
- As documents different in function are usually prepared by different groups of people, the set for a contract should be co-ordinated by one person.

Contract management
- Establish self-control of a contract through a single manager who has experience of the potential conflicts of interest that can arise and the authority to decide how to avoid problems.
- Assess your suppliers' representatives' real power over resources.
- Study the contract. Note the general obligations and rights of all parties.
- Recognize that objectives and priorities change during most contracts.
- Keep records, notes of reasons for decisions, and use routine headings.
- Distinguish between legal rights and commercial interests. Consider whether enforcing a right to damages or other compensation is in your best interests overall, but be aware of immediate pressures.
- Contracts should be a means to an end.

Further reading

Barnes, N.M.L., 1996, How contracts can help project managers, *Proceedings, International Project Management Association Congress, Paris* (IPMA).

Bommer, M., *et al*, 1993, Technology transfer utilizing vendor partnering and a self managed project team, *Project Management Journal*, XXIV (2): 27–33 and 48.

Boyce, T., 1992, *Successful Contract Administration* (Hawksmere).

CII, 1991, *In Search of Partnering Excellence*, Special Publication 17-1 (Construction Industry Institute, Austin).

Construction Industry Board, 1997, *Partnering in the Team* (Thomas Telford).

Loraine, R.K., 1994, Project specific partnering, *Engineering, Construction and Architectural Management*, 1 (1): 5–16.

Merna, A. and Bower, D.A., 1997, *Dispute Resolution in Construction and Infrastructure Projects* (Asia Law & Practice).

Merna, A. and Smith, N.J., 1996, *Projects Procured by Privately Financed Concession Contracts*, 2 volumes (Asia Law & Practice).

Merna, A. and Smith, N.J., 1990, Project managers and the use of turnkey contracts, *International Journal of Project Management*, 8 (3): 183–189.

Smith, N.J. and Wearne, S.H., 1993, *Construction Contract Arrangements in EU Countries* (European Construction Institute). (Includes lists of abbreviations and definitions of words used in engineering and construction contracts.)

Ward, S. and Chapman, C., 1994, Choosing contractor payment terms, *International Journal of Project Management*, 12 (4): 216–221.

Wright, D., 1996, *An Engineer's Guide to the Model Forms of Conditions of Contract* ('the Purple Book'), 2nd edition (Institution of Chemical Engineers).

Appendix: model conditions of contract

Model Form of Conditions of Contract for Process Plant Suitable for Reimbursable Contracts (known as 'the Green Book'), 2nd edition, 1992 (Institution of Chemical Engineers).

Model Form of Conditions of Contract for Process Plant Suitable for Lump Sum Contracts (known as 'the Red Book'), 3rd edition, 1995 (Institution of Chemical Engineers).

Model Form of Conditions of Contract for Process Plant — Subcontracts (known as 'the Yellow Book'), 2nd edition, 1997 (Institution of Chemical Engineers).

Model Form of Conditions of Contract for Process Plant — Minor Works (known as 'the Orange Book'), 1998 (Institution of Chemical Engineers).

Model Form of General Conditions of Contract, Home or Overseas Contracts — With Erection, Model Form MF/1, 2nd edition, 1994 (Institution of Mechanical Engineers, Institution of Electrical Engineers and Association of Consulting Engineers). (Model form MF/2 is for equipment supply without erection.)

The New Engineering Contract — A Form of Contract for Engineering and Construction Projects, 1993 (Institution of Civil Engineers). (Core set of conditions plus options, and matching conditions for professional services.)

Conditions of Contract for Civil Engineering Works, 6th edition, 1991 ('ICE 6'), and *Conditions of Contract for Minor Works*, 2nd edition, 1995 (Institution of Civil Engineers).

Conditions of Contract for Design and Construct, 1992 (Institution of Civil Engineers).

JCT Management Contract, 1987, and *Works Contract 3*, 1987 (Joint Contracts Tribunal for the Standard Building Contract).

There are other models published by trade associations and many sets of model terms for specialist work and subcontracts.

Guidance notes and model terms of subcontract are published with most of the engineering institutions' model conditions of contract.

International

Client-Consultant Model Services Agreement ('the White Book') (Fédération International des Ingénieurs-Conseils — FIDIC).

General Conditions for the Supply of Plant and Machinery for Export (alternatives for supply with and without erection) (United Nations Economic Commission for Europe — ECE).

Conditions of Contract (International) for Electrical and Mechanical Works ('the Yellow Book') (FIDIC).

Conditions of Contract (International) for Design-Build and Turnkey (FIDIC).

Conditions of Contract (International) for Works of Civil Engineering Construction ('the Red Book') (FIDIC).

Project organizations

19

Stephen Wearne

Projects large and small depend upon the temporary services of people. The authority to use people and other resources needs to be allocated, communicated and implemented, as well as responsibilities and accountability. An organization structure is a system of formal communications and of authority over resources. A standard system of organization that suits all demands has not yet been evolved. Probably it never will be, because companies and their projects vary in their objectives, culture, work and circumstances. This chapter reviews choices in selecting organization structures to suit the type of project.

Organizations

Structure

Organization is a means of enabling people to achieve more together than they could alone. Or it should be. How and how much to organize departments and project teams therefore depends on how and how many people need to work together. How far to define a structure of jobs should be decided on the basis of the work to be done and how people are dependent on each other to do it. An organization structure should be designed to link everyone who takes part in decisions on the objectives, scope, standards, design, economy, financing, timing, methods, safety, control and acceptability of a project. It should help to motivate people. It should convey facts, ideas and understanding. It should also feed back data useful for controlling projects and for improving future performance.

Sometimes everybody working on a small project can be located together. If so, they are able to share information easily, and also understand each others' intentions and interests. More commonly, most of the people contributing to a project are employed in specialist functions. Many are in separate organizations and in them located in separate departments. As a result they may fail to keep others informed of new information and potential problems. Separated groups of people also tend to interpret information differently. People employed in specialist functions are particularly likely to do so. They tend to concentrate on their own work and its importance as they see it. Specialization by departments and individuals has the longer-term advantages that they can build up expertise and be spread economically over many projects. A disadvantage is that many specialists may be involved in only their part of a project. They may not know about or understand the needs of the project as a whole. And if treated as advisers rather than as members of project teams, they may also tend to concentrate on quality rather than delivery times and budgets. A system of organization is therefore needed to link them.

The need to plan these relationships and the information system does not mean that organizations should be bureaucratic. They should be flexible and informal in order to be able to perceive and solve problems and adapt to the changing needs stage by stage through projects.

Economic allocation of resources

The demands for the expertise of people and other resources required to carry out a project (or to alter one) are transitory. To be economic, these resources must be used on a series of projects and as continuously as possible. Continuity in the use of resources and the development of skills may not suit the order of their use that is ideal for a project. An organization structure therefore has to serve two objectives:

* achieving the sequence of activities essential to each project;
* distributing resources amongst a variety of projects.

Therefore most projects have to share resources. At the feasibility study stage alternative projects may be under consideration and competing for selection. Those selected are then likely to share design resources with others which may be otherwise unconnected, but therefore be in competition with them for the use of these resources. A similar situation may exist through all the subsequent stages in the cycle. The relationships between the people working on a project therefore need to be planned and reviewed regularly.

Project teams

Client project team

The 'WHIZZO' project team described in Chapter 3 illustrated the formation of a client's team by the temporary allocation of engineers and others to the team from engineering and other specialist functions in the company. This is typical of many projects.

A 'PROJECT TASK FORCE' SHOULD CONCENTRATE ATTENTION AND HELP MOTIVATE ALL TO MEET THE CUSTOMER'S NEEDS.

An organizational problem is that most of the projects in hand in such a company are not large enough for people to be dedicated to only one project at a time. Attention to each project may therefore be interrupted by the needs of other projects or by delays from a customer or other parties. The consequent loss of continuity and risks to motivation and efficiency may be costly, especially if few of the people allocated to a project are located together.

Very small projects may need some or all of the time of perhaps only one person plus some services from others, but their short time-scale makes it difficult to predict when the services will be required. Certain categories of project may follow a similar pattern and call on much the same expertise, but regular relationships are interrupted. The organization therefore needs a system for setting priorities to employ people effectively, rather than a formal structure which separates them into groups or project teams.

The people allocated to a project need the expertise demanded by the nature of the projects, the problems and the risks, plus experience of applying this expertise to the type of customer and the range of work. An engineering department therefore needs its specialist technical experts, but with the flexibility and the ability to work on more than one project at once. An engineer may have several roles — leader of one or more projects, expert in a subject, and the person knowing most about a particular production system or client.

One means of achieving attention to each project and its objectives is to dedicate people to a project from start to finish. The larger the project, the more it may be practicable to do so. Putting together all the people and resources required for a project directly under a manager responsible only for meeting the objectives of that project to form what is known as a 'project task force' concentrates attention and helps motivate all to meet the customer's needs. It has disadvantages, one being that it requires people to work themselves out of a job by completing their stage of the work. Another is that skills and other resources are not shared between projects, which can be wasteful at the time and fail to accumulate experience for future projects.

Contractor's project team

Contractors and design organizations have the same needs as clients to achieve the sequence of activities essential for each project and distribute their available resources amongst a variety of projects. A customer may demand that a contractor designates a team dedicated to that customer's project, because of his concern that the contractor should allocate the resources needed to complete his commitments. This can be an uneconomic arrangement to the contractor, and therefore may have to be imposed by the client.

Choice of this system is clearly logical as a means of concentrating on clients' and customers' objectives, as projects are the productive work and all other activities have value only as a contribution to a project. It puts together the people dependent upon information and decisions, and should therefore be coherent in reacting to demands and to new problems. Designating a separate project team involving all affected can also be a means of achieving an organizational transition, utilizing people's interest in the technical novelties or other features of a project to draw them into a changed system. It is the system that most tests the project managers, as each has the range of responsibilities of a general manager. This can be a useful part of a company's scheme for developing top management.

On the other hand the needs of a project for various skills, etc are only temporary and may fluctuate. Sharing of these needs between projects, rather than having self-sufficient project groups, may therefore be much more economical. Experience can then be shared and reserves of resources drawn upon when required. Grouping entirely by project is a principle that is appropriate for a 'one-time undertaking … that is infrequent or unfamiliar … complex … and critical', as concluded in an early study of some examples in companies in the USA. A dedicated project team or 'task force' located together is appropriate for a project which is urgent, important, complex or unique. Except in these conditions it is more logical to give preference to a system for sharing resources, adding to this a secondary means of linking the decisions for each project.

Project co-ordination and control

Project managers

The lesson of all experience is that every project needs someone responsible for it from start to finish. Whether formally called the project manager or not, the role is required to achieve leadership, championship of the project and continuity of knowledge of it, as discussed further in Chapter 22. The role can change from person to person from stage to stage through a project because of individual workloads or suitability. For small projects this can be part of the role of the engineer responsible for defining or designing a project. For larger projects it can be nearly a full-time task and a separate role.

The structure of the company and its contracts with others provide the formal basis for generating and communicating authority and decisions. A project may also need its informal system for the project manager to obtain ideas, get early warnings of problems and check that information has been received and understood. This need varies according to the number of people employed on a project, the interdependence of their work, the extent of unexpected problems, whether they are located together, and whether most are familiar with these conditions.

The project role in a management structure

The simplest arrangement is to add the co-ordinating role to the tasks of a person already working on the project, and so not make communications more complicated.

If the size of a project makes its co-ordination a full-time task, a separate person can be given the role on behalf of the manager controlling the resources essential to that project, in a 'staff officer' position as indicated in Figure 19.1. The 'line' manager remains formally in control of the resources. One or a small team of people can be used in this position to provide a temporary project management team. (Safety officers and other specialist advisers are in the same 'staff' relationship to line managers.)The important principle is that the staff position is not an additional level in the hierarchy. Its effectiveness may be limited by the role being that of co-ordinating other people, rather than being their boss in the formal managerial system.

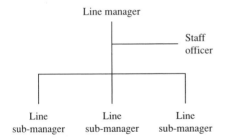

Figure 19.1 Line and staff roles in a management structure

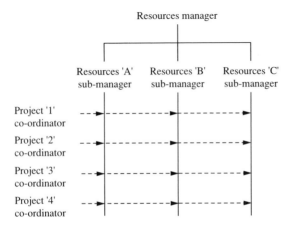

Figure 19.2 A 'weak' matrix system of responsibilities for resources and projects

In theory people in staff roles act only as an extension of the line managers' capacity. They have to be accepted as givers of decisions authorized by the line managers. Like anything logical, the line-and-staff arrangement works when all concerned understand it. In times of conflict or uncertainty it may be limited in its effectiveness because decisions remain dependent upon the line members of the hierarchy of authority.

Matrix systems

Companies and public authorities have evolved what are called 'matrix' systems of management to achieve leadership of a set of projects which share the resources of groups of specialists. An instance of this is shown in Figure 19.2. The people and other resources needed for the projects are based in three

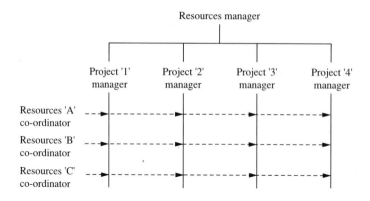

Figure 19.3 A 'strong' matrix system of responsibilities for resources and projects

departments — A, B and C — each headed by a manager. Their work for each particular project is co-ordinated by a separate person.

Figure 19.2 shows what is known as a 'weak' matrix because the permanent resource managers of A, B and C are in the hierarchy of authority over resources. The alternative of a 'strong' matrix is shown in Figure 19.3. In this, the resources are in 'task forces' responsible to the project managers. The project managers are then the line managers. The role of the resource managers is to co-ordinate the use of the specialist resources, operating across the project teams to provide expert guidance and advise the top manager on the allocation of resources between the projects.

A matrix structure is a system for sharing resources between projects and concentrating the information about each project in its project manager. A matrix system is appropriate if people and other resources located in different functional departments have to be shared amongst a set of projects, but to be successful it requires planning of their allocation to each project and undivided authority and responsibility for standards, safety, costs and delivery.

Matrix systems can be more complex and organic, particularly in the extent of the formal authority of the project managers relative to that of the resources managers. The project managers and the resources managers should theoretically all influence decisions in a matrix system. In some organizations the project managers are responsible for quantitative decisions affecting the cost and programme of the projects, whereas the resources managers are responsible for qualitative standards in allocating people and other resources to each project. If so, the resources managers have to act as consultants to members of their sections once allocated to a project. A matrix system thus provides opportunities to employ leaders with different skills and knowledge in these two types of managerial roles.

The matrix principle is awkward to try to depict in the two-dimensional diagrams used to show systems of organization. The usual convention in drawing organizational diagrams is that the line of authority is vertical. Collaboration is thus horizontal. In a matrix these are compounded. If authority is meant to be shared between the project and resources managers, the matrix is drawn on the skew.

Matrix management or internal contracts?

Observations of matrix systems indicate that there can be problems in them between the project managers and the resources managers about the allocation of resources to a project and the quality, cost and timing of the work to be done by them. The resources managers should earlier have agreed on specifications, budgets and schedules for every project, but may have done so some time before a project starts and then only in sufficient detail to get a budget or a contract to proceed. This may not ensure that adequate resources are available when a project calls for them.

One means of avoiding most or all such problems is to treat the work for a project to be done by each specialist group of people as in effect a contractual commitment between their resource manager and the project manager. If it was to be purchased by contract from another company there would normally be a prior process of investigating the potential supplier's capacity and understanding of the work required, followed by an invitation to offer to do it for a price and specified quality and delivery. Procedures for progress reporting, inspection, changes and resolving problems would also be established before they might be needed. The same are in effect needed within organizations, not through legally enforceable documents but by agreed definitions of what is expected of others rather than assuming that commitments are known, agreed and understood.

Final comments

The potential problems can be minimized if an organization structure is designed on the following principles:
- least separation of the people working on a project;
- those who control resources are responsible for delivering the project.

The proportion of unforeseen and uncertain problems of projects in all industries has increased because of greater uncertainties in predicting markets, technological changes, public controls and the continuing growth in the complexity and the economic risks of new projects. A project can less and less be defined once and for all at the start and the subsequent decisions delegated amongst groups classically divided under a hierarchy of managers. As a result, more problems require continued co-ordination at the level of management that has the authority over the use of resources.

In all but the very smallest companies the working relationships between people should therefore be reviewed regularly. For engineering managers this means that their responsibilities for what may be the answers to project problems and technical questions must be extended to attention to how the decisions on these are made.

Further reading

Briner, W., *et al*, 1995, *Project Leadership*, 2nd edition (Gower).

Handy, C.B., 1985, *Understanding Organizations*, 3rd edition (Penguin).

Martin, A.S. and Grover, F. (eds), 1988, *Managing People* (Thomas Telford).

Morris, P.W.G., 1989, *Managing Project Interfaces, Technical Paper No 7* (Major Projects Association).

Rutter, P.A. and Martin, A.S. (eds), 1990, *Management of Design Offices* (Thomas Telford).

Smith, N.J., *et al*, 1995, *Engineering Project Management*, Chapters 8 and 9 (Blackwell).

Wearne, S.H., 1993, *Principles of Engineering Organization*, 2nd edition, Chapters 8 and 9 (Thomas Telford Publishing).

Project information

Jack Loftus and Stephen Wearne

Projects large and small depend upon everybody contributing to them knowing what is required and why. Objectives and priorities need to be defined and understood, as well as what has to be done and when. This chapter provides check-lists of the information and documents which may be required for a project.

Project definition

The following check-list gives guidance to everyone involved on what information and decisions are needed to define a project before becoming committed to it. The minimum information required for all projects is indicated in bold type:

- customer's requirements and expectations, **function required**, type of equipment, purpose, payload, throughput, duty cycles, specification, operating envelope, special safety risks, environment, and parameters of performance, reliability and availability;
- customer's name, **authorized representative**, contact names, phone/fax numbers and e-mail addresses, and locations;
- scope of supply, spares, manuals, drawings, responsibilities for installation, testing, commissioning, training, limits of scope — for example, site preparation work by client or other contractors;
- preferred suppliers, **restraints** on selection of subcontracting and purchasing of materials and services, free issue of materials, testing and quality control by customer;
- information requirements, submissions of design, statutory data, test data and QA records, for approval and project close-out audit;
- intermediate and **final dates for delivery**, handover and tests;
- whether standard, customized or special components required, to British, European Union, US, customer's or other standards;
- site location, interfaces with existing plant, **power supply, services, amenities**, interfaces with others, site access by land or sea, site constraints;

- site safety rules, legal requirements (overseas), vehicles;
- **terms of contract**, special conditions, **price** and pricing schedule, budget, basis of payment, **damages liabilities**, financing, bank guarantees, warranties, insurance;
- cost — what can the customer afford, what will the market stand, what extras may be required, is there competition in providing spares and service?

Initially every item listed here plus others specific to a project should be agreed before becoming committed to a project. More than the minimum information will be needed for the average project, and for a large, high-risk project consider all the items on the list carefully.

Contract commitments

The following check-list is a guide for everyone involved in sales and negotiating contracts on what commitments should be defined before entering into a contract with a vendor or a contractor:

- objectives and scope of contract, process, equipment, services and structures; free issue of materials;
- specification — covering purpose, process, licensing, materials, capacity, standards, performance criteria, treatment, quality, hazards, instrumentation, services, inspection, installation and testing;
- exclusions from client's scope and specification; status of pre-contract design and test data;
- preferred or nominated suppliers;
- programme — showing dates for start, milestones, approvals, tests, partial/complete handover and commissioning;
- likelihood of changes to any of the above; variations and claims procedures and culture;
- client's budget; contractor's sales policy, contract price make-up and minimum acceptable profit;
- site layout, power, water and other services, access, storage, security and environmental controls; termination points of site services and interfaces with other suppliers and contractors;
- site working conditions, safety and employment rules and welfare services;
- training requirements and facilities;
- client's contract, safety and quality control procedures;
- criteria and responsibilities for tests;
- insurance, defects and maintenance liabilities;
- terms of payment, contract financing, responsibilities for escalation and payments to subcontractors; bonus, incentives and liquidated damages terms;

- client's and contractor's management and service personnel; client's and consultant's style; powers and name of 'the Engineer' or 'the Project Manager';
- exporting or importing conditions, dates and procedures, responsibilities and quality of agents; liabilities for insurance and for currency risks.

Project documentation

Every stage of a project depends upon information from the previous stages, and the information becomes more voluminous through its development from first ideas to handing over to operations. Memory alone is a poor filing cabinet, and is lost when personnel replace others. Project data should therefore be recorded. Usually more should be recorded than seems necessary at the time, so that facts are available to guide unexpected problems. All project teams should therefore produce and maintain, as a minimum:

- definition of project objectives and scope;
- a project execution plan (see Chapter 3);
- a project completion or 'close-out' review.

These documents need consist of only a page or two for a small project which was similar to previous ones and limited in its risks. The project execution plan can consist of only a statement that established procedures will apply.

THE CUSTOMER'S BRIEF NEED CONSIST OF ONLY A PAGE OR TWO.

Using company or others' standard documents for each of the bulleted items can save much time but should be followed only after giving attention to whether they are appropriate for the nature, risks, priorities and organization of the particular project.

For a large or novel project many more separate documents may be needed so that each one is small and concentrated on a single purpose:

Project authorizing documents:
- customer's project policy and brief;
- statement of project objectives;
- reports of project studies and investigations;
- project authorization instruction.

Engineering briefing documents:
- front end design brief;
- list of front end deliverables (the 'frozen design' documents);
- project scope;
- standards;
- project specification;
- basis of process;
- process specification;
- operating principles;
- maintenance principles;
- commissioning plan.

Procedural documents:
- project execution plan;
- programme for statutory approvals or equivalents in a country;
- procedures and reporting manual;
- QA manual;
- safety policy directive;
- communications guide — names, addresses and other contact details of sponsor/customer's representative, the project manager and all managers and contacts in departments, contractors and other organizations responsible for work for the project;
- software and IT protocols.

Project control documents:
- the health and safety file (or equivalent national requirement);
- site rules, space allocation and permitry;

- programmes and schedules;
- work breakdown structure and budgets;
- manpower and materials supply data;
- drawings;
- contracts and subcontracts;
- change control system (see configuration control notes below);
- progress reports covering:
— progress, productivity and trends compared to targets
— earned value, committed cost and trends compared to budget
— use of contingency
— forecast final cost
— period highlights
— next period objectives
— actions on forecast critical problems;
- minutes of meetings;
- project diaries;
- project bulletins and press releases;
- logs of documents received and documents issued.

Deliverable documents:
- introduction to the project;
- operating manuals;
- maintenance manuals;
- commissioning procedures;
- completion documents;
- the final health and safety file;
- list of project records;
- project review and list of reasons for successes and problems.

Some of these can be combined for less complex projects. Use these lists to check whether each class of information is recorded for a project and, if not, whether it need be.

Whatever the type of project or the urgency of the moment, the project manager should impose rules to ensure that all documents — formal or informal — are dated, show their source, and include a distribution list.

Project information centre – configuration control
The performance requirements, design, layout and sometimes the location of a project can change as it is developed from the first definition of objectives to handing over the completed plant to operations.

'Configuration control' is a formal name for a system of maintaining up-to-date information at one point for use by everyone on the project. On a large or complex project it may consist of the master copy of all the documents already listed. The minimum need only be:

- definition of the performance requirement;
- name, address, etc, of the project manager;
- layout drawing;
- summary of the design data;
- record of changes.

Everyone working on a project needs confidence that the information is up to date. The system should therefore never be bypassed by the project team or senior managers. It includes a procedure for recording proposed design and other changes and for circulating the results of the decisions to allow or to refuse a change.

Whatever the size of the project, one person should control this information. For a small project it is the job of the project manager or equivalent. For a very large project it should be delegated to the leader of a dedicated document management team.

Acknowledgements

The check-lists used in this chapter were compiled with the aid of engineers, managers and others when attending project management courses run by the Institution of Chemical Engineers and the UMIST Centre for Research in the Management of Projects.

Further reading

Lock, D., 1996, *Project Management*, 6th edition, Chapter 24 (Gower).

Open University, 1990, *Software Project Execution*, M355, Block IV, Unit 14 (Open University).

Project Management Institute, 1997, *PMI Book of Project Management Forms* (Project Management Institute, Upper Darby, PA).

Stallworthy, E.A. and Kharbanda, O.P., 1986, *A Guide to Project Implementation*, Appendix A (Institution of Chemical Engineers) (out of print).

Turner, J.R., 1993, *The Handbook of Project-Based Management*, Chapter 16: Project administration (McGraw-Hill).

Section 3 – Skills and knowledge

Peter Iles-Smith

The first two sections of this book discuss the scope of a potential project and the specific tools necessary for its execution. Section 3 reviews some of the more general skills and knowledge required by the project manager, and considers the ways in which real projects differ from the ideal.

Chapter 21 considers the personal skills and organization that lets a project manager work effectively. Chapter 22 outlines the importance of communications and project administration and Chapter 23 introduces the basics of accountancy. The section finishes with an introduction to value engineering in Chapter 24 and, in Chapter 25, a brief discussion of the different types of project that may be encountered in a project manager's career.

Personal skills and the organization

Peter Iles-Smith

People who run projects are a unique breed. Whether they are called project managers, project engineers or something similar, they generally have an impact across an entire organization without necessarily having the formal managerial authority one might expect. The basic tasks of project management — control of time, cost and quality — require the ability to interact with people and organizations successfully.

There are few careers where the content of the next day is so uncertain. Consider this: it is 4:30 pm on Friday, and you have just been told that the new pump you were expecting today to complete the current project phase has fallen off its transport. You were not driving the vehicle, but the problem and the solution are yours.

In many ways, good organizational skills are the project manager's greatest attribute. Meticulous planning will come to produce nothing of value if the individual concerned cannot organize to achieve the final result. Good management of individuals — either inside or outside the company — are essential to the success of any project.

The project manager's position in the organization

Before considering the project manager's skills, it is useful to consider the position of the project manager in the organization. In many companies, there is a strong distinction between the line (or functional) and project organization. Even when the project manager operates within one particular department, there is undoubtedly a need to work with construction, maintenance or other support functions, as illustrated in Chapter 3 and discussed further in Chapter 19. Typically these departments do not report directly to the project manager and the problem of responsibility without clear authority can increase the 'stress' of the situation and have an impact on the running of the project.

The success of a project is usually measured by comparing the outcome to the requirement. The success of a project manager can be measured in much the same way. Unless you and your management have a clear understanding of your position within the organization and the limits of your authority before the project starts, the result may be muddle and uncertainty. This can be a particular problem if, as a new project manager, your role is part-time or the responsibilities between, say, engineering and project management are blurred.

One of the biggest challenges to the management of projects within most organizations is the concept of responsibility without authority. This is particularly true of situations — for example, manufacturing plant — where the primary role of the company is not in project work. Under these circumstances, the ability to influence, persuade, cajole and even threaten is crucial to success; in short, leadership is an important attribute.

THE RESPONSIBILITIES OF A NEW
PROJECT MANAGER CAN BE BLURRED.

Managing people

Project management involves the co-ordination of resources to achieve a goal. A critical resource is the project personnel who need to be built into a team. There is nothing more uninspiring than working on a project where there is little communication or co-operation between participants, the goals are unclear and there is no recognition.

Teams

There are a number of golden rules to observe in the establishment and management of teams:

Avoid large teams

Large groups tend to fragment into smaller subgroups of five or fewer people. Aim to create the logical subgroups before inappropriate de facto groupings appear. This is one objective of the work breakdown structure — see Chapter 16.

Look out for 'group think'

Organizational behaviour studies show that close groups of people tend to think alike and avoid challenging the consensus. Within any project, this can affect decision-making.

Don't 'do-it-yourself'

As a practising engineer with a high degree of skill, you can do the job quicker, better and more professionally than anyone else. Avoid the temptation: in anything but the simplest activity either the cost, schedule or quality will suffer. Manage or engineer, don't try to do both.

Management by walking about

This is a concept advanced by management guru Charles Handy and is very good sense for any project manager. In any project management role, it is easy to fall into the trap of communicating by reports only. Since most people tend to be optimistic with regard to progress estimates, this can be very misleading (that last 10% of the work seems to take 90% of the time). You will only appreciate what the team is doing if you pay close attention to the team's work and do that by literally 'walking about'. Don't confuse this with doing the job yourself or scything through other peoples' responsibilities.

Goal setting

Like the project, the team needs clear, achievable goals. These should be set *and communicated* at the beginning. When the project priorities change, make sure that the goals are changed accordingly. Without goals, the team members will set their own objectives and progress accordingly.

People and motivation

Different people are motivated by different things — a self-evident comment, but one that can be frequently overlooked within the project team.

The project manager works with a range of individuals, from unionized labour through technicians to professional engineers and ambitious managers. The drives and motivations of these individuals need to be understood.

People are not necessarily driven by a desire to see a good job done. Nor are they driven by pay, though inadequate pay can be a demotivator. People need to be managed in a way that ensures that the project objectives are not subverted to personal agendas or functional rivalry. They are also not (generally) impressed by a manager's job title or position. This can place the project manager in a difficult position, particularly if the project manager is outside the 'line'. The concept of position power or respect therefore comes into play.

The project manager's authority derives from:

• being seen as concerned with what is best for the project, rather than self-interest or exploiting problems to others' disadvantage;

• knowledge of the project, facts rather than rumour or guesswork, leading to value as a guide in solving problems;

• access to top management and their support;

• experience — as a basis for asking meaningful questions, but not necessarily having fixed answers;

• leadership, enthusiasm, drive and energy;

• being trusted to give decisions which may not be the best for every party involved, but are the best for the project.

Far more can be achieved by a quiet chat with a technician than by dictatorial orders. Do not be complacent, but realistic to the project demands and the limits of your authority.

Managing within the organization

Organizations vary from the highly structured and bureaucratic to the open and entrepreneurial. The project manager needs to be able to accommodate the organization structure and requirements, and still get the job done.

Highly bureaucratic organizations tend toward rigid control systems where the adherence to regulation becomes an end in itself. Such organizations are characterized by a demand for control and an emphasis on reliability of behaviour — this can lead to unintentional problems of rigid behaviour, subsequent difficulty with clients and defensive postures being taken.

At the other extreme, entrepreneurial organizations tend to be flexible and responsive, but can lack structure and have much of the power concentrated in a small number of individuals. Imposition of the structure and discipline required of a project can be difficult.

There are no fixed and firm approaches to managing within an organization, other than the benefit of experience. Many companies are a combination of organizational types based around departments and functions — if you wish to explore the matter further, consult the further reading section at the end of this chapter.

The project manager needs to be aware of the political drives and demands of the organization and the inevitable conflicts that arise between departments – for example, maintenance and production. The most important thing, however, is to try and create a project team that can function across the organizational boundaries and thereby achieve its objectives. Once the representatives of your team are 'on board' the project, it is then possible to use the inside track to get around a lack of co-operation and achieve what the project wants.

The final point of call in any organizational conflict is the project sponsors, who may be the company's senior management. But this is somewhat like referring to the terms and conditions of the contract — the initiative has been lost and a solution may need to be imposed.

Managing suppliers

The management of suppliers is a critical part of the success of a project. In many cases, the formal selection and negotiation may be the remit of the purchasing department. But the project manager needs to establish a working relationship for critical purchases during the project.

This relationship needs to be built by the project manager on two levels — technically, so that issues can be discussed, and commercially. One of the cardinal rules is that there must be an opportunity to tackle issues such a cost escalation, programme slippage and poor quality without jeopardizing the technical relationship.

If you act as project manager and technical lead, then it can be difficult to divorce the two requirements — perhaps your purchasing group could handle the commercial areas. On larger projects with a team, nominate yourself as primary point of contact for all correspondence and make sure that it is clearly understood that scope changes can only be authorized by you. Then nominate a discipline engineer to act as primary technical contact. Make sure the limits of authority are understood, and that any changes are communicated to you when they first occur.

Managing the client

Your client — whether an external customer, your manager or another part of your company — is the customer, and the customer is always right. A key part of managing the relationship is to ensure that the client really is right and that the client receives what is actually wanted, which is not necessarily what was asked for. As project manager, you should:

- check that the requirements have been thought through. This should really happen at the project proposal/feasibility stage;
- challenge given information — is it what you need to complete the project? What else is required?
- state what you believe to be the objectives of the project and the priorities, and get them confirmed. A good mutual understanding at this stage will certainly help later;
- remember that priorities and in some cases objectives change during all but the shortest of projects;
- what are the acceptance criteria? Do not assume that just because the operations group works for the same company that it will accept the project. Get the acceptance/handover criteria established at the start of the project, and update them if the objectives change;
- involve the client in the project where feasible. This can be a highly sensitive area, especially on fixed price contracts, but nothing can assure the failure of a project more surely than that the client's first view of the project is when it is finished.

As project manager, try to establish a good working relationship with the client by being as open and honest as possible. This is one area where your technical competence and communication skills come to the front. But remember that no-one likes to be proved wrong in public; this is especially true if you are paying the bill. Be sensitive to people's egos — it will help in establishing the relationship.

Take care when pressurized by client demands. Nothing will undermine your credibility more (especially with your team) than agreeing to unreasonable demands. There are times when a determined position will benefit everyone, including ultimately the client — remember Theodore Roosevelt's comment, 'speak softly and carry a big stick; you will go far'.

Negotiation

The ability to negotiate underpins much of the project manager's success. There are many approaches to negotiation and many texts on the subject (see further reading). There are a number of essential points to think about:

- prepare for a negotiation;
- list what is essential to your side;
- list what is preferable to your side;
- establish the limits of your authority;
- list what is essential to the other side;
- list what is preferable to the other side;
- establish the limits of the other side's authority;

- if you enter a negotiation as a team, who will make decisions and speak from your side? One person must be the decision-maker, and none of the others may make concessions;
- avoid confusing technical understanding with commercial agreement. Saying that something is possible is not the same as agreeing to supply it — get commercial agreements clarified;
- when answering questions, give yourself time to think. Try to avoid giving detailed technical answers in commercial discussions — they only serve to complicate and you may give away more than you intended;
- watch out for 'cherry-picking' — taking the good bits and leaving the rest. How is the offer structured, what will happen if only one part is accepted?
- aim to win-win on the essentials;
- don't crow when you win; you may need a favour tomorrow;
- if you intend to be adversarial, are you prepared for the negotiation to fail?

Further reading

Briner, W., *et al*, 1996, *Project Leadership*, 2nd edition (Gower).

Handy, C., 1985, *Understanding Organisations*, 3rd edition (Penguin).

Karras, C.L., 1974, *Give & Take* (Thomas Y Crowell).

Martin, A.S. and Grover, F. (eds), 1988, *Managing People* (Thomas Telford).

Wilson, D.C. and Rosenfeld, R.H., 1990, *Managing Organisations* (McGraw Hill).

Information management

Peter Iles-Smith

22

This chapter outlines some of the important considerations in communications and project administration. It is not intended as a guide to meetings or letter writing as there are alternative sources of material, one key example of which is cited at the end of this chapter.

Meetings

With meetings, the first question that has to be asked is, 'why bother?'. To many engineers, meetings can be a tedious distraction from work. But communication is crucial to the success of a project, and meetings run by the project manager are one of the main forms of communication.

Types of meeting

Projects generally have four main types of meeting:
- with the client;
- with the team;
- with suppliers;
- with the management.

Although there are similarities in all meetings, the style and goals can be very different and the project manager, who will often chair such meetings, needs to be sensitive to these differences.

Chairing meetings

Well-run, focused meetings can be a major aid to the project manager in ensuring that the customer, team and suppliers are working toward a common goal. Badly-run, loose meetings can be expensive, time consuming and meaningless. Be aware of how much the meeting is costing. Every hour of a meeting with senior members of a project team can cost from £200 to £500. Meetings can be very informative, but make sure you plan and control them.

The key to making the meeting a success is the chairman. Since this will often be you, the project manager, there are some important points to keep in mind:

- make the objective of the meeting clear (for example, 'Progress review for project XYZ', not 'Design discussion on pumping techniques, etc');
- set the agenda before the meeting and let the attendees see it;
- keep the attendees to the minimum necessary (lead discipline engineers, rather than the whole team). If engineers with specialist knowledge are required at some point, call them in rather than have them waiting in the meeting;
- keep the meeting short. If you cannot review the pertinent issues in under one hour, the agenda or the objectives need to be re-examined;
- avoid taking sides. Be fair and even-handed. Meetings are not the place to identify scapegoats or punish offenders;
- read the minutes of the last meeting, *before* the start of the meeting. If information is required, bring it to the meeting;
- take short, contemporaneous minutes during the meeting. If possible do this yourself and have them typed up immediately afterwards;
- ensure that key actions are summarized and responsibilities allocated at the end of the meeting.

BE FAIR AND EVEN-HANDED IN MEETINGS.

Agenda and minutes

Most project meetings follow a similar agenda and it is useful to develop a standard format to make things go as smoothly as possible. The main agenda items should include:

1. Review of actions from last meeting.
Rather than review all the minutes, concentrate on the action points only.

2. Progress from last period.
Compare forecast progress against actual and update any plans.

3. Forecast progress for next period.
What does the current plan show, and what are the implications of any delays? (See 2 above.)

4. Resources.
Identify current resources used and any issues arising (people leaving, utilities required that may not be available).

5. Problems/issues.
Highlight any technical or commercial points that may have an impact on the schedule. *But do not try to solve a technical issue unless it is trivial* — call a separate meeting to discuss the options, review the risks and specify actions.

6. Correspondence.
Highlight any outstanding correspondence that needs to be answered or is contentious.

7. Commercial.
Review change orders, invoicing and any other commercial points outstanding.

8. Review action list.

The preceding agenda items should have generated actions. Make sure everyone agrees and responsibilities for the action items are clear.

The second most important part of a meeting is the minutes; remember, if it isn't written down, it didn't happen. Wherever possible, try to keep the minutes of a meeting concise and meaningful to other people. Long records of discussion are not useful or appropriate in a project meeting — the minutes should record decisions and actions. It is also important to remember that minutes of meetings between customer and supplier are commercially important and may be used to support subsequent disagreements — so if you don't mean it, don't say or record it.

The layout of minutes should follow wherever possible the agenda structure, and each minute should be uniquely numbered; a new item for discussion should create a new minute. Based on the agenda already outlined, a typical minute would be:

5.0 Problems/issues.
      5.1 Late receipt of engineering drawings
           Brief outline of the problem, implications and actions arising
      5.2 Another item

The meeting action item can then be referred to by a combination of meeting date and minute number — for example, 191098/5.1.

It is helpful to record all the actions in summary form at the end of the minutes in the form of a table setting out action number, due date and responsible person. If this is maintained as a 'running' list with action status, it becomes a useful *aide-mémoire* for the project manager.

Correspondence

As a project manager, you are likely to find your working day rapidly filled by project correspondence in all its forms — letter, fax, e-mail and telex. Being clear, accurate and managing this flood of information is an important skill.

Writing letters

In this context, *all* project correspondence should be treated alike. Just because you use e-mail does not mean the same thought and care should not go into a piece of writing as if it were a letter. For the remainder of this section, 'letter' is used interchangeably with other written forms of correspondence.

There are some basic points to keep in mind when writing project correspondence:

- who you are writing to (the client, a supplier, a colleague);
- what the objective of the letter is (asking for a change order, requesting action);
- do you intend to make a commercial statement (for example, varying the delivery date on an order)? This can be difficult to control, but be aware that an innocent comment on a changed delivery date could be construed as acceptance;
- what authority you have. Can you commit your company to a purchase order?

- do not respond in the heat of the moment. There is a view that rapid responses generate errors; this is especially true when bad news or critical comment lands on your desk. Read it, generate some notes and then leave it (possibly overnight) before finishing your response with a more clinical detachment.

Having thought about the basics, write the letter remembering to:
- write clearly and stick to the point;
- read what you have written — does it say what you mean?
- get the addressee's name and title right;
- check your grammar. Many engineers fail to pay attention to simple elements of a letter that, incorrectly done, detract from its content;
- be accurate. Do not make unsubstantiated comment;
- keep confidential material confidential. Do not be tempted to reveal what you do not need to;
- type it, unless you have copperplate handwriting;
- keep a copy and file it in an accessible system;
- ensure the correspondence has a reference number and a date (and that the date is correct — do not just rely on the word processing package);
- add the correct closure ('Yours faithfully', 'Yours sincerely', etc);
- sign it.

There is a school of thought that project correspondence should be addressed formally between companies, for example:

Ref:
Date:

Mr Joe Bloggs
Your Company Ltd
Address

Dear Sirs,

The Subject

The letter content

Yours faithfully,

Carol Brown, Project Manager

A formal structure such as this helps enforce the commercial discipline and separation that is useful to a project manager, though it is not essential.

Managing correspondence

In a later section of this chapter, the use of administration systems is discussed. This subsection is concerned with how you as project manager are to cope with the information flood.

All project correspondence received should be logged and held on file. The project manager then needs to decide on how to handle that information. A useful technique is known as TRAF:

Trash

It is unsafe to throw away any project correspondence. If you continually receive information that is not worth keeping, then tell whoever sends it to stop!

Refer

The document needs to be referred to another for action.

Action

Action is required.

File

Consign to the project files.

Each document that passes across your desk should be 'TRAFfed' as soon as it arrives. Review the document and decide on what category it falls into, then move onto the next document. Do not address each document until you have cleared the complete set.

Once you have completed the initial review and allocation of the correspondence, return to the action items, prioritize and then work through them. The objective of this approach is to cut through the volume of paper and make positive progress. Information overload is the surest way to bring a project to a grinding halt.

Reports

Regular reporting is part of a project manager's job. You will almost certainly be expected to produce a report on the state and trends of the project for the client and for your management. If this is not required, it makes good sense to do it anyway as the discipline of regular report writing ensures you take a regular look at the overall project.

A typical project report need not be long. In fact, exception reporting is likely to reduce the effort required significantly. Typically, the progress report is very similar to the progress meeting agenda:

1. Overview.

A single paragraph highlighting major successes, failures or problems. Here is the proper place to state the completion date and reaffirm overall costs (that is, 'the project remains on schedule and costs within budget').

2. Progress since the last reporting period.

3. Progress planned for the next period.

4. Correspondence outstanding.

5. Problems/issues.

6. Commercial.

One of the best tools to cover a large part of this report is the project plan. Modern planning tools can generate useful progress reports and forecasts — so keep the plan up to date and use it.

One area that any project manager needs to treat sensitively is the inevitable problems/delays or cost overruns. For a supplier in particular, when and how to tell the client can be worrying. It is usually not good practice for the first sign of significant project trouble to be announced (or worse still hidden) within a project report — for no other reason than that the report tends to be widely circulated. On the other hand, the report should be kept honest — otherwise you may become discredited.

Telephones

Telephones are convenient, easy to use and, if you are busy, a nuisance. The project manager needs to allow significant time to handle telephone calls — many of which are unpredictable. Time management courses tend to expound the virtue of scheduling telephone time around your working day. As a project manager you are more likely to schedule your working day around the telephone, so here are a few pointers to simplifying life:

• answer a ringing telephone. Nothing is more irritating to a client than hanging on to a ringing telephone, waiting for someone to answer it;

• give your name and company. Just saying 'hello' is not very helpful;

314

- make sure you know who you are talking to. If the caller is enquiring about your business, get his or her name, company, telephone number and any other details and then pass it on to the relevant person — it could mean business;
- take notes, and keep them;
- avoid making snap decisions during a telephone call. At the very least take down all the details and offer to ring back with an answer;
- if you say you will ring back, do so. This is especially important if you are taking a message for someone else;
- if it isn't written down, then it didn't happen. Confirm in writing all conversations that achieve a decision in writing;
- if a caller is angry and frustrated, try to stay calm. Listen to their point of view and offer to investigate and call back. Remember that one person's point of view may be inaccurate, so do not commit to anything in response to a shouted complaint until you fully understand the problem from all angles;
- if you are busy, politely make it clear and offer to ring back as soon as possible — then do so.

There are a number of other issues depending on the nature of your job, but for a project manager, the key ones are to stay polite, think before you act, keep a record and actually do something if you say you are going to.

Project administration

Chapter 20 covers the major areas that a project information system should consider. This section is concerned with the mechanics of administering the information required in the project.

Project records

Everything produced within a project forms part of the project records and therefore needs to be filed in a manageable way. Most organizations have some form of document filing system for projects, this may range from the simple to the labyrinthine. The principal features are:

- a unique reference number for the project (for example, UK97004);
- a unique document type number or prefix (for example, L02 for letters);
- a unique document number for each item (for example, 001, 002, etc).

The resulting document can then be referenced as, for example, UK97004–L02–001. If the project files are organized along similar lines, then the documents can be filed and retrieved just as easily.

For most projects, it is desirable to have a clerk perform the routine document filing tasks on a regular basis. This frees the (usually more expensive) project team to more productive work.

315

Areas for special consideration and review are:

- purchase orders (your accounts department may need a copy or even the original for the sales/purchase ledger);
- technical drawings and specifications. If these are new or changed they need reviewing and acting upon. There must be only *one* master reference document that the team is using;
- certificates of conformity or material certificates. These will almost certainly be required for document dossiers at the end of the project. Make sure they are filed correctly in the first place;
- bank guarantees. File them so that they can be easily retrieved at the end of the project.

Check what your company rules and the contract say about keeping records. Some (notably offshore) require that suppliers keep the original records for ten years — how will this be achieved? Many companies require commercial paperwork to be kept for up to seven years.

Project administration systems

Any project administration system should meet the following objectives:

- keep information in such a way that it can be retrieved. If you cannot find and recover the information, then you may as well not keep it;
- allow change to be tracked easily. Keep old specifications and summarize changes from one to the next;
- meet the legal requirements of your company;
- meet the requirements of ISO 9001 or a similar quality system;
- meet the regulatory requirements of the industry — for example, nuclear or pharmaceutical;
- be traceable and auditable. If you have developed a process design to the point of mechanical plant, it should be possible to show from the project records what information was used to support the end result. This is desirable in all industries; in some it is essential to getting an operating licence.

Computer-based engineering tools and packages are a major part of the project information generation system. Whilst providing great assistance, they generate some problems of their own:

- if the project documentation is produced by a supplier on an obscure CAD/CAM or word processing package you may not be able to change the documentation to reflect site modifications. The same problem can occur if well-known and very expensive packages are used that you do not have access to. Insist on your standards for documentation;
- version/revision control for electronic documents can be difficult. If you do not use an electronic document management system, then take great care in

ensuring that the electronic version matches the approved paper version — perhaps backup files should be taken at the approval point;

• consider retrieval five or ten years from now. The packages and even the media may not exist — the US space agency NASA experienced problems with 10–15 year old space probe data that could not be read because the tape reading machines were obsolete and no-one was left who understood the old technology.

Computer-based systems are undoubtedly the future for most project engineering activities. A number of initiatives and developments are under way, including PISTEP (common standards for data exchange), workflow systems (for example, Lotus Notes) and electronics signatures that are aimed at streamlining project information flow. It is unlikely, however, that the volume of information and the decisions required will do anything other than increase.

Further reading

Communication Skills for Engineers and Scientists, 2nd edition, 1994 (Institution of Chemical Engineers).

Basics of accountancy and shipping

Peter Iles-Smith

23

As engineers, many of us are reluctant to become involved in the intricacies of business accounts. Project management inevitably increases one's exposure to money and its impact on the business.

This chapter outlines some of the key aspects of accountancy and some of the areas the project manager needs to be aware of.

Accountancy

The profession of accountancy originates in the need to keep a record (literally an account) of financial transactions. As in any other field, there are specific rules governing the way in which these accounts are maintained and reported, many of them having statutory authority. Whilst the new project manager is unlikely to have direct involvement with the company accounts, the project runs on money and the actions of the project manager will have an effect.

Accounts can be divided into two broad categories, financial and management.

Financial accounts are generally those which appear in company reports and must by law be made publicly available. They purport to show the financial standing of the company *at the time they were prepared*. Since they are published, they may show the minimum information to satisfy the law.

Management accounts are usually prepared on a monthly basis and are far more detailed in that they break down the business to its lowest reasonable level. Management accounts are frequently produced on a business unit basis and it is here that the project will have the most visibility.

The structure of accounts

Both management and financial accounts have the same basic structure and comprise a balance sheet and a profit and loss (P&L) account. There are also (in published accounts) statements on the source and application of funds (that is, where the money comes from and where it goes to), but these are less significant in day-to-day business management than the other data.

The balance sheet

The essence of a balance sheet is to match the total assets of a company (what it owns or is owed) against its liabilities (what it owes). The elements of a balance sheet and their significance for a project are outlined below:

- fixed assets are items owned by the company and used in its primary business. For example, the process vessel owned by a manufacturing company is a fixed asset. However, if a process vessel is purchased by a contracting company in the course of a project, the vessel is not a fixed asset of the contractor (because it is not used in the contractor's primary business as a process vessel);
- current assets are items which can be readily converted into cash (or liquidated) — for example, raw materials, short term or trade debtors (customers who owe the company money), cash on hand or at the bank;
- current liabilities are money owed by the company and these include trade creditors (money owed to suppliers), bank loans and so on;
- 'financed by' indicates where the money used in the business originates from — share capital (the owner's money), retained profits.

Profit and loss account

The balance sheet records the assets and liabilities of a company. Whilst this is a useful view of the financial strength and stability of a company, the P&L account is regarded as a more instant view. Before outlining the elements of the P&L, there are two key factors to remember:

- the P&L account is a snapshot in time. It shows the financial performance of the company at a particular moment. It is not a forecasting tool (other than showing known accruals for sales and debts) and it can be manipulated (legally) to present an advantageous view of a company's performance;
- profit or loss is not the same as cash. Usually the profit a company declares goes to two things — dividends to shareholders and retained earnings (shown on the balance sheet). Frequently, the retained earnings are used to fund the business by capital expansion — so the increase in retained earnings is matched by an increase in assets. There is no actual cash left.

The structure of a typical P&L account is shown in Table 23.1 (page 320). It is also important to note that the time at which items are entered on the P&L account do not necessarily coincide with the payment and receipt of cash. For example, sales are usually entered at the point of delivery and invoice — the payment period for the invoice could be up to 120 days. The outstanding invoice becomes a trade debt, but profit can be declared well before the money is received. The obvious result of this approach is that a company can declare significant profits and have no cash, resulting in a cash-flow crisis and subsequent difficulties.

PROFIT AND LOSS IS NOT THE
SAME THING AS CASH.

Table 23.1 Structure of a typical P&L account

Sales	£10,000	
Less cost of sales	£8000	Note (a)
Gross profit	£2000	
Less expenses	£500	Note (b)
Net profit before interest and tax	£1500	
Interest		
Net profit before tax		
Taxation		
Net profit after taxation		
Dividend		
Retained profits for the year		

Notes:
(a) The costs normally only cover the actual, direct costs associated with sale. These
include labour, materials and a proportion of overhead consumed by the activity.
(b) Expenses include all those things not directly associated with the sale.
These include management costs, professional expenses, sales staff, etc.

Impact of the project on the accounts

Disregarding the fact that all projects have the ultimate aim of contributing to the financial well-being of a business, there are some direct effects a project can have.

The need for cash

A project may provide a future benefit, but it needs cash to operate now. If the project is financed by bank loans, then there will be a financing cost that the project manager may not directly see. If the project is late, or promised payments are not received, then the financing costs increase. Companies with extended indebtedness can be restricted in the business they wish to pursue. Ensure that you know how the project is being financed and what are the commercial impacts on the business of changes to payment or schedule.

The need for profit

This is usually something that affects suppliers or contractors more than end-user companies. In any company where the business is the supply of equipment and services, revenue and profit are only realized at the time of delivery or acceptance (the two may not be at the same point).

Whilst the project may have an agreed slippage to accommodate a change, if this pushes delivery over a financial year-end, the company may not find it acceptable. In simple terms, it would mean that the revenue and profit forecast in one year move to the next. The internal pressures on a project manager that this generates should not be underestimated — the failure of a company to deliver on its financial promises can be difficult for all and will inevitably result in significant project management effort being expended on trying to recover the situation.

On rare occasions, the company may need to move revenue and profit out of a good period into the next. The project management effort in manipulating the project to achieve this can be significant.

Investment appraisal and project financing

The initial decision to proceed with any project will have taken into account the benefits and costs. Almost all projects require capital expenditure by the end-user, however, as a way of acquiring, producing or enhancing the fixed assets of a company. This capital expenditure has a knock-on effect through other organizations; this section concentrates on the initial financial decision-making process that results in the original project.

Investment appraisal

The vast majority of projects are initiated to provide future benefits to the company. Usually, those benefits are realized in financial terms in the future — so-called 'payback'.

Investment appraisal techniques attempt to relate expenditure to future benefits in order to assist with the decision-making. There are a number of projects which are initiated to overcome legal, regulatory or environmental problems. Whilst these appear to have no immediate advantage, they do have an effective negative benefit of non-conformance which can be used to support investment decisions. Note that these techniques are a guide, not a precise analytical answer — it is impossible to predict future events well enough to be very confident of the decision. Techniques include:

Payback

The payback method simply estimates when the returns from a project will have paid for the investment. Simply dividing the investment by the operating return yields the payback period. It is an extremely crude technique, however, as it ignores the fact that the timing of receipts and payments affects their value (£100 next year is worth less than £100 now).

Since the technique ignores long-term costs, short payback periods may be chosen despite the fact that other solutions may offer better long-term profitability.

Discounted payback

Discounted payback is an extension of the payback method in which the cash receipts in the future are discounted to yield a more accurate current worth. Apart from this refinement, the same limitations apply as for the simple payback method.

Accounting rate of return

Accounting rate of return compensates for the payback method's cash-only view by calculating a rate of return based on the profit an investment generates measured against the capital.

Care needs to be taken in determining what the profit actually is. It is normal to consider the gross profit before interest and tax — such are the complexities introduced by these last two. But bear in mind that the cost of capital may appear in the interest charges payable and perhaps needs to be included.

In order to use the technique, it is necessary to average the profit, and perhaps the capital employed, over the life of the plant. No account is taken of the value of money over time.

Net present value and internal rate of return

The net present value and internal rate of return techniques are similar in that they consider the current (or net present) value of future returns. For net present value, the approach is:

- calculate the annual net cash flow for the lifetime of the plant;
- select a rate of interest or return;
- discount the annual cash flows at the selected rate and sum them. This gives the net present value (NPV) of the cash flows;
- compare the NPV with the capital employed;
- if the NPV is less than the capital estimate, then the project is probably not viable. If it is higher then the project is probably viable.

The internal rate of return (IRR) technique is similar, though the calculation result is the rate of return required to match the investment exactly (iterative calculation is required to do this, though simple spreadsheet tools exist). If the IRR is below the company's required value (perhaps the current bank rate) then the project is probably not viable.

Note the use of the word 'probably'. Both of these techniques require a significant degree of estimation of future returns and costs. The techniques can therefore only provide guidance and information for investment decisions.

Life cycle costing

All of the techniques defined so far are based on an appraisal of capital against future returns. This results in a decision based solely on the initial project costs and not on the long-term operating costs. Increasingly, the concept of life cycle costing is being used to guide investment decisions.

Life cycle costing models have the disadvantage of being difficult to employ because they need significant consideration of:

- capital cost;
- scheduled and unplanned down-time;
- operating costs;
- spares costs;
- maintenance costs;
- project strategy (risk and reward schemes can affect the future profit stream if they are too biased toward the supplier);
- expected production level and efficiency;
- market prices for the products;
- and others.

This information, combined with NPV costing, can then be used to determine the impact of reliability and down-time on the life cycle costs of the project.

It is unlikely that this sort of detail will be available at the initial project appraisal phase. Life cycle costing is therefore more likely to be applied to assist in decisions on particular technologies or supplier offerings. Typically, the approach can show that higher capital investment in critical areas can yield more reliable operation and longer maintenance intervals and therefore lower life cycle costs. But bear in mind that acceptance of life cycle costs is not general in many organizations and lowest capital cost is frequently the deciding factor.

Project finance

Most companies have four sources of funding for projects — retained earnings (that is, previous profits), issuing new shares, long-term borrowing or short-term borrowing (overdraft).

For all but the largest of investments, the use of retained earnings or short-term borrowing will be the principal choice. The ability of a company to undertake projects is therefore constrained by its profitability and its credit-worthiness — hence the impact that project extensions can have on the accounts.

The value of a capital investment does not appear in the P&L account as an expense. The P&L account does not show investment in this way — only the cost of capital, usually as an interest charge. The capital investment appears in the balance sheet as an increase in assets and liabilities (for the loan).

Such capital-based approaches continue to be dominant for most asset-based businesses — typically end-users and manufacturers. Many organizations are, however, looking at leasing and hire purchase as financing methods for many projects. This has the advantage of removing the need for large loans for capital and replacing it with an expense-based business. The disadvantage is that, for many larger companies, the cost of capital is lower than the interest charges for the lease or hire purchase deal. There has been a significant move to leasing or outsourcing for many non-core (and some core) businesses — for example, catering, computing services and combined heat and power stations.

Getting paid and paying for things

Carrying out a project requires ultimately an exchange of funds to pay for the goods and services. The potential problems of being paid late have been discussed in an earlier part of this chapter. This section outlines the issues that you need to be aware of as project manager.

Payment terms can be confusing. The first and most important thing is to find out what your accounts department uses and expects. Deviating from this will be difficult and require further time and effort to ensure that things happen when you want them to.

324

Typical payment terms that appear on orders are 'nett monthly' or '30 days' or '60 days'. Nett monthly means the invoice will be paid in the month after the receipt of the invoice, not one month after the invoice. 30 days and 60 days mean what they say — the invoice will be paid 30 or 60 days after receipt. Many companies operate on the nett monthly approach and have a set day for invoice payment. If that day is missed, then the payment will slip for a complete month. Do not, therefore, promise payment terms that you cannot deliver, and make sure that any purchase enquiries and orders include details of your payment terms.

Another area of difficulty in payment is ensuring that the milestones for payment are clear, unambiguous and not open to interpretation. So, for example, payment on ex-works delivery should mean just that, not payment on arrival on site or after certain documentation has been received. As project manager you have an influence on issuing an invoice at the appropriate time and for approving payment for purchased goods. There is nothing more stressful than attracting the attention of your credit controller because an invoice is overdue (and the milestone has not been completed) or perhaps even worse your supplier's credit controller because you have neglected to pay an invoice.

For many supplier organizations, the payment of invoices by their customers is a closely monitored ratio — something known usually as the debtors ratio or days sales outstanding. The latter term equates the business turnover to the invoices due and represents it as the average number of days to collect debts. For many businesses 30 to 60 days is good and 60 to 90 days is typical. Values over 90 days are likely to attract the attention of senior management, particularly if they are due to a large unpaid invoice on your project!

Business abroad

In an increasingly global economy, it is highly unlikely that all the project materials, services or even the project will be in one country. For example, pressure vessels from Italy, valves from Hungary, pressure transmitters from Singapore ... for a project in Saudi Arabia.

It may be possible to purchase all the items locally from suppliers' offices in your country, but sometimes it is necessary to purchase, ship, install and pay for equipment abroad.

In conducting business abroad, there are some key areas to consider:

Currency exchange

Operating a project in foreign currencies introduces complexity and can have a significant impact on its viability. For example, a £100,000 project with foreign costs of £65,000 will see those costs rise to £68,000 with just a 5% currency swing; consider the impact of 10–20% currency swings.

The solution is quite simple — wherever possible, use only one (your national) currency. If this is not possible, then nominate the project currency, preferably one that is stable and international. This is why the US dollar tends to be the dominant currency in international business.

Require all your suppliers to quote and deal in your nominated currency — they take the risk — but be aware that if they have any sense they will have priced in the risk or limited the variations in currency. Evaluate the risk and benefit of this approach just as you would for any other project cost.

If you have to deal in a foreign currency, get familiar with your company's policies. Do not agree something with your supplier or client that your financial rules do not allow. Also be aware that a significant number of currencies are unconvertible (that is, they can only be exchanged within the country), are tightly exchange controlled or are extremely volatile. Managing currency in these circumstances is the domain of financial experts, not project managers, so get expert assistance.

Where a project has to deal with more than one currency, it is advisable to convert all foreign currencies at some notional exchange rate (perhaps at the time of order) and fix them for the purposes of cost control. If necessary, record the effect of currency fluctuations outside the normal cost control applied to the project. This will prevent currency fluctuations distorting the true project costs.

Movement of goods

Once you have purchased your goods, it is necessary to move them across national borders. For some parts of the worlds, notably the European Union (EU) and North American Free Trade Area (NAFTA), harmonization of customs rules means that the movement of goods is relatively easy — with correct (and simple) documentation.

Goods coming from outside free trade areas almost always attract duty and may require comprehensive and specialized paperwork. This usually includes a packing list and shipping invoice as well as a certificate of origin which needs to be attested by an official body like the Chamber of Commerce. Key points to bear in mind are:

- has the duty been considered in the costing? (5% is typical, but for some countries and equipment 12% or higher is common);
- the shipping paperwork can only be done when the goods are packed and ready for shipment and may take between one and two weeks. Has this time been allowed for in the project plan?
- what are the customs requirements and who will handle them?

Professional assistance from your organization or a specialist shipping company is almost always worthwhile.

Shipping terms

Within export or import contracts, you will undoubtedly see a number of shipping terms that need to be explained. These terms are standards set by the International Chamber of Commerce and are known as Incoterms (1990).

Ex-works

Cost of goods only at the factory gate.

FCA (free carriage alongside)

Cost of goods and delivery to ship for export — but not loading, shipping or insurance.

FOB (free on board)

Cost of goods, delivery and loading onto ship — but not shipping or insurance.

CIF (cost, insurance and freight)

Cost of goods, freight and insurance to port of discharge — but not duty or final delivery.

DDP (delivered duty paid)

Cost of goods, freight, insurance and duty delivered to a named destination.

Shipping restrictions

There are restrictions on shipping materials that need to be borne in mind. These fall into two categories — hazard related and governmental.

Limitations on shipment of hazardous goods are well documented for bulk chemicals, but remember that they also apply to seemingly innocuous items like touch-up paint or lead-acid batteries — neither of which can be urgently flown anywhere.

Governmental restrictions are much more problematic and it is wise to seek professional advice from within your company or the Department of Trade and Industry (UK) or Department of Commerce (US).

There are a number of companies with which it is virtually impossible to do business. In fact there are criminal sanctions for shipping certain types of equipment or technologies (including design drawings or manuals) to proscribed countries. In many cases these are high technology items, but specific restrictions apply to process plant and equipment that could be used in the production of nuclear, biological or chemical weapons. Make sure you are aware of them.

There are also rules, particularly in the US, regarding boycotts by other countries. As US law treats anyone employed by a US company or using US technology as a US citizen, regardless of location, the scope of such rules is wide. The sanctions can be the removal of the right to use or resell US technology. A further confusion is that within the UK and EU some of the rules are different and, in fact, adherence to US rules may be regarded as a breach of EU rules. If in doubt, ask.

Letters of credit

Many of the criteria for payment and getting paid with foreign business are similar to those previously discussed. There is a major concern, however, with regard to the ability of the country to pay, particularly if the currency is weak. One method used to overcome this is documentary letters of credit.

A letter of credit is a bank instrument which guarantees that an amount of money is lodged with a mutually agreed bank and that this money will be paid on demand with suitable shipping paperwork. The shipping paperwork is normally the shipping invoice and the bill of lading for the ship.

There are two forms of letter of credit — revocable or irrevocable. A revocable letter of credit can be cancelled or amended at any time without the exporter being notified. They are therefore highly undesirable. An irrevocable letter of credit can only be amended or withdrawn if all parties agree. An irrevocable letter of credit can also be 'confirmed' or 'unconfirmed'. If it is 'confirmed' then the bank has added its own undertaking to pay under the terms of the letter. An 'unconfirmed' letter means the bank will not undertake to pay and merely notes the letter.

To conduct business safely an irrevocable, confirmed letter of credit is required. Without this, the letter of credit may not be honoured.

Bank guarantees and retentions

A retention is where a proportion of the contract price — usually 5–10% — is invoiced to the customer, but the payment only becomes outstanding at a later date, usually the end of a warranty period. A bank guarantee is where money is received, but a guarantee is made available for a specified amount, usually 10%, with the guarantee period being equivalent to the warranty period (see also Chapter 18).

There are other forms of guarantee — performance and advance payment — which are similar in format but serve different purposes. The performance guarantee is usually provided at the start of the project and can be drawn upon in the event that the supplier breaches the contract. The advance payment guarantee is intended to cover the issue of stage payments made before the goods are received.

Form of words

Most organizations have a standard form of words for a bank guarantee, and it makes little sense to invent a new form. In many cases, the bank needs to approve the format before issuing. The major points to be aware of are:

● the guarantee is available for a specific reason and is 'on demand'. This means that the guarantee can be called by the holder without notification;

● the guarantee is limited in value and duration. A statement needs to be included on the expiry of the guarantee, because things like this tend to go missing after the project is complete;

● the guarantee is constituted under your local law (for example, English).

Costs

Banks charge for setting up a guarantee (typically £250) and then charge a percentage, typically 1–2% per annum. It also needs to be understood that guarantees are a company liability and you may have limits on the value available to guarantee.

Finally, although guarantees have expiry dates, the bank will continue to charge until they are returned.

Further reading

Barnes, N.M.L., 1990, *Financial Control* (Thomas Telford Publishing).

Brennan, D., 1997, *Process Industry Economics* (Institution of Chemical Engineers).

Dyson, J.R., 1994, *Accounting for Non-accounting Students*, 3rd edition (Pitman Publishing).

Value engineering

Peter Iles-Smith and Peter Gulliver

24

Getting good value for money is something close to all our hearts; we apply it to most of our everyday purchases. For a project, value can be critical, as cost is one of the trinity of factors the project manager must control (the others are time and quality). Delivering value for that cost may be the true measure of project success.

This chapter outlines two formal approaches to the problem of gaining value. Although from different bases, both approaches have the same aim — to identify the minimum cost to deliver the quality and performance required.

Design to cost

Design to cost approaches the problem from the perspective of designing for low element cost. The technique is almost as old as modern manufacturing and is prevalent in the consumer goods industries. It is becoming more important, so much so that the US Department of Defense requires the application of such principles to major development projects.

Design to cost is essentially a management philosophy that aims (in the process industries) to focus on the total project costs, perhaps including operating and decommissioning costs. It is an important part of the design to cost concept that cost is given equal weight with schedule and performance on the project: cost should not be automatically sacrificed to recover schedule slippage or achieve a performance target. For example, a desirable (but not essential) feature may be lost to recover a programme slip and maintain the costs. Such an approach can be difficult for many engineers who instinctively want to provide the best solution.

If a formal design to cost approach is adopted on a project, then it is the project manager's responsibility to meet the cost target (this is different from controlling costs). It is therefore incumbent on the project manager to ensure that:

- a cost plan is developed within the project plan;
- actions and responsibilities for cost targets are clearly defined;

- a design to cost review and reporting procedure is defined;
- the design to cost target cannot be easily breached for expediency.

Figure 24.1 outlines the methodology.

The process of design to cost has at its centre the idea that costs are largely designed into, or out of, a project. It follows therefore that design engineers have the most influence and responsibility for achieving the design to cost target. The process is iterative and to some extent continuous. Changing requirements during the process life will need the same attention to detail as the initial design.

Once the cost goal is set for the individual sub-targets, the overall project target cost can be reassessed. Reporting and monitoring mechanisms are most important with the design to cost approach. Each item should be monitored at regular cost review meetings and a design to cost status report produced (Figure 24.2, page 332), used to record changes.

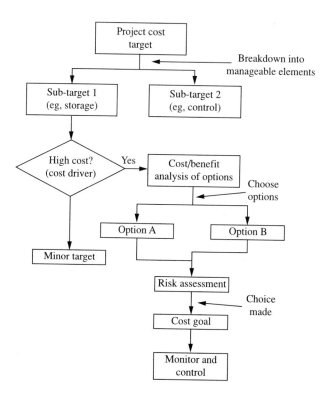

Figure 24.1 Design to cost methodology

Project:				Date:
Project manager:				
Item	Target	Current estimate	Variance	Remarks

Figure 24.2 Sample design to cost report form

Value engineering

Design to cost is concerned with ensuring that the individual elements of a project are designed with the minimum cost. Value engineering is a discipline concerned with ensuring that the value obtained from the constituent items is maximized. Perhaps the biggest distinction between the approaches is that design to cost works on the basis that features of the project can be traded to maintain cost constraints decided at the start of the project.

Originally developed by General Electric in the USA, value engineering is a process for the systematic and disciplined analysis of a product or service to determine the optimum performance at the lowest cost. This definition encompasses a wide range of activities and immediately raises a host of questions which need to be addressed before a potential user can successfully apply this most exciting technique. This section is intended to help you achieve that first success.

Value for money

The concept of 'value for money' is widely applied in day-to-day life. Many purchases are made by the application of this process, albeit often no more profoundly than picking up the article in question, assessing its usefulness, suitability and cost and deciding on the spot either to buy or not. This apparently simple analysis contains all the ingredients of value engineering:

Fit for purpose

As the customer, and with knowledge of the application, you have assessed whether the article will perform in the desired manner.

Reliability

Based on your experience, you have gauged whether or not the article will be able to sustain its performance over the anticipated life span.

Cost

Finally, you have balanced these factors in relation to the cost of the article and the cost of similar competing devices. This assessment will also include the test of, 'Can I afford it?'.

In this analogy, you made all of these judgements based on your experience and knowledge. This is an imperfect process and can lead to disappointment later — a feeling we have all experienced at various times.

We can all relate to the pitfalls associated with even the most simple of purchases. It is therefore not difficult to imagine how much more complicated the decision-making process becomes when the article in question is a process plant.

You are now faced with the expenditure of substantial sums of money, the deployment of many disparate groups of people, and a process which rapidly seems to gain a relentless momentum of its own. Decisions are often made in haste by individuals ill equipped to make them.

Value engineering is aimed at just this situation, and its application is intended to minimize the potential damage both in cost and time which can so easily result from the inevitable pressures a project generates.

Value engineering in project execution

A project is from start to finish a continuous process of making decisions. The project manager is a key element in this process and is required to make, or be responsible for, many of the important decisions which will determine the success or otherwise of the project.

It is impractical to review every decision critically. The first task of the project manager is to identify the key project events where a value engineering session would be most effective. If the session is held too early in the project event cycle then insufficient technical and cost information will be available to review. If the session is too late, then the implementation of any improvements identified will be costly in rework and changes.

Timing is therefore important. A typical programme of value engineering for a project might include the following sessions:

Conceptual design phase

This session critically reviews the basis of design, process configuration and process performance. The cost implications of any changes are based on preliminary budget costs only.

Feasibility study

By this time, the process definition is broadly in place and the project team is moving into the engineering development phase. This session could consider a review of such items as:

- site selection;
- preliminary engineering flowsheets;
- equipment specifications.

Detailed engineering

The project is now well defined. A site has been selected and all the major process decisions have been made. This session focuses on the details of plant layout, engineering specifications and standards, equipment specifications and vendor options and alternatives.

This list is not exhaustive. In practice, many project activities can benefit from value engineering and the decision to implement a session is very much at the discretion of the project manager.

Value engineering – composition of the team

An effective decision-making process requires:

- an assembly of as much information as possible, both technical and commercial;
- a process to review this information critically;
- a decision on the preferred option.

The composition of the team to carry out this process is critical and the project manager will need representatives of each of the key elements involved in the final decision. Thus, in the session during the conceptual design phase, the team could include:

Project manager

As custodian of the project, the project manager is responsible for the implementation of any decisions taken by the team, and ensures that these decisions are consistent with the project's objectives.

Process engineer

The process engineer contributes knowledge of the process options and alternatives.

Sales and marketing manager

Any decisions affecting the process yield or product specifications may require a sales or marketing input.

Research manager

The value engineering process may well consider novel or unproven process steps. The research manager will be able to assess any inherent risks in these options.

Cost estimator

The estimator has a unique role in value engineering. Cost is important in the decision-making process. The cost implications of all options must be estimated and any decision that does not include a cost implication is fundamentally flawed. The costs need not be accurate as the process is seeking comparative costs. It is important that costs are consistent across the alternatives under consideration.

For the smaller project, much of the information-gathering and analysis will fall to the project manager rather than a team. Expert input in terms of the feasibility of alternatives is still very important, particularly in providing challenges to assumptions made during the value engineering process.

Value engineering – organization of the session

The project manager has now fixed the timing of the session and the composition of the team. The final ingredient is the organization of the session. Opinions differ on the length of the session but, bearing in mind the need to evaluate the cost implications of alternatives, it is unlikely that a session will be less than two or three working days.

The first concern is the assembly of an information package. The team requires this in advance of the session; the package should include both technical and cost/commercial information.

The information package for the session held during the conceptual design phase could include:

- process flow diagrams (these could be in block form);
- preliminary basis of design, including feed and product flows and compositions;

- preliminary utility consumption data;
- initial heat and material balances;
- budget costs, including an identification of the key cost items;
- a statement of the project guidelines;
- an agenda for the session.

Armed with the information package, the team assembles at the designated location and the project manager opens the session with a statement defining the purpose of the meeting. This statement sets the objective of the meeting and provides a reference point for the subsequent discussions.

The purpose of the value engineering sessions is to review critically the data available and to look at options and alternatives using the combined knowledge and experience of the team. To achieve this purpose it is essential that the discussions are structured and that all ideas and suggestions are recorded. Brainstorming techniques are frequently employed, with the facilitator recording all the ideas for subsequent analysis. The session should be directed towards the identification of one or two alternatives for subsequent technical/cost evaluation.

The cost implication of the short-listed options should be evaluated outside the meeting and preferably within the time frame of the session. Again, costs need not be accurate.

The final session includes a review of the cost/benefits of the options and concludes with a clear instruction to the project manager and the project team to make any changes to the project specifications.

Conclusion

Value engineering is an established practice in the processing industries and it is widely used by both operators and contractors. It has the unique feature of putting together the important players in the project to review and agree the way ahead collectively. It is commonplace for sessions to record significant cost savings and/or process improvements with wide-ranging implications for the benefit of the project.

Summary

There are a number of important things to keep in mind regarding the value engineering process.

Value engineering is not cost-cutting. The intent is to provide the same functional value at a lower purchase price (a car for the price of a bike).

Value engineering needs team and management commitment. If management and members of the project team are not committed, then apathy sets in and ultimately the exercise will be seen as cost-cutting and undermining the efforts of the design team.

Time spent on value engineering should be kept in proportion. Typically for a £100,000 project the value engineering exercise will require a team of 2–4 people meeting once or twice (for half a day) to establish the best value direction.

Finally, a number of initiatives have appeared in recent years associated with either cost reduction or adding value. Perhaps the best known of these is CRINE (Cost Reduction Initiative for the New Era) undertaken for the UK Continental Shelf oil and gas industry.

CRINE was established to meet the challenge of increasingly marginal fields in ever more difficult locations. Broadly speaking, the CRINE recommendations fit very well into many projects. The key ones are:

- use standard equipment — do not reinvent the wheel or design specials;
- use functional specifications — state what is required, not how it should be achieved;
- use criticality analysis to determine documentation requirements — if it is of no use, don't ask for it;
- simplify and clarify contract language and eliminate adversarial clauses;
- rationalize industry regulations;
- raise the credibility of quality accreditation.

Interestingly, one of the key issues identified during the CRINE study was the entrenched North Sea culture. A challenge for any project manager is to apply value analysis in spite of resistance to change!

Further reading

Creating Value in Engineering Projects, 1996 (Thomas Telford Publications).

Different projects

Peter Iles-Smith

25

It is a truism that all projects are unique and therefore different. Some are, however, more different than others. This is particularly the case when either the project deliverables or the way of working are different to those 'normally' experienced.

This chapter outlines some of those differences, and the areas that the new project manager should be aware of.

Fast-track projects

Any project is a balance between time, cost and quality. In an ideal world, there is a sufficiency of the first two elements to ensure that the third is adequate. When the balance is distorted, frequently by a constraint on the available time, the challenge for project management increases.

Time versus cost is more broadly described as 'economy versus urgency'. It is usually possible to accelerate a project by spending more money, up to a limit. Finding the right balance involves consideration of issues outside the project. These include:

• time to market. Is there an economic advantage to achieving completion as quickly as possible? Very often, new products in the pharmaceutical and consumer industries can generate significant revenue if they are introduced to market quickly;

• emergency. Replacement of damaged or failed equipment, the failure of which is costing money in, for example, lost production;

• operational windows. Weather, production shutdowns and seasonal business demand (for example, in the sugar industry) can dictate the project time-scale.

Managing a project where the time-scale is shorter than the norm can present a greater project management challenge:

• change can threaten the whole project rather than just one small part of it. Controlling change is therefore much more significant;

- measuring and monitoring progress are significant challenges. Any slippage may be virtually impossible to recover. Good objective criteria for progress measurement are important;
- team co-operation is essential. Pressures on individuals on a short time-scale project may be great and if the team relationship breaks down progress can be affected;
- quality can suffer. The balance is not simply time versus cost, but also includes quality. Quality may be sacrificed unintentionally in the pursuit of completion on time.

Brownfield projects

Brownfield projects vary in that they are replacements of existing plant or the site was previously used for other purposes. What they all have in common is that they may require demolition and cleaning work, with the associated risks and demands, and care has to be taken that the demolition work does not affect other facilities.

If the site has been abandoned for some time, the initial planning and budgeting of the new project should include extra allowances in case data on previous uses, chemicals and other hazards is unavailable or unreliable.

Projects to reuse abandoned industrial land can attract public grants for decontamination and other preparatory work, but the grant may then tie the project to following its proposed plan precisely.

Shutdown projects

Projects to shut down major production units and systems for maintenance and improvements are amongst the largest and most critical projects on operating sites.

Speed of work is usually the priority during a shutdown in order to minimize loss of production, but the control of quality is also important because any resulting defect could require another shutdown. Shutdown projects are therefore usually 'fast track' but planned and managed by a dedicated team representing operations, maintenance, project engineering, quality assurance, environmental protection, employees, corporate objectives and any other stakeholders.

For speed, safety and accuracy of communications, the client should employ most (if not all) designers, vendors and contractors directly, rather than in a supply chain of employing them through a main contractor. Project specific partnering (see Chapter 16) can be suitable to create the team needed. Whatever the mix of employing internal and external resources, communications should be systematic to avoid errors and having to change faulty actions.

Design changes during a shutdown should be limited to those found essential in opening up the system, to avoid ill-thought, unplanned and potentially hazardous proposals.

A shutdown of part of an operating site can be a proper opportunity for access to other systems, units and services to carry out maintenance and improvement work on them, but the extent of this needs to be planned in detail because it can create many parallel critical paths and be taken as an opportunity for other work which is not financially justified. 'Opportunity' work added to a major shutdown can also overload technical, safety, management and other resources.

Redfield projects

Some fast-track projects include on-line work to alter operating plant. They are classified as 'redfield' projects. They need dedicated permits-to-work to control access. They also need unified management, as once started they must be finished and throughout controlled to meet operational demands and safety risks.

Demolition work

All demolition work in the UK, however small scale, is subject to the Construction (Design and Management) Regulations 1994 (see Chapter 11).

The disposal of materials can be difficult, costly and subject to statutory approvals. In old buildings and sites the amounts of toxic, valuable or reusable materials are uncertain.

All proposed methods of demolition should be subject to hazard analysis because, apart from safety questions, a failure in method that results in partial demolition can be very expensive to complete.

Software projects

Software projects are unique in many ways because the deliverables can be hard to determine and the project progress almost impossible to measure. Unlike a construction project, the progress of a software project cannot be measured simply by lines of code written or similar criteria. Some of the most significant disasters in software projects have not come to light until the point of final testing or even commissioning.

For the project manager involved in a software project (including those in the traditional IT arena, but increasingly process control system projects), a clearly structured methodology is required to ensure control. This is frequently known as the software life cycle (see Figure 25.1, page 342). Within this life cycle, a number of important points need to be borne in mind:

• there needs to be a clear statement of requirements for the project, usually known as a user requirements specification (URS). This dictates what is required, but not how it should be achieved. Without a clear URS, a project will fail to meet time, cost or quality criteria;

• avoid requirement creep. Once a specification is agreed, freeze it unless there are good, quantifiable reasons to change;

• the supplier should produce a functional design specification (FDS) defining how the requirements are to be achieved and clearly stating the limitations. This document does not replace the USR, but is an interpretation of it for a specific solution;

• test specifications need to be written stating how the requirements in the URS (*not* the FDS) are to be met. Testing must be as realistic as possible and as exhaustive as practical. Figure 25.2 (page 343) shows the specification/test relationship;

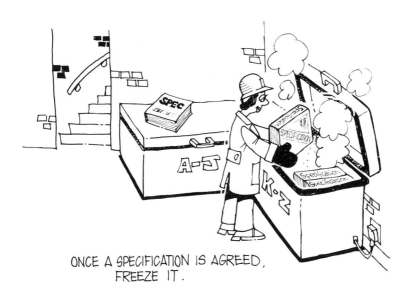

ONCE A SPECIFICATION IS AGREED,
FREEZE IT.

- project implementation needs to be modular, with milestone objectives being met as modules are completed and tested. This avoids the experience of being 80% of the way through the project before it becomes apparent that only 20% progress has been made;
- insist on prototypes so that the actual implementation can be studied prior to committing major development funds;
- involve the actual users in review of specifications and prototypes. Getting 'buy-in' at an early stage helps at the acceptance stage;
- software engineers tend to be optimistic in their assessment of progress and work to complete. Objective criteria based on completion of measurable activities (which should be of relatively short duration) need to be in place;
- no complex piece of software will be free from defects. Testing should eliminate the critical defects, but cannot simulate all the permutations of live use. Ensure that maintenance is available to correct defects rapidly when they are revealed.

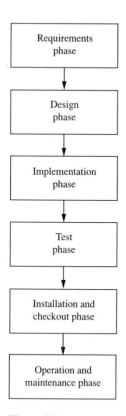

Figure 25.1 Software life cycle

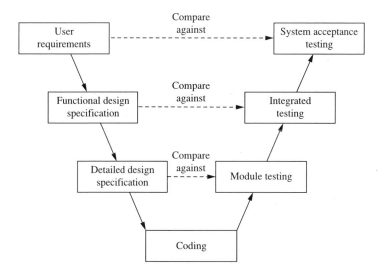

Figure 25.2 Software development framework

EPIC projects

Engineer-procure-install-commission (EPIC), often known as EPC or fixed price lump-sum-turn-key (LSTK) projects are those where an engineering contractor or supplier organization is given the job of providing a complete solution and meeting specific performance criteria for a fixed price. The vast majority of large chemical engineering construction projects throughout the world are EPIC projects.

For the end-user companies, the major advantage of this approach is the limitation of risk. Provided the scope of work is well defined, the EPIC contractor has to deliver a solution for a fixed price; there are usually penalties associated with the performance criteria. Management of the EPIC contractor is therefore reduced and the end-user's engineering team relegated to the role of monitoring.

There are disadvantages to this approach, however, particularly for the project manager. These can be summarized as:
- the need to define the requirements adequately;
- loss of 'control' over the offered solution. Since the contract scope is fixed, any attempt to influence the specification by the end-user tends to result in claims for variation;
- limited ability to influence key items of supply. If the specification is too detailed, then the purpose of the EPIC contract is lost.

For the contractor companies, the major disadvantage tends to be in managing the project within tight constraints and controlling variations. A key challenge is what approach to take to the end-user (customer) engineers. Trying to include those engineers in the contractor team can result in increased costs on the project, without any formal change order to accompany it.

Validated projects

Pharmaceutical companies wishing to market a product in either domestic or foreign markets must apply for a licence from a regulatory authority — for example, the US Food and Drugs Administration (FDA) or the UK Medicines Control Agency (MCA). Part of the approval process for receiving a licence is proving that the process follows current Good Manufacturing Practice (cGMP). This approval process is frequently known as validation.

Validation is a simple concept that can appear difficult and costly to apply, particularly when the technology is new or unfamiliar. The essential elements of validation are:

- decide what you intend to do and document it;
- implement what you decided to do, documenting any deviations;
- test what you implemented to show it does what you intended;
- document the results.

These elements are part of any good quality system, though the existence of a quality system does not mean that a process can be validated.

The overall responsibility for the validation of the process lies with the end-user who is accountable to the regulatory authorities. Equipment vendors are not responsible for cGMP compliance, but can only assist the end-user to achieve validation compliance.

As is common with many industries, pharmaceutical validation has developed special terminology to describe the validation process and project life cycle. The key elements and the way in which the project and validation process fit together are shown in Figure 25.3.

Joint ventures, consortia and alliance projects

Joint ventures (JVs) are an increasingly popular way of promoting and executing large projects, but not the only or most common way. JVs vary greatly in their form and legal status, but all of them are systems for co-operation as distinct from amalgamation to form one company. They are selective in that the partner companies continue with other business activities independently, sometimes in competition.

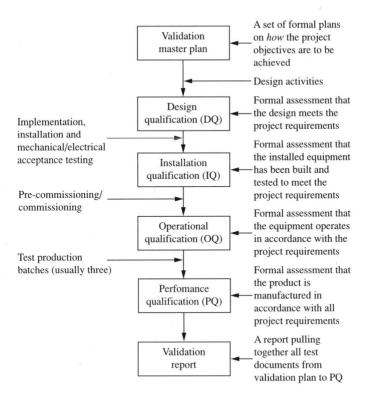

Figure 25.3 The validation process

JVs are subject to the normal risks of any organization — for instance, the risks of buying and selling. As mentioned in Chapter 14, JVs have some special risks, but most of the risks and problems are predictable and can be avoided or controlled by forethought. All but minor and brief JVs between experienced partners require formal attention at the outset to the organization and management of the JV itself. A horizontal collaboration can be simple to operate if the partners have similar expertise and interests and can divide the work into independent packages. Parallel operation of their normal systems of organization can then be effective in achieving sufficient linking of decisions during the project. To achieve consistency, a single channel of communications with a customer is always better for all parties, but control of the partners' operations need not be centralized unless some resource has to be shared between them.

Vertical or more complicated collaboration may require formal linking and overlapping of the partners' systems of organization, not necessarily on a large scale, but starting before commitment to a project so that joint decisions are possible in a way unusual in their normal work. A legally unincorporated JV can be adequate for this if all partners are familiar with the system. If not, incorporation may be needed, or the JV replaced by one partner taking control and the others working for it as subcontractors.

Research and development projects

Research is the process of searching for ideas for a solution to a problem or market demand. Development is the process of taking a solution to a commercially viable product. Both of these projects (or phases of a project) have a great deal in common with engineering projects. Briefly, they contain:

- a requirement or demand (a better mousetrap or a new drug therapy);
- defined start and end points (possibly with many years between them);
- a budget (£500 or £5 billion);
- a need for resources, including people;
- a uniqueness (the search for a solution is unique).

Research and development (R&D) projects also need to be planned carefully, have specifications and identifiable deliverables — even if those deliverables are negative results of the research.

Perhaps the most significant difference between R&D projects and most engineering projects is that although the demand or requirement may exist, the mechanism to find the solution may not. The project process therefore tends to be heavily concentrated on the initiation, requirements and detail specification stages. Perhaps some ideas need to be explored before the specification can be progressed. Looked at in this light, research projects can be broken down into parts as much as any other project and managed using the same techniques.

The most likely problems to be faced are in failure of the research to achieve its desired end. This is not the same as failure of the project itself, and by tackling the research project with the same rigour as a capital engineering project, the project manager's goal is to avoid wasted effort as early as possible.

Further reading

Briggs, M., Buck, S. and Smith, M. (eds), 1997, *Decommissioning, Mothballing and Revamping* (Institution of Chemical Engineers).

Decommissioning and Demolition — Third International Conference on Decommissioning Offshore, Onshore, Demolition and Nuclear Works, Manchester, 1992 (Thomas Telford Publications).

Hartman, F., 1996, A positive revolution in software development, *Proceedings, Seminar/Symposium, Boston* (Project Management Institute).

Jones, D., McQuitty, N. and Thompson, P.A., 1992, Timber yard: a collaborative initiation leads to a successful environment project, *International Journal of Project Management*, 10 (3): 171–174.

Wearne, S.H. and Wright, D., 1996, Organizational risks of joint ventures, consortia and alliance partnerships, *International Journal of Project and Business Risk Management*, 2 (1): 45–58.

Glossary

Terms and phrases used in project management may have a clear meaning to their users but may have unknown or even different meaning to others. This glossary attempts to explain many of them, but if someone uses a phrase which is new or ambiguous (as always in good project management), seek clarification.

ACTIVE
Achieving Competitiveness Through Innovation and Value Engineering (sponsored by the UK onshore oil, gas, process and energy industries and the Department of Trade and Industry).

Activities
Identifiable items of work for a project.

ACWP
Actual cost of work performed to date.

Adhesive or adherent terms of contract
The party proposing them does not intend to consider any alternative terms.

Admeasurement
Apportioning of quantities or costs. See also 'Remeasurement'.

Alliance
Co-operative management by client and contractor of the work to be done in a contract, based upon a formal agreement to share the benefits and dis-benefits ('win-win'), also sometimes including one or more major subcontractors. See also 'Joint venture' and 'Partnering'.

Anticipated final cost (AFC)
A prediction of the final cost of a project.

Approvals or Approved for construction
Submission of the contractor's design, construction programme or other information to the client or his representative for 'approval', but the approval not usually relieving the contractor of liability for the satisfactory performance of the contract.

Award of a contract
Announcement by a client that a tender has been accepted.

Back-to-back terms of contract
Terms of a contract matching those of another contract, particularly the terms of a subcontract matching those of the main contract.

Base date
If contract price adjustment is a term of a contract, a date stated in the invitation for bids for the tender prices to be based upon the costs of the relevant labour and materials on that date.

BATNEEC
Best Available Techniques Not Entailing Excessive Cost.

Battery limits
The boundary at which a project meets existing plant, services, utilities and so on.

Battle of the forms
A process of offer, counter-offer, counter-offer, etc of proposals for the terms of a contract, often consisting of exchanges of printed forms which have conditions of contract or terms of sale printed on their reverse side.

BCWP
Budgeted cost of work performed.

BCWS
Budgeted cost of work scheduled.

BDEP
Basic design and engineering package.

Bid
= 'Tender'

Bill of materials (BoM)

List of the types and quantities of materials the designers expect will be required in construction.

Bill of quantities (BoQ)

List of the expected quantities of items of work to be done by a contractor with prices ('rates') per unit quantity of each item.

BoD

Basis of design. A document which describes the purpose and nature of a proposed project.

Boiler plate terms

See 'Adhesive or adherent terms of contract'.

Bond

Undertaking by an insurance company or other third party to recompense a party to a contract for a specified fault by the other party. See also 'Guarantee'.

Bought-in packaged equipment

Complete unit of equipment supplied by a vendor — for example, a materials handling unit.

BPEO

Best Practicable Environmental Option.

Breach of contract

See 'Conditions of contract'.

Brownfield site

Area containing operating or abandoned systems, structures or materials, and perhaps requiring their revamping, adaptation, treatment or removal. Design, site layout and access are therefore restricted. See also 'Greenfield site' and 'Redfield site'.

Ceiling price

Upper limit to the amount to be paid. See also 'Guaranteed maximum price contract'.

Change

Change from the project scope originally agreed between the client and contractor which occurs during design development, construction or commissioning. See also 'Variation order'.

CIF

Carriage, insurance and freight. A shipping term.

Claim

Demand or request, usually for extra payment and/or time by a supplier from a client, or by a subcontractor from a contractor. In most building and civil engineering in the UK a 'claim' is assertion of a right in a contract, but in others it is the opposite, a request outside the terms of the contract.

Client

The company which will own and/or operate the plant at the end of the project.

Commissioning

Preparation and start-up of a new or modified project. See also 'Mechanical completion' and 'Pre-commissioning'.

Commissioning manager

Person responsible for planning and directing the commissioning of a project.

Completion of equipment

Technical readiness for testing or commissioning. Handover may be another stage in a contract.

Compliant

A tender meets or is required to meet all the terms of an invitation to tender.

Conceptual engineering

Design work to study possible schemes and options for a project. Some people use the phrase to mean design to provide the basis for a feasibility study. Others use it to mean the next stage of design.

Conditions of contract

See also 'Model conditions of contract'. In English law 'conditions' means all the terms of a contract which are fundamental to the intentions of the parties, so that failure to comply with a condition is a serious breach of contract, but in engineering and other industries in the UK documents often called 'conditions of contract' are sets of general and commercial terms comprising conditions and warranties.

Consideration
In English contracts 'valuable consideration' means payment.

Consortium
Contractual collaboration or formation of a joint subsidiary by two or more organizations, usually for one project, sometimes for a series of projects. See also 'Joint venture'.

Construction management
Used with a special meaning in the USA and the UK to mean the employment by a client of a construction contractor to help plan, define and co-ordinate design and construction and to supervise construction.

Construction (Design and Management) Regulations (CDM)
UK legislation designed to ensure that the safety hazards of construction and demolition activities are considered from the start of design and through to the completion of the work.

Consultants
Advisers on projects, design, management, techniques and technical or other problems.

Contract
Agreement enforceable at law.

Contractor
See also 'Vendor'. Supplier of goods or services (including design or management services) to a client. 'The contractor' means a party to a contract, as distinct from any contractor. The word 'the' is important in English practice as identifying the particular contractor. In some other countries where the English language is used in contracts the practice is to write 'Contractor' or <CONTRACTOR>. The contractor may be a consortium or a joint venture of two or more companies.

Contract price
Amount to be paid to a contractor for performance, as distinct from what the work costs the contractor.

Contract price adjustment or fluctuation (CPA)
Payment to a contractor for changes in national costs of materials or labour.

Cost
See 'Contract price'.

Cost estimate
Estimate of the cost to carry out a certain piece of work or to provide a service.

CRINE
Cost Reduction Initiative for the New Era (sponsored by the UK Offshore Operators' Association).

Critical activity
An activity for a project in the sequence of activities (the critical path) which governs the total time expected to be required for a project.

Damages
Compensation for loss. See also 'Liquidated damages terms'.

Dayworks
Work done by a contractor as instructed and to be paid for by the client on the basis of rates for the resources used — for instance, labour per hour. This is a particular form of reimbursable terms of payment.

Defects correction period
Period for a contractor to remedy defects after handing over a project. Also known as the 'Maintenance period'.

Deliverables
The intended products from work — for instance, a pump from a vendor, or the complete project.

Design house
Contractor or consulting engineer employed to supply design services and design management.

Detailed design
Production of the drawings, specifications and other information needed for the procurement of equipment and services, demolition and site preparation, construction, testing, commissioning and plant operation and maintenance.

Determination of a contract

Termination by completion of all obligations, or by agreement, frustration or breach.

Deviation

Used by process industry contractors to mean a change to the quantity, nature or timing of work for a client. See also 'Variation'.

Direct contract

Contract between a client and a contractor, as distinct from a subcontract.

Direct labour

Own employees employed on construction, sometimes under the internal equivalent of a contract, otherwise as a service department.

Direct works

Construction by direct labour.

Domestic subcontractor

Subcontractor selected by a main contractor — that is, not nominated by the client.

Earned value

Value of work completed at any time during the progress of a project (usually compared with the value of the work which it was planned should have been completed by that time).

EFC

Estimated final cost.

The Engineer to a contract

Person nominated the role of 'the Engineer' as specified in the contract, usually as the channel of communications between client and contractor. In some countries use of the title 'engineer' is controlled by law.

Engineering

The work of designing a project, specifying all procurement, and planning construction, installation, testing and commissioning.

Engineering definition or Engineering specification
Documents detailing the technical requirements for a proposed project. It is typically produced to form the basis for estimating project cost sufficiently accurately for submitting the proposal for sanction.

Engineering level
Percentage available of the final engineering information required for a project.

Enquiry
Invitation for tenders.

EPCI
Engineer-procure-construct-install contract,
or
European Institute of Advanced Project and Contract Management.

EPIC
Engineer-procure-install-commission contract. See also 'Turnkey contract'.

Equipment
The process and control items required to form a production unit.

Escalation
Changes in contract price due to inflation — that is, rises or falls in national or regional wage rates or materials costs,
and/or
Changes in the contract price due to variations or claims.

Estimate
Calculation of the cost, resources or time required for the part or whole of a project.

Estimate grade or tolerance
Accuracy of an estimate.

ETC
Estimated/expected time of completion.

Excepted risks
Events which may entitle a contractor or subcontractor to extra time or payment.

Express terms
Written terms in a contract — that is, expressed, not implied.

Facility
The completed structure or system resulting from a project.

Fast tra(c)k
Not a precise phrase, but usually meaning design and construction of a project faster than at minimum capital cost.

Feasibility study
Engineering, estimating, marketing and other work carried out on a proposed project or alternatives to provide the basis for deciding whether to proceed.

Firm price
Varies in its meaning, but is often used to indicate that a tendered price is offered only for a stated period and is not a commitment if it is not accepted within that period.

Fixed price
Usually means that a tender price will not be subject to escalation, but it may mean that there is no variations term. Like other words used in contract management, 'fixed price' has no fixed meaning. What matters in a contract are the terms of payment in that contract.

Flow sheet
Drawing showing the main plant items, instruments and controls, and the flow rate, pressure, temperature and so on of each of the process streams or batches.

Force majeure
Overwhelming event beyond the control of the parties to a contract, such as war.

Forms of contract
In the UK 'forms of contract' is used to mean model forms of agreement and performance bond published with sets of general conditions of contract.

Frame agreement
Agreement between two or more companies stating the terms for an 'Alliance' or 'Partnering'.

Free issue
Materials purchased by a client and issued to a contractor to use in constructing a project.

FEED
Front end engineering design.

FEEP
Front end engineering package. Another term for 'Engineering definition'.

Functional engineer
Engineer employed in a specialist engineering discipline — for example, control engineering or civil engineering.

Gantt chart
Method of representing a programme using horizontal bars to represent activity time-scales.

General conditions of contract
See 'Model conditions of contract'.

General contractor
= 'Main contractor'

Greenfield site
Area free of previous construction and which can be temporarily handed over to a new project. Design and site layout can therefore be optimized to meet the objectives of the project. See also 'Brownfield site' and 'Redfield site'

Guarantee
In finance a guarantee means an undertaking by a bank or other third party to recompense a party to a contract for a specified fault by the other party,
or
In engineering a guarantee can mean a warranty from a seller to a customer for the performance and safety of a design, system, equipment or similar.
See also 'Bond'.

Guaranteed maximum price contract
Contract which combines the firm price and target principles such that the client and the contractor share savings but the contractor alone meets all costs incurred above a specified maximum ('the ceiling').

Handover

Handing over of the ownership of part or all of a project. See also 'Taking over'.

Hazard

Situation with the potential to cause harm to people, property or the environment.

Hazard study (Hazop)

Hazard and operability study. A formal and systematic analysis to ensure that hazards are identified, understood and eliminated or controlled.

Head contract

= 'Main contract'

Hook up

Connecting equipment after installation to form a complete system.

House contractor

Contractor regularly employed by a client.

Implied terms of a contract

Terms which are part of a contract by law but are not expressed. In contracts under English law they can include:
- the duty to exercise skill and care;
- fitness for purpose (where the purpose has been made known to the supplier and is not overridden by an imposed specification);
- responsibility of a contractor for its subcontractors;
- compliance with statutes (EC Regulations, Factories Act, Construction Regulations, Health and Safety at Work, etc Act);
- furtherance of purpose — both parties will do their best to perform the contract;
- liability of a contractor to carry out work at reasonable speed.

In house

Within an organization.

Joint venture (JV)

Collaboration between two or more organizations, usually for one project, sometimes for a series of projects.

Letter of credit

Document issued by a bank stating that it holds money from a client to pay for work.

Letter of intent

Letter from a client to a contractor stating the intention to enter into a contract and requesting the contractor to continue negotiating the proposed contract,
or
Letter from a client to a contractor stating the intention to enter into a contract and requesting the contractor to commence the work to be done under the proposed contract.

Level

The amount of detail shown or available. See 'Engineering level' and 'Level one plan'.

Level one plan

The master plan for a project. For all but small projects progressively more detail is given in level two, level three, etc plans.

Line manager

Classically a manager responsible for part or all of the resources needed for production. The term is now used to mean the person with management responsibility for an individual, whether or not also responsible for the tasks which that individual may be carrying out — for instance, if the individual is temporarily seconded to a project team.

Liquidated damages terms (LDs)

Liability in a contract to pay a specified sum for a specified breach of contract, such as being late in completing construction.

Long lead item

Item to be ordered at the start of a project because of the time the supplier requires to obtain materials and/or do the work.

LSTK

Lump-sum-turnkey-contract. See also 'Lump sum payment' and 'Turnkey'.

Lump sum payment

Single payment for all the work done under a contract, but often used to mean fixed price.

Main contractor

Contractor who undertakes the construction of all or nearly all a project, but usually employing specialist contractors and others as subcontractors.

Maintenance period

See 'Defects correction period'.

Main plant items (MPIs)

Units of equipment required for a project which have the main influence on space and services required, building layout, installation methods or cost — for example, vessel, agitator, pump.

Making a contract

Entering into a contract. Agreement to enter into a contract may include a term that the contract does not come into effect until some later date or action. Or that the work is not to start until the contractor is so instructed.

Management contractor

Contractor employed by the client to help plan, define and co-ordinate design and construction and to supervise construction.

Managing contractor

A 'Main contractor', as distinct from a 'Management contractor'.

Mechanical completion

Equipment/systems are complete, inspected and checked as correct to design and specification,

or

Equipment/systems are complete, inspected and checked as correct to design and specification, and pre-commissioning tests and trials are complete.

See also 'Pre-commissioning'. In either case mechanical completion can be a milestone when a payment becomes due to the contractor and can be the time for contractual handover to the client.

Milestone

Event of significant value in the progress of a project.

Model conditions of contract

Sets of contract terms on general matters likely to be required by clients in any contract for a class of work, usually defining words used, the responsibilities of the parties, procedures, liabilities for damage and injuries, mistakes, failure of contractor or subcontractors, delays, changes in legislation such as taxation, frustration of contract and termination. These general terms are designed to be used with a specification, drawings, schedules and other documents which state the particular terms of a contract. They are also called 'general conditions of contract', 'model forms' or 'standard forms'.

MTO
Materials take-off.

Nominated subcontractor
Subcontractor chosen by the client or his representative, usually for specialist work.

Offer
= 'Tender'

Open tendering
Any interested contractor can tender. See 'Selective tendering'.

Operational window
Opportunity for work at a plant shutdown (for example, for maintenance and/or because of a seasonal lack of demand) or when weather permits.

Order
= 'Purchase order'

Organization breakdown structure
= 'Work breakdown structure'

Ownership
Commitment to the objectives of a project.

Parties
The 'persons' who offer and accept the terms of a contract. (A company or corporation has the legal status of a person.) 'Third parties' are any others who are not parties to that contract.

Partnering
Co-operative management by client and contractor of the work to be done in a

contract or a series of contracts jointly so as to anticipate and overcome problems in achieving mutual goals. The word does not mean a formal legal partnership. See also 'Alliance' and 'Joint venture'.

Payback period
Time taken for the investment in a project to be paid back by the cash it earns in use.

Penalty
Under English law what is called a 'penalty' in a contract may not be enforceable. See 'Liquidated damages terms'.

Performance
Completion of all obligations.

P&ID
Piping and instrumentation diagram. A drawing of symbols showing equipment, pipework and instruments, for all or part of the project.

Planned payment
Scheme for payment to a contractor for achieving defined stages or percentages of an agreed programme of work.

Plant
System of equipment and services which comprise a production unit. Also used by contractors to mean equipment used in demolition and construction work.

Practical completion
The project or a section of it is sufficiently complete for the client to take it over or begin to use it.

Pre-assembled unit (PAU)
A sub-system or section of equipment assembled off-site and transported and installed as a single unit.

Pre-commissioning
Preparation of completed plant for start-up. See also 'Commissioning' and 'Mechanical completion'.

Pre-engineering
= 'FEED'

Preliminaries
Miscellaneous and preparatory work by a contractor for which payment will be made, such as ordering materials, mobilizing resources, running the site and providing services to the client's representative.

Pre-qualification or Pre-selection
Selection of contractors to invite to tender for a contract. See 'Selective tendering'.

Price
See 'Contract price'.

Prime contract
= 'Direct contract'

Principal contractor
= 'Main contractor'

Procurement
Purchasing of services, materials or equipment. 'Procurement' is now also used in the construction industry to mean a client's actions in employing a contractor to construct a project.

Produit en main
The contractor is in control of the completed facility.

Programme
Diagram or table showing proposed dates for starting and completing activities. See also 'Schedule'.

Project breakdown structure
= 'Work breakdown structure'

Project champion
Manager with the authority and ultimate responsibility for the successful implementation of a project.

Project data book
A collection of the relevant project information handed over to the client at the end of a project.

Project engineer

See also 'Project manager'. Person responsible for establishing and achieving the objectives of an engineering project, particularly for a small project,
or
An engineer responsible for one or more work packages for a project, responsible to the project manager.

Project estimate

Estimate of the cost of a whole project.

Project execution plan or Project implementation plan (PEP or PIP)

Document stating who is to be responsible for all the activities necessary to carry out a project.

Project manager

See also 'Project engineer'. Person responsible for establishing and achieving the objectives of a project.

Project management contractor

Contractor employed to plan, define and co-ordinate design and construction, and supervise construction.

Project review or Review report

The process of collecting and examining data and experience on a completed project from those involved in the project, to be used as learning for the future.

Project services contract (PSC)

Used in the offshore industry to mean the employment by a client of a construction contractor to help plan, define and co-ordinate design and construction, and supervise construction. The role can include co-ordinating the client's internal departments' decisions and other contributions to a project. The construction work is carried out by other contractors employed by the client. See also 'Construction management' and 'Project management contractor'.

Project sponsor

= 'Project champion'

Promoter

= 'Client'

Punch-list
List of outstanding activities to be completed before work will be accepted.

Purchase order
Contract for smaller purchases.

Qualified acceptance
Limited, modified or restricted acceptance of an offer to enter into a contract, and therefore a counter-offer, not an acceptance.

Qualified bid
Limited, modified or restricted offer, not compliant with all the terms proposed in an invitation for tenders.

QS
Quantity surveyor.

Quantum meruit
Literally the amount it deserves, meaning a reasonable price.

Quotation
A 'quotation' may be an offer to enter into a contract or only an indication of price.

Redfield site
Area with hazards due to operational systems, materials or structures. These hazards should therefore govern the planning and control of any project work in the area. See also 'Brownfield site' and 'Greenfield site'.

Reimbursable
Means 'cost-reimbursable'.

Remeasurement
Calculation of the actual quantities of work ordered on the contractor for payment to the contractor. Remeasurement is also known as 'measure-and-value'.

Remoteness
Not being a party to a contract.

Reservation

A defect in a contractor's work. See also 'Punch-list'.

Retention = Retention money

Part of the payment due to a contractor for progress with the work which is not paid until the contractor has discharged liabilities to remedy defects for a period after the taking over or acceptance of the works.

Sanction of a project

Decision by the appropriate body in the client organization to authorize expenditure of resources on a project.

Schedule

Diagram or list showing the proposed starting and completion dates for activities,

or

Any list.

Schedule of rates

List of approximate quantities of items of work to be done by a contractor with prices ('rates') per unit quantity of each item.

Selective tendering

Inviting tenders only from selected contractors, usually those considered to be qualified by their resources and their performance on previous contracts.

Seller

= 'Contractor'

Serial contract

One contract agreed for the construction of a series of projects or separate instalments of work. See also 'Term contract'.

SHE

Safety, health and environmental protection.

Simple contract

Under English law a contract not under seal and made orally or in writing by:
- offer;
- acceptance;

- valuable consideration (usually payment);
- identity of intention;
- intention to make a legal relationship;
- possibility.

Speciality contract
In England a contract made under seal.

Standard forms
See 'Model conditions of contract'.

Start-up
Usually means the commissioning (see 'Commissioning') of a completed system or facility, but is also used to mean the process of making a new project team effective.

Statute law
Law made by the EC or Parliament.

Steering committee
Group formed usually for larger projects to guide the project manager on behalf of all stakeholders.

Subcontractor
Company providing services, goods and/or management services to a main contractor and not in contract with the client.

Subletting
Employment of a subcontractor by a main contractor.

Substantial completion
= 'Practical completion'

Supplier
= 'Contractor' or 'Subcontractor'

Supplier data
Information such as drawings, calculations and data sheets produced by a supplier.

Supply chain

The sequence of contracts client → main contractor → subcontractor → materials supplier, etc, and the subsequent reverse flow of deliverables.

Take-off

Calculation from drawings of the quantities of materials and so on required for work.

Taking over

When the use or the ownership of the works passes from contractor to client.

Tender

Offer to enter into a contract, indicating costs, time, etc.

Term contract

Contract for providing construction or other work when ordered by a client at any time within an agreed period (the 'term'), usually based upon descriptions of types of work which may be ordered but without quantities being known in advance. Used in some 'Partnering'.

Termination of a contract

= 'Determination of a contract'

Terms of a contract

All the obligations and rights agreed between the parties, plus any terms implied by law. In English contracts the terms may consist of conditions and warranties.

Terms of sale

= 'Terms of a contract' or 'Conditions of contract'
Terms of sale is more typically the phrase used for small contracts such as in purchasing materials or plant.

Test schedule (also sometimes includes acceptance tests)

A list of the tests and inspections necessary to indicate that the project has met the agreed performance requirements. Acceptance tests are those which the client may want to witness before accepting handover of the project.

Third parties

See 'Parties'.

TIC
Total installed cost.

Tie-ins
Connections between existing systems and new systems installed for a project.

Turnkey contract
Comprehensive contract in which the contractor is responsible for the design, supply, construction and commissioning of a complete building, factory or process plant, usually with responsibility for fitness for purpose, and perhaps also to train client's staff and pre-commission and commission the plant.

Validated project
Project which meets approvals necessary for the product to satisfy statutory regulatory requirements — for example, pharmaceuticals.

Valuation
Calculating the amount of payment due under a contract.

Variation
Change to the quantity, quality or timing of the works which is ordered by the client's representative under a term of a contract.

Variation order
Instruction from the client or his representative for an addition, omission or alteration to the scope or timing of the work to be done by a contractor.

Vendor
Company or person contractually committed to providing goods (either direct to the client or through a contractor).

Vendor information
Design information from a vendor that is essential to the client or contractor for the design of the project.

Weather window
= 'Operational window'

Work breakdown structure (WBS)
Division of the work for a project into defined packages or sub-projects,

showing the responsibilities for the management, reporting and control of each package.

Work package

A particular piece of work for a project as defined in a work breakdown structure.

Work package owner

A person responsible for a work package.

The works

What a contractor has undertaken to provide or do for a client. Defined in UK construction contracts as the work to be carried out, goods, materials and services to be supplied, and the liabilities, obligations and risks to be taken by a contractor.

Bibliography

Andersen, E.S., *et al*, 1995, *Goal Directed Project Management*, 2nd edition, ISBN 0 7494 1389 1 (Kogan Page).

Cleland, D.I. and Gareis, R., 1993, *Global Project Management*, ISBN 0 07011329 7 (McGraw-Hill).

Graham, J.H., 1996, Machiavellian project managers: Do they perform better?, *International Journal of Project Management*, 14 (2): 67–74.

Harrison, F.L., 1992, *Advanced Project Management*, 3rd edition, ISBN 0 566 09100 3 (Gower).

Kerzner, H., 1995, *Project Management: A Systems Approach to Planning, Scheduling and Controlling*, 5th edition, ISBN 0 442 01907 6 (van Nostrand).

Lock, D. (ed), 1995, *Project Management Handbook*, 3rd edition, ISBN 0 566 07391 9 (Gower Press).

Lock, D., 1996, *Project Management*, 6th edition, ISBN 0 566 07738 0 (Gower Publishing).

Merna, A. and Smith, N.J., 1996, *Projects Procured by Privately Financed Concession Contracts*, 2 volumes, ISBN 962 7708 73 9 and 962 7708 74 7 (Asia Law & Practice).

Morris, P.W.G., 1997, *The Management of Projects*, revised edition, ISBN 0 7277 1693 X (Thomas Telford Publications).

Morris, P.W.G. and Hough, G.H., 1987, *The Anatomy of Project Management*, ISBN 0 471 91551 3 (John Wiley).

Reiss, G., 1992, *Project Management Demystified*, ISBN 0 419 16920 2 (Spon).

Whittaker, R., 1995, *Project Management in the Process Industries*, ISBN 0 471 96040 3 (John Wiley).

Journals

International Journal of Project Management, ISSN 0263 7863 (Elsevier Science).

Project, ISSN 0957 7033 (Association for Project Management).

Project Manager Today, ISSN 0957 1853 (Larchdrift Projects Ltd).

Project Management Journal, ISSN 8756 9728 (Project Management Institute, USA) .

Useful addresses

Association for Project Management
150 West Wycombe Road
High Wycombe HP12 3AE, UK
Phone: 01494 440090, Fax: 01494 528937
E-mail: secretariat@apm-uk.demon.co.uk
www.apm.org.uk

The APM Group Ltd
85 Oxford Road
High Wycombe HP11 2DX, UK
Phone: 01494 452450, Fax: 01494 459559
E-mail: apmgroup@compuserve.com
www.apmgroup.co.uk

The Library
Institution of Chemical Engineers
Davis Building
165–189 Railway Terrace
Rugby CV21 3HQ, UK
Phone: 01788 578214, Fax: 01788 560833
E-mail: library@icheme.org.uk
www.icheme.org

Project (magazine of the Association for Project Management)
Financial and Business Publications
95 Wigmore Street
London W1H 9AA, UK
Phone: 0171 935 4959, Fax: 0171 935 5833
E-mail: jo@fbpl.demon.co.uk

Project Manager Today
PO Box 55
Wokingham RG40 4XN, UK
Phone: 0118 976 1944/1399, Fax: 0118 976 1944
E-mail: ken_lane@compuserve.com

International Journal of Project Management
Elsevier Science Ltd
Bampfylde Street
Exeter EX1 2AH, UK
Phone: 01392 251558, Fax: 01392 425370

Association of Cost Engineers
Lea House
5 Middlewich Road
Sandbach CW11 9XL, UK
Phone: 01270 764798, Fax: 01270 766180

International Project Management Association
PO Box 30
Monmouth NP5 4YZ, UK
Phone: 01594 531007, Fax: 01594 531008
E-mail: ipma@btinternet.com
www.ipma.ch

Project Management Institute
130 South State Road
Upper Darby
PA 19082, USA
Phone: 001 610 734 3330, Fax: 001 610 734 3266 or 3270
E-mail: pmieo@pmi.org

Index

376